GETTING SHIT DONE:

The No-Nonsense Framework for
Closing the Strategy-Execution Gap

Thank you to my loving (and patient) wife, Hannah.

Thank you to my father-in-law for reviewing and editing.

Thank you to my three dogs for being perfect in every way.

Thank you to everyone in my network who supported me and provided guidance throughout this project.

CONTENTS

PREFACE

Organizations all over the world continue to struggle in achieving their strategies. If and when they eventually succeed, most of these efforts come in over-budget and well past the deadlines.

Not that this is a new problem, but the pace of competition and innovation today has substantially raised the stakes of the game. In the past two decades, our world has witnessed a monumental shift in technology, globalization, and productivity. For most organizations, no longer is it enough to offer a good product at a fair price and with reasonable customer service levels- no, today, companies must seek to be the absolute best in whatever they do and whoever they serve to retain their competitive edge. What worked yesterday may not work today, and an organization needs to be dynamic enough to choose new courses of action and make them a reality.

Although organizations and industries can identify what needs to change, most strategy-execution efforts fail. Those strategy executions that don't fail outright will limp forward. Staggering price tags, incomplete deliverables, and a demoralized workforce usually lie in the wake of many change efforts. Change now occurs at a faster pace and from more directions at once. Existing competitors are cut-throat, suppliers are clever, buyers are fickle, better substitutes exist in the market, and new entrants seem to pop out of nowhere to steal market share.

Staying in business means having a dynamic strategy, the ability to quickly shift to adapt, and the means of doing so. Rather than a nice to have, it is here that we begin to understand that strategy-execution is a core competency of the most successful companies we know today.

Each year, organizations go through the same ritual where the executive teams design their strategy and then pass it down through their organizations to be translated and implemented. But it is somewhere in the middle between creating the plan (strategy) and carrying it out (execution) that critical elements get lost. Most don't plan to fail, but a lack of understanding finds organizations inevitably falling back into the same trap over and over again. Researchers have long acknowledged that even the most brilliant strategy is worthless if it isn't executed well.

> "Companies, on average, only deliver 63% of the financial performance on their strategies promise."-Harvard Business Review [2]

> "82% of Fortune 500 CEOs feel their organization is effective at strategic planning. Only 14% indicated to be effective at implementing the strategy."-Forbes Magazine

> "Executional Excellence is the number one challenge facing global corporate leaders."-Harvard Business Review [2]

> "Slow strategy execution is the top challenge for 2019; 70% of executives say they had little confidence in their ability to solve the problem."-Gartner [1]

> "50% of well-formulated strategies fail to deliver expected results because of poor execution."-Harvard Business Review [2]

> "Only 2% of leaders feel confident that 80-100% of their goals will be executed." - Bridges Business Consultancy

Conversely, lacking the ability to execute is often a precursor to a company's demise. It is fair to go so far as to say that a lack of execution is one of the most significant problems facing businesses today. With it, you can overcome many deficiencies; without it, you're dead. Understanding and bridging the strategy-execution gap up to this point has been an ambiguous and murky exercise. Without a clear framework, organizations are left to guesswork to fill in the strategy-execution gap that spans from expectations to deliverables. [3]

Add it all up, and the conclusion seems obvious: 1) Execution is essential both strategically and operationally, 2) Regardless of industry sector, we must be better at it, and 3) Poor execution is a leading cause for concern among organizations.

We are in the middle of an ongoing crisis where the sky-high rate of execution failures in achieving organizational change remains one of the most pressing challenges for employees, managers, and executives. Organizations must find a way to be great at both setting the strategy and sustaining core competencies with a long-term perspective. Still, most organizations are only focusing on one piece of the puzzle at a time. Although the execution gap is a daunting problem, there is hope. For those willing to look inwards and improve, the prize for closing the strategy-to-performance gap is enormous—an increase in performance of anywhere from 60% to 100% for most companies. [2]

By reading this book to understand the causes of strategy-execution failures and remedies, individuals and leaders at all levels of an organization can better understand their role and contribution to an organization's success. It has been assumed that strategy is what the executives do for far too long, and execution is for everyone else to figure out.

That changes today.

WHAT IS THIS BOOK?

The genesis of this book is the following:

Why does the strategy-execution problem still exist?

Getting Shit Done is a book designed to be a comprehensive guide on understanding what it takes to break strategy down into meaningful milestones for people at all levels of the organization, not just executives. The structure follows an unconventional path to help readers understand the critical ingredients for success. Instead of talking about what executives at Apple or Microsoft supposedly did, this book seeks to bring new energy and interest to the subject by exploring strategy-execution throughout our shared history and various cultures.

While this book is not the first to explore the disconnect between the formulation of strategy and execution, **many books before have a fatal flaw- they talk about what other people must do to make things happen.** In a nutshell, too many other books focus the wrong message on the wrong people.

Too many other books in the strategy-execution realm are written from the lens of a high-level executive or professional consultant who has spent decades away from doing the actual work. Even worse, many of these books are lazily disguised as marketing tools to sell even more training and consulting services to you later on. GSD is not written from the viewpoint of consultants, "gurus," or "thought leaders" worried about how to change others. Instead, GSD examines the world differently by stepping away from the lens of the outsider looking in or the executive looking down. The real and untapped potential lies through the eyes of the insider looking all around for answers.

It's painful to see that so many books are written just for the CEO and executive team's privileged eyes in the realm of strategy and execution. What about the rest of us? Don't we, those who do the work, matter?

Image1- "Tommy & Tammy Talker"

This book is for those living through strategy and execution's everyday challenges- the core workers, staff people, supervisors, managers, and executives- anyone who wants to do better. This book is for the frontline workers and people in support roles who have decided that their organization needs to change but doubts whether they are on the right path in creating accountable and committed workplaces.

Doesn't work

Consultant tells executives what other people need to do

Executives tell managers what other people need to do

Supervisors tell workers what they need to do

Image2- The Consultant Circle of Life

Too many resources on strategy-execution fall short in explaining what happens next after a strategy is set and assume that implementation is a given- something waiting to be willed into existence. After a strategy is declared, how does everyone else in the organization know who will take responsibility for disseminating the strategy down to the individual tasks and milestones that must be accomplished? How do we coordinate resources and teams to meet the strategy-execution goals on time and budget?

To answer the "what comes next" questions, GSD prescribes actionable insights and exercises to help you become a better leader that others will be proud to follow. Not only will we explore what works, but we will call out the systems, attitudes, and management fads that have contributed to the current mess. **Closing the strategy execution gap starts by acknowledging that execution is a distinctive discipline and skillset built over time.**

Many of the building blocks of effective strategy execution already exist- there is nothing new under the sun. Strategic planning and strategy execution tools have been developed and available for decades. However, what is lacking is a comprehensive framework to integrate all these tools to build alignment and synchronization.

In our learning journey, rather than following a group of companies' performances over time in a format that mirrors Jim Collins's "Good to Great" or Tom Peter's "In Search of Excellence," GSD takes a different approach. I avoid examples that quickly go stale; most of the stories and examples come from our shared history. Truly, the world has been transformed by leaders who have followed the principles espoused in this book.

You will come to find that execution isn't the job of the elite or privileged few, but rather everyone in the organization. The world needs fewer people who merely think- and more people who can think differently and then move to bold action. Let's start here and now to move past the generality of strategy and learn how to think and act like true operational leaders.

Image4- The People Who Do Matter

The world doesn't need another book on strategy and execution; we need the right book. Business education shouldn't put people to sleep, nor should it focus on 1% of the people who must hear the message. By learning how to set better targets, align resources, lead at all levels, deliver results, and build controls around processes, we learn to build a system that ensures what gets done, stays done.

Welcome to Getting Shit Done.

WHO AM I TO WRITE THIS BOOK?

Image- Ben Wann

In the last decade, I've had the opportunity to experience a vast assortment of roles and employers in the manufacturing industry. Beginning in 2012 as a cost accountant and currently working as an Associate Director/Operational Controller for a biotech start-up, I can count on having no less than ten managers, six employers, and seven job titles and roles during my tenure, a testament to the pace of change in today's world. This variety of positions and roles, especially the last three where

I have worked directly with the executive teams, has shown me that no matter where I worked or what my responsibilities were, there is always a persistent problem with strategy-execution at all levels of an organization.

Experience has shown that each organization has its own backlog of inefficient, inaccurate, and wasteful processes with seemingly no one willing to step up and do something about it-it was always someone else's problem. Sensing an opportunity, I've built my career around studying and experimenting with the skills, discipline, and principles necessary to be the person who could rebuild processes, tackle the challenges others let fester and implement automation tools to save substantial amounts of both time and money. Instead of maintaining the status quo, I've focused on building my brand around identifying problems and then Getting Shit Done. I don't care what the problem is, why an improvement failed before, how big or nasty the challenge is, or the level of difficulty... if there's work to be done, you can put my name on the line.

I've become deeply passionate about understanding the strategy-execution gap and the elements that drive it. I've studied and implemented various programs and ideas to understand what needs to be done and how to get it done. My passion has been to understand the mindset, the soft skills, the hard skills, and the methodologies that produce results. To that end, aside from personal experience, I've endlessly researched the subject, and the result of these efforts is this book.

On its own, you'll find that executing strategy and tasks is a challenging, complex, and dynamic responsibility that is usually a distinct career path. However, as organizations have become leaner and meaner, many professionals who already have "day jobs" and other core responsibilities are frequently asked to step into leadership roles to help their organizations drive change.

My overall aim in writing Getting Shit Done is to:

1) Raise organization awareness around the strategy-execution gap and its remedies and

2) Inspire other professionals to strengthen their careers by mastering the discipline of strategy-execution.

This book is written to share the best practices around execution so that when the challenge presents itself, you too can rise to the occasion and find success. We all have good ideas- the hard part is just making them happen.

Enjoy.

-Ben

THE QUESTIONS TO BE ANSWERED

Getting Shit Done is about designing a framework for effectively thinking through and tackling each critical question that involves people and processes. To make it simple, every challenge around execution boils down to just three main questions, which can be summarized as the following:

Who Will do What and by When?

It's the mission, the motto, the mantra, whatever else you want to call it. If every task is approached with just these three questions and clear answers in mind, you'll be set up for a lifetime of success.

The remaining execution questions fall into a distribution that follows the Pareto Principle- roughly 80% of the effects are derived from 20% of the drivers.

In total, 12 key questions should be answered when working to Get Shit Done. The first three questions (20%) around Who, What, and When deliver 80% of the execution impact. The remaining 11 questions are essential and fill in the gap of everything else.

The three core questions of GSD:

1. Who will do the work?
2. What work needs to be done?
3. When will the work be done?

Supporting questions of GSD:

4. Who owns the problem, and who owns the solution?

5. Why isn't the work getting done?

6. Why isn't the work getting done on time?

7. Does each person in the organization understand What needs to be done?

8. Does each person understand How the work will be done?

9. Are we communicating as effectively and efficiently as possible to facilitate excellence?

10. Are you learning like a leader?

11. Are you thinking like a leader?

12. Are you executing like a leader?

WHO NEEDS TO DO WHAT AND BY WHEN?

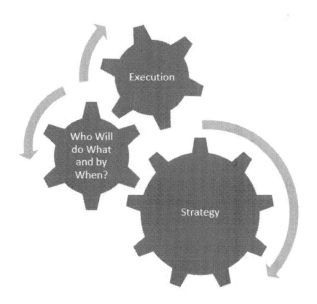

Image5- Strategy-Execution Machine

CHAPTER 1

GETTING SHIT DONE: THE STRATEGY-EXECUTION GAP

"Vision without action is a daydream. Action without vision is a nightmare."

- Japanese proverb

"I don't care whether the cat is black or white so long as it catches mice."

- Deng Xiaoping, former leader of China

"Real strategy lies not in figuring out what to do, but in devising ways to ensure that, compared to others, we actually do more of what everybody knows they should do. Strategy is not about understanding something-or planning to get around to it. It's about having the courage to make it happen."

- David H. Maister [8]

WHAT IS STRATEGY?

**"The essence of strategy is choosing to perform
activities differently than rivals do. Trade-offs are
essential to strategy. They create the need for choice
and purposefully limit what a company offers."
- Michael Porter [26]**

**"Strategy is the great work of the organization... it is
a unifying theme that gives coherence and direction
to the actions and direction of an organization."
- Sun Tzu, The Art of War [43]**

Strategy, what the heck is strategy?

It's one of those questions where no one person will give you the same answer, yet each person believes they're right. It's a hot buzzword that generates interest just about everywhere and anywhere. At the same time, it's a bit funny because this is perhaps the question central to all commercial enterprises. The wealth and health of whole economies depend on how well the people and organizations can understand and articulate the concept.

However, to save time (and avoid more philosophy), we'll begin by focusing on one of the best answers to the "What is strategy question?" which came from acclaimed author Michael Porter in his seminal HBR article (cleverly titled), "What is Strategy," which was first published in 1996. The article was such a hit that it still rings true today; it is commonly required reading material for most MBA programs.

While the original article can be a bit lengthy and dense to read through, it helps to break down the main arguments and takeaways into bitesize pieces.

If you remember nothing else about strategy, Porter tells you to remember this- **You can boil all strategies down to one of two alternatives:**

> a. **Do what everyone else is doing (but spend less money doing it), <u>or</u>**
>
> b. **Do something no one else can do.**

You can't do both- It's one or the other. To determine which strategic option to pursue, organizations must have a solid understanding of their core competencies and unique activities, which can be bucketed into the ability to either:

> 1. Satisfy a customer's needs,
>
> 2. Satisfy a customer's accessibility issues, or
>
> 3. Provide an unparalleled variety of products or services. [26]

Easy enough, right?

Porter made a point in the article to emphasize that operational excellence is not the same concept as a strategy. While both strategy and execution are essential elements for a company, they are separate topics.

Strategy <> Execution

Porter points out that customers do not purchase a company's products or services because an organization is efficient at what they do. Instead, customers purchase a company's products or services because of the unique value offered. It doesn't matter if you sell the world's most clever computer for $100 if it costs you $110 and arrives three weeks late. The fit between strategy and execution becomes essential to superior performance because unique product offerings cannot be sustained unless an organization is efficient at what they do.

Selecting which strategy to pursue then becomes an exercise in introspection to ensure that the organization's operational core work creates value for their end customer; that the core value stream is correctly designed.

Strategy= Doing the right things= Choosing what to do= Choosing what not to do

The final point that Porter offered in his article was that strategy and execution have very different characteristics.

Porter shared three critical characteristics of strategy:

1. Long-term focus; 3-5 year minimum; often a decade-plus.

2. Requires trade-offs and choices- You cannot be all things to all customers or people. Must purposefully limit what to offer.

3. Strategy setting activities include defining a unique position, making clear trade-offs, and tightening fit.

A company can outperform its rivals in both the short and long term only if it can identify and preserve a unique differentiating factor in the marketplace. Not only must an organization know where it wants to go, but it must also have the capabilities, functions, and people in place to help it get there.

The strategic plan involves a continual search for ways to reinforce and extend a company's position around what it does best. Just as a good strategy is based on a sound concept or idea, failure to construct a cohesive strategy makes it impossible to implement. A strategy is a compass pointing to where a company wants to go. For a strategy to be understood by the organization, the key is that it should be simple, unambiguous, and understandable to all. **Best-in-class organizations understand that doing something is not the same thing as doing the right thing.** Having a bias towards action is good, but don't be tempted to do something if it doesn't add up to anything.

In so many words, says Porter, a strategy is choosing what business to pursue.

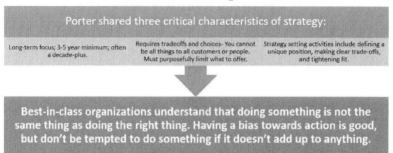

Porter shared three critical characteristics of strategy:

Long-term focus; 3-5 year minimum; often a decade-plus.

Requires tradeoffs and choices- You cannot be all things to all customers or people. Must purposefully limit what to offer.

Strategy setting activities include defining a unique position, making clear trade-offs, and tightening fit.

Best-in-class organizations understand that doing something is not the same thing as doing the right thing. Having a bias towards action is good, but don't be tempted to do something if it doesn't add up to anything.

Image6- Defining Strategy

What Is Execution?

Execution is the excellence found in all the operational and support activities of an enterprise. Execution can be seen in what appears to be the mundane and ordinary: the janitor who cleans the halls so that they sparkle and shine, in the manager who coaches their team until they operate at their best, in the coder who makes sure their work is bug-free, and the project manager who builds accountability into each piece of a project, leaving no room for assumptions. Collectively, each person doing their best work each day becomes a powerful engine inside an organization. Execution and operational excellence become very difficult, if not impossible, for a competitor to copy.

Execution: How to pursue and sustain operational excellence

In "What is Strategy," Porter defined the three elements of Operational Effectiveness (Execution) as follows:

- A daily, continuous focus is required.

- No trade-offs between alternatives are required.

- Activities include constant change, flexibility, and

relentless efforts to achieve best practice.[26]

Execution= doing things right= How work is done

In other words, execution means ensuring that work is completed with mastery. Over time, execution leads to operational excellence, which then leads to consistent higher-quality outputs. High-quality outputs then decrease costs and increase productivity by minimizing rework and other non-compliance costs. As a result, profitability increases as operational excellence delivers products or services to customers in the most efficient manner possible while ensuring high-quality products, services, and support. Operational excellence and execution are not about cost-cutting or minimizing waste but doing things right all the time.

STRATEGY + EXECUTION = FIT= RESULTS

**"Without a strategy, execution is aimless.
Without execution, strategy is useless. "**

- Morris Chang
**"Efficiency is doing things right; effectiveness
is doing the right thing."**

- Peter Drucker

**"Any business that tries to deliver all four virtues of
quality, cost, variety, and speed is doomed to failure."**

- David Maister [8]

Think of strategy without execution as a boat paddling with a clear sense of direction but manned by a crew who doesn't know how to or can't row the boat.

Image7- Clear Direction, Not Capable

Think of execution without a strategy as a boat paddling quickly but spinning in circles and going nowhere fast.

Image8- No Direction, But Capable

Strategy-execution and fit is an Olympic rowing team, where leadership provides clear direction, and the crew is individually strong and competent.

Image9- Clear Direction & Capable- Photo by Quino Al on Unsplash

In today's fast-paced business world, the difference between great companies and not-so-great companies comes down to their ability to execute the best strategic plan.

As we understand from Porter, strategy is a system of activities, not a collection of parts. **The best approach towards creating a sustainably profitable company is identifying a unique offering and ensuring the operational excellence and execution are in place for the support activities throughout the value chain.** To find this sweet spot, an organizations' leaders hold a critical responsibility role in defining a company's strategy by creating a market position, negotiating trade-offs, and then forging fit among activities. The key is to find the sweet spot between where the two concepts overlap; this intersection is known as fit.[26]

Maintaining fit between operational excellence and strategy locks out imitators by creating a robust value chain. Just as with the legendary phalanx formation that we will learn about later, the combination forms a perfect offense/defense.

However, if a fit is not found among the support activities, no distinctive strategy can be sustained. A competitive advantage can only come from the unique intersection of strategy and core competencies that fit together and reinforce each other. Fit is especially crucial because discrete activities often affect one another.

To better understand fit, consider the exercise below to compare which two companies have a higher execution score. We can assume that both are pursuing the same strategy.

Company A: (focused/excellent)

Activity 1: 90%

Activity 2:80%

Activity 3:95%

Activity 4: 100%

Total Execution Score= (90% * 80% * 95% * 100%) = 68.4%

Company B: (unfocused/distracted)

Activity 1: 70%

Activity 2:90%

Activity 3:60%

Activity 4: 80%

Activity 5: 50%

Total Execution Score= (70% * 90% * 60% * 80% * 50%) = 15.12%

The difference between the two companies is enormous- an execution score of 68.4% for Company A vs. an execution score of 15.12% for Company B.

As you can observe, each low score from multiple activities drags down the average for company B. Having more activities and performing them worse than a competitor increases complexity, reduces speed, and increases costs. As more and more value for companies is derived from the skills, knowledge, and capabilities of the people who work there, it is unlikely that company B can make quick changes to build the same or better competencies as company A.

A rival will struggle to match and imitate the interlocking activities of a competitor's salesforce, mirror a process technology, or replicate product features. Competitive positions built on systems of interlocking activities are far more sustainable than those built on individual activities. No amount of money or stomping, kicking, or screaming, will fix this problem. Ultimately, Company B faces what looks to be an insurmountable disadvantage. [26]

In his article, Porter shared the example of the Japanese economy's outperformance in the 1980s to accentuate the potential of excellence through execution. During this time, Japanese firms found themselves far ahead of their competition because of their substantial operating efficiencies over their US rivals. Whether in car manufacturing, camera technology, or computer chip manufacturing, the Japanese could just do it better, faster, and at a lower cost.

However, after more than a decade of impressive gains, many Japanese companies began to face diminishing returns. Gradually, company leaders let operational effectiveness supplant strategy. As a result, organizations often mirrored the capabilities of their competitors. They then found themselves in a dismal zero-sum competitive environment, static or declining prices, and economic pressure that compromised their ability to think or invest in the long term. Doing something efficiently was not the same as doing the right thing efficiently, and the Japanese suffered from two decades of low to no growth (the lost decades). Success leads to laxity and bloat, and eventually, to decline. Few organizations avoid this tragic arc over the long-term.

Developing a bold but executable strategy begins with ensuring leaders have addressed the questions of "What are we great at?" and "What can we achieve?" It's not enough to simply have good capabilities; all companies have them, or they couldn't compete. A genuinely winning company manages itself around a few differentiating capabilities- and deliberately integrates them. [29]

As the Japanese example shows, while continual improvement in operational effectiveness helps achieve superior profitability, it is not sufficient as a standalone means of competitiveness. Execution cannot make up for strategy, just as a strategy cannot make up for lack of execution.

Too many organizations assume that their historical baseline is correct and that their core capabilities are valid. They have the right employees, the right customers, and the right products. There is a stubborn belief that managerial force of mind is all that is required to generate profits.

For these reasons, improving operational effectiveness and execution capabilities becomes a critical part of management's job. **Leadership cannot be fooled into thinking that they are paid the big bucks just to set the strategy.** Instead, leadership plays a vital role in making sure that all the necessary pieces fall into place.

Great leaders can articulate the few differentiating capabilities that the company must excel at to realize the strategy. Establishing alignment on who is working on which strategic objective and what each of those objectives is will empower their people to drive the priority over nonstrategic objectives. [29]

Fit is found when companies make choices about who they are and what they do- and don't do- by using their strengths as a guide to move through the rapidly changing world. An actual strategy expresses what your organization does exceptionally well and why it matters.

The fit premium reflects the reality that distinctive capabilities are difficult to build; they are complex and expensive, with high fixed costs in human capital, tools, and systems. No matter how large and well-managed a company may be, it can only compete at a world-class level with a handful of distinctive capabilities. Organizations that organize core capabilities in a mutually reinforcing system and apply it to everything they do have an economic advantage.

A sign that Strategy & Execution are aligned for fit:

1. People at all levels of the organization bring their whole selves to work and feel mutually accountable for results by developing collective mastery.

2. All employees at all levels are willing to spend time energy to achieve both individual and organizational goals. Individuals are willing to work with others to help meet and surpass goals.

3. The company has identified a unique market position for which there is demand, and the company is very good at producing that product or service.

Overall, organizations that miss on strategy-execution are too SLOW.

Strategy is misaligned with reality and core competencies.
Leaders are misaligned with priorities and their people.
Organizations are misaligned with decentralization.
Workers are misaligned with critical skills and empowerment.

Getting Shit Done is the framework that builds Fit and gets organizations back up to speed. There is no good strategy and failed implementation. If an organization is not aware of its core capabilities and limitations and moves forward anyway, the strategy was flawed.

THE STRATEGY-EXECUTION GAP: WHO NEEDS TO DO WHAT AND BY WHEN

"No implementation can save a strategy, and no strategy can save an implementation, probably neither of which were feasible nor sound to begin with. A failure to think through the strategy makes it impossible to implement, except by chance."
-Hussey, 1996 [25]

In many books that cover strategy and execution, there's often this hilarious idea you'll come across where the writer portrays a caricature-like scene where the executives are a group of blundering idiots. Without understanding how the real world works, authors imagine company leadership perched up high in their C-suite lofts, bumbling along, and attempting to set the strategy by throwing darts at a wall. Will it be mergers & acquisitions? Organic growth? Layoffs and furloughs? New products and services? Close your eyes, spin three times, and chuck that dart!

First, to be clear, executives are not overpaid, Dilbertesque buffoons. Instead, executives are good people with extensive experience in their fields, trying their best in imperfect organizations with imperfect information to make good decisions.

Just like you, executives are frustrated by the lack of visibility into the cost and profit drivers, so they often make do with the best information available at the time. Like you, they trust people to carry out the strategy's execution steps but are often faced with disappointment. The main difference is that if they mess up, their faces appear in the news and yours doesn't-that's why they get paid a bit more.

At the same time, employees are not lazy people, goofballs, or complacent drones. Most people want to do the right thing and aim to produce their best work; they often don't know what is expected. They don't understand What needs to get done, and the confusion often begets chaos and more frustration—misleading signals and reward structures often contradict each other.

It is here, in the messy middle, where we find the strategy-execution gap—and where we often find executives thinking, "Why doesn't everybody else understand what we must do." And, at the same time, the people closest to the work are thinking, "Why doesn't leadership share what needs to get done and help us get our jobs done better?"

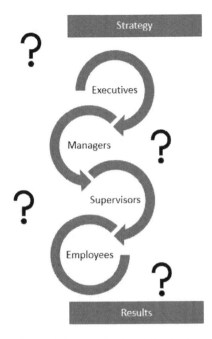

Image10- Organizational Confusion

The Strategy-Execution Gap is the missing piece between strategy and execution that determines Who Needs to Do What and by When. The people in the organization feel that they are working just to tread water and survive, and the people at the top feel frustrated when they set a strategy that most people never hear about or do anything about. Without a clear direction and alignment on direction and differentiation between the activities that matter and those that don't, the people in an organization send themselves into a flurry trying to tackle what they each think should be done.

This book is about bridging the Strategy-Execution Gap.

In the following pages, you'll learn how to make sure everyone in your organization knows Who Needs to Do What by When. There are five elements involved in answering this question, the first three being *Who, What,* and *When.* To get employees to commit to understanding and acting on Who Needs to Do What by When they'll need to understand the *Why.* And

39

finally, employees with the best motivation won't execute if they don't know the *How*. These five elements — Who, What, When, How, and Why — will constantly thread throughout the book.

The Strategy-Execution Gap is illustrated in the image below, where the "???" represents all the stuff that should have been said, done, or explained but wasn't done or wasn't done right. It falls into the realm of assumptions and someone else's problem to deal with. Somewhere between the two different levels of the organization, top and bottom, much gets missed or forgotten.

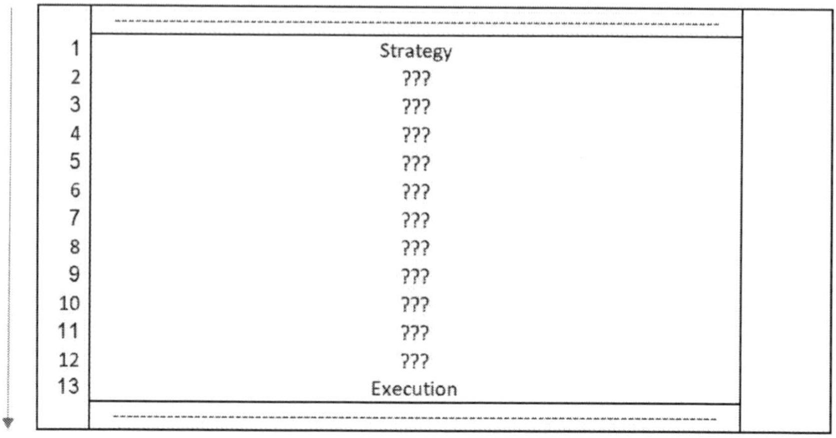

1	Strategy
2	???
3	???
4	???
5	???
6	???
7	???
8	???
9	???
10	???
11	???
12	???
13	Execution

Image11- Strategy-Execution Gap Illustration

To bridge the Strategy-Execution Gap, leaders and organizations need a clear intellectual framework to guide strategy as a necessary counterweight to fill in the execution gap. The bridge linking Strategy and Execution consists of the eleven themes that we'll be covering in this book:

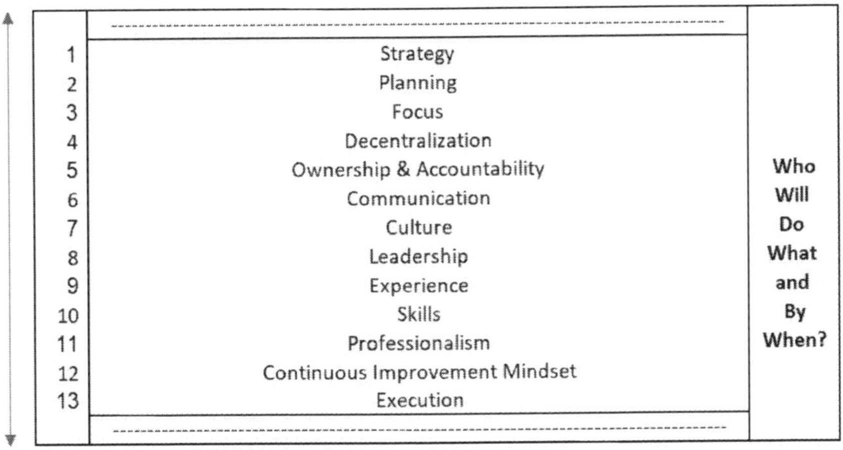

1	Strategy	
2	Planning	
3	Focus	
4	Decentralization	
5	Ownership & Accountability	Who
6	Communication	Will
7	Culture	Do
8	Leadership	What
9	Experience	and
10	Skills	By
11	Professionalism	When?
12	Continuous Improvement Mindset	
13	Execution	

Image12- Strategy-Execution GSD Framework Illustration

1. STRATEGY

2. Planning

3. Focus

4. Decentralization

5. Ownership & Accountability

6. Communication

7. Culture

8. Leadership

9. Experience

10. Skills

11. Professionalism

12. Continuous Improvement Mindset

13. EXECUTION

These thirteen themes, woven throughout this book, represent the crucial capabilities that link strategy and execution to close the execution gap. These elements serve to operate as a framework for all to see and embrace, making fit possible.

You'll notice that not one of these ideas or themes is new. Instead, they are fleshed out in a way that makes them memorable and interesting. Whenever you or your team feels a bit lost, the framework will serve to reorient your direction and a sense of purpose.

The Who, What, When, How, and Why (WWWHW) elements are interwoven throughout these twelve themes. Ownership and Accountability, for example, is focused on the Who. "It's not my job; it's his" is a classic expression of lack of Ownership and Accountability. Focus is about the What — what should be done and what should not be done. As we cover each of these themes, we'll bring in the five elements.

It's essential to resist the temptation to codify Who Needs to do What and by When mechanically. Instead, a learning framework serves to help people get used to the recipes and routines of excellence and adapt them to their circumstances while remaining true to the identity and capabilities that the entire organization needs. As organizational learning specialist Robert Putnam put it, "The learning of skills begins with recipes. Without practice, the concept won't be second nature. But until it's second nature, you can't practice with it effectively. So, you can short-cut the dilemma by following a set of rules" – at least at first, until you don't need the rules anymore.

You want to promote ownership of the knowledge embedded in the capability and encourage innovation while operating. By improving your recipe, opportunities follow many others to advance toward master chef status, practicing the steps until they no longer need the recipes. If you can make it work, you will create a whole enterprise of skilled enough people to make their own valuable variations, understand how they fit the value proposition, see their place in the capabilities system, and continually learn from each other.

Great restaurants don't have one master chef who knows

all the best recipes; instead, teams of passionate and driven people come together to create out-of-this-world experiences.

TAKEAWAYS:

- An organization needs a unique strategy that serves a need in the overall market that competitors cannot copy.

- Strategy is choosing what to do and what not to do.

- Executing strategy is circular, not a linear process.

- An organization needs a core set of competencies that make achieving the strategy possible in the short and long-term. It's not enough to get one or two competencies right- Linkage between those and strategy is crucial.

- Fit occurs when the strategy and core competencies are aligned.

- Fit is extremely difficult for competitors to imitate and is the path to sustainable long-term profitability.

- The strategy-execution gap is the disconnect between a strategy being set and people closest to the work knowing what the strategy is and what they must do to help achieve it.

- There is no good strategy and failed implementation. If an organization is not aware of its core capabilities and limitations and moves forward anyway, the strategy was flawed.

REFLECTION:

Build the strategy:

- Are you clear about how you add value to customers in a way that others don't?

- What business or opportunities will you say no to?

- Is your strategy realistic?

Building Core Competencies

- Does your organization understand its core competencies?

- Do all people in the organization understand the strategy and their role in it?

- What are the specific core operational capabilities that enable you to excel at that value proposition? What are the 3-6 things that do you do better than your competitors?

- What activities must be eliminated, outsourced, or cut so that the company can focus on what it does best?

- Are you enabling employees to work together across organizational silos to tackle the cross-functional challenges that allow the company to win?

- Are you keeping track not just of your performance but of how you're building and scaling up those few key capabilities to create value for customers in ways that others cannot?

- Is your whole management team engaged in building and executing the strategy—not just by measuring results but by continually challenging the organization and supporting it in improving its key capabilities? Do you set your team's sights high enough for what they must accomplish, and by when?

Forging Fit:

- Does the organization possess the capabilities required to achieve the strategy? Who is responsible for maintaining and enhancing the core capabilities?

- Have we identified the underlying processes, systems, skills, and structures critical to driving performance for each capability?

- Is the operating model transparent so that we know which core capabilities drive the most value to customers?

CHAPTER 2

Why Shit Doesn't Get Done on Time

"Lost time is never found again."
- Benjamin Franklin
"The key is in not spending time, but in investing it."
- Stephen R. Covey
"You can either get stuck or get results. Period. Case closed."
-The Oz Principle [5]

INTRODUCTION

The fact that anything gets done in many organizations is impressive despite our best efforts to the contrary. Whether we are working on a project or a task, we often begin our efforts knowing that we will never meet the expectations.

Because we know that "something" always occurs to derail us or make our time disappear from the outset, we discount the chances of not just getting the work done but also done on time. You don't have to look far to see the evidence in all corners of the world. A study by PWC, for example, reviewed 10,640 projects from 200 companies in 30 countries and across various industries and found that only 2.5% of the companies completed 100% of their projects. Another study published in the Harvard Business Review, which analyzed 1,471 IT projects, found that the average cost overrun was 27%, and the typical schedule/time overrun was almost 70%. [11]

When we do manage to Get Shit Done, we often don't get Shit Done on Time.

Painful.

The root cause of this problem is that many of us approach our work with a default "take it as it comes mentality" without much awareness. We'll complicitly bend to the circumstances around us and allow the ingrained organizational culture and other people's poor attitudes and habits to warp our productivity and happiness. For some reason, we let the environment we work in dictate how we approach our work and our degree of assuming ownership. Without a more thoughtful and conscientious awareness of how best to approach and handle work, we throw ourselves into the chaos of chance. Is it any wonder that we have issues with strategy execution in a world like this?

Part of the problem is that we also confuse being busy with being productive. Lots of people, emails, and meetings do not define operational effectiveness or excellence. But without knowing how best to work, we set ourselves up for disaster. It only takes a few rogue waves from unseen obstacles to broadside and flip our unsteady execution vessel.

What causes our pain? What are the main drivers of Shit not getting done on time?

Experience, history, and research have revealed that the two main drivers around why Shit Doesn't Get Done on Time are:
1. Poor Planning
2. Poor Time Management

Poor Planning Leads to Unrealistic Expectations

"Executives say that they lose 40% of their strategy's potential value to breakdowns in execution. In our experience at Bain & Company, however, this strategy-to-performance gap is rarely the result of shortcomings in implementation; it is because the plans are flawed from the start. [30]
-Harvard Business Review

While there are certainly steps that organizations can take to enhance their capabilities, nothing can happen overnight. Defining core capabilities, building competencies, and establishing ownership and accountability all take time. Moreover, even in organizations that operate with excellence, there is still a cap on what can be achieved. It's always a nice idea to add a little disclaimer that objectives must be tied to reality in defining what needs to get done.

To implement the strategy effectively, the strategy needs to be realistic, based on a sound idea, and be well thought out. **No**

implementation can save a strategy, which is not feasible or sound to begin with. There is nothing worse than a misunderstood plan than an unrealistic plan, and many strategy executions often fail because the strategic plan was a delusion.

Image14- Caution- Photo by Justus Menke on Unsplash

What happens with unrealistic plans is that they create the expectation throughout an organization that plans are all talk and that no one expects them to be fulfilled- it's just lip service for the investors. As employees begin to realize that keeping and fulfilling commitments isn't part of the job, ownership and accountability die on the spot. As a result, commitments at all levels cease to form binding promises because there are neither real expectations nor real consequences.

Even more, with unrealistic plans, leaders quickly pivot their attention and focus on fighting fires instead. Leaders cease leading their teams and instead start spending more time and effort to defer others' eventual outcomes. Rather than stretching to ensure that commitments are kept, leaders, expecting failure, seek to protect what they can. More time and energy are spent covering their tracks rather than identifying actions to drive execution performance. As the organization gradually becomes less self-critical and less intellectually honest about its shortcomings, execution gaps appear, and the capacity to perform, ultimately, the strategy-to-performance gap fosters a culture of underperformance, which is very difficult to reverse.

Go too fast, and people become discouraged and burn out. On the other hand, if you go too slow, the Sense of Urgency is lost, and complacency grows. If leadership selects a strategy that most people find unrealistic or stupid, people disengage. The trick is finding the balance that still challenges and motivates people but can also be achieved.

As organizations have become larger and more complex and diversified, we should adjust by spending more time building clarity and milestones into any strategic plan. The strategy includes both strategic thinking and tactical elements. If an organization sets the strategy as: "Company X will enter the ABC market and own a 30% share within five years," the assumptions to build the model that led to the strategy and targets must be clear, visible, and understood and the core competencies must be in place to support those activities.

If teams face aggressive target timelines that they didn't agree to, they will become demoralized and stop measuring themselves against the targets. Setting realistic expectations and avoiding unrealistic expectations will ensure that a plan that is well calculated and communicated by your team will be the one most likely achieved. Poor planning is ignoring their inputs. If you stand by your teams' side, support them, and refuse to bow to unrealistic expectations, then you will be set up for long-term success.

The final point on unrealistic expectations concerns the lean organization. It can be tempting to cut costs across the board to meet challenging targets. If new sales and products didn't materialize, then the next place reviewed is the operational and structure costs that hit the organization's bottom line or profitability. As we had learned about fit in the previous chapter, cutting costs that affect core competencies irreparably damages fit and turns a situation from bad to worse. What was once almost manageable is now a complete fiasco.

Executives often treat support units and corporate staff functions as discretionary cost centers focused on cost reduction rather than value addition. As a result, support units' strategies and operations do not align well with those of the company and business units they are supposed to support. Successful strategy execution requires that support units align their internal strategies to the company's overall strategy.

The trouble with short-minded thinking is that starving key capabilities doesn't help organizations build or maintain their core competencies. To the people closest to the work, this action feels like getting a leg chopped off and then being told to run faster... If you cut too deeply into fat, you destroy muscle that cannot be replaced or takes years to repair.

Failing to cut costs responsibly leaves an organization severely malnourished. A reputation takes a long time to earn and a few shitty actions to destroy. If people hear whispers that your company has no idea what it's doing or where it's going, potential employees will avoid it like the plague.

Good leaders are forthcoming in contesting timelines and expectations that run contrary to long-term results. We know in life that we cannot always sprint to our destinations. Sometimes we walk, sometimes we jog, sometimes we rest. Getting Shit Done on and Done on Time comes down to understanding how to work sustainably. Life is too short to burn ourselves out, and we have little to show for it.

Instead, organizations are better off spending more than anyone else does on what matters and then as little as possible on everything else. Pet projects, gone. Muddling IT projects, gone. Any functions that can be performed better and at a lower cost outside the organization, gone.

Instead of insisting on unrealistic targets, those who set strategy would be wise to pursue a sustainable competitive advantage and avoid cannibalization that could destroy the business. Do less, prioritize your objectives, concentrate your resources, and you'll accomplish more.

Please recognize that hope is not a strategy.

POOR PLANNING METHODOLOGIES

"Plans are worthless, but planning is everything."

-Dwight Eisenhower

"Man Plans, and God Laughs."

-Unknown

Despite our most careful and detailed planning efforts in life and work, we often find that our world is unpredictable. We wanted A to happen, but we got B. We tried our best, but an unforeseen obstacle jumped into our path. It happens constantly. It's a common adage to hear that the only constant in life IS change.

While we might have a well-planned course-of-action and timeline for reaching a destination, we must anticipate obstacles and prepare for the unknown to alter the course. Depending on your perspective, the best plans in life can be upended by unexpected changes, which could be either disappointing or exhilarating. On the other hand, fate can provide unanticipated good fortune or lesson learning experiences.

The first quote above, "Plans are worthless, but planning is everything," embodies the proactive planning theme's spirit. Planning for work to get done and done on time is about building flexibility and contingencies into our lives and work. As our plans must be flexible, we also need people who can be flexible.

However, as you may have noticed, a strategy is often poisoned at the planning level when it comes to many projects and becomes nowhere near realistic in the execution stage. If executives declare that they want a project completed by the end of the year, but the people below them know that reality is light-years away, there is no chance of an organization meeting this goal. After the two perceptions collide, deadlines are missed, and additional resources are hastily spent can a poorly planned project move forward. Often, in cases like these, too much damage has already been done to the project.

Before we can improve the problems around poor planning and re-planning, the first step is to acknowledge that traditional planning has a major flaw: Humans are awful at estimating the time to complete tasks- this is known as the Planning Fallacy.

PLANNING FALLACY

The term Planning Fallacy was first coined in 1977 by psychologists Daniel Kahneman and Amos Tversky. Kahneman later expanded on the original idea in his 2011 book *Thinking Fast and Slow*. In it, he argues that we can attribute two factors to estimation mistakes:

1) We fail to consider how long it's taken us to complete similar tasks in the past.
2) We assume that execution/projects won't encounter any complications/ delays. [18]

Since this chapter is about why Shit Doesn't Get Done on Time, we must look at all reasons to explain gaps in assumptions or actions. The Planning Fallacy is unique because it is a concept that applies to all people, in all environments, in all organizations. Each day, we are faced with countless opportunities to either plan our individual or team contributions for the day.

The problem is that too many of us fall short of our initial time estimates and don't adjust. Then we show up the next day and do it again. What we think should take five minutes actually takes thirty minutes- an hour becomes two hours- a day becomes three- a week becomes a month. The problem compounds at a faster rate when multiple people and teams are involved. Bottlenecks grow and become unmanageable.

Enough is enough.

We've all heard the famous Einstein quote that applies to this situation: "Insanity is doing the same thing over and over again and expecting different results." Assuming that we are all not insane, we must start working and thinking differently to address our tendency to underestimate the time required by tasks. Whether we are working on a significant strategy implementation or just trying to get our jobs done, relying on inaccurate estimates will delay progress and make it so that nothing gets done on time. Flawed assumptions for time requirements hurt not just your performance but the rest of the organization, as the compounded inaccuracies derail strategies with utterly unrealistic execution timelines.

Adopting measures to create accurate time estimates will give you and the people around you the confidence to move forward and better communicate deadlines and milestones. The Planning Fallacy's critical insight is that we must understand our inherent weaknesses in creating accurate time estimates and then determine a better approach to deal with the issue directly. Planning is useful but blindly following plans is stupid.

THE US CIVIL WAR ALMOST ENDED EARLY

Before we transition from describing poor planning factors to exploring remedies, a quick bit of history is worth adding here.

As we will learn throughout Getting Shit Done, leadership is a critical factor in successful strategy-execution. However, the Confederate forces lacked one at the battle of Bull Run (First Manassas).

Here's what happened:
The engagement began when about 35,000 Union troops marched from the federal capital in Washington, D.C., to strike a Confederate force of 20,000 along a small river known as Bull Run. As the Union forces loomed on the horizon, Confederate General P. G. T. Beauregard commanded the defense. From the start, his lack of leadership was evident. The battle plan and its language were vague. First, he would assemble available brigades into two groups. One was assigned to General T. H. Holmes and the other to an undesignated "second in command." General Holmes was not notified of either decision.

Beauregard issued orders at 6:00 A.M. that were either read or were interpreted by each of the affected officers as follows:
"(1) Longstreet should cross Bull Run and attack; (2) Ewell should await word to launch a diversion toward Centreville; (3) Holmes should support Ewell, though

orders had not reached Holmes; (4) David Jones should follow Ewell; (5) Cocke and N. G. Evans should stand to the last in defense of the left-center and left; and (6) Early should take position to support either Jones or Longstreet." [78]

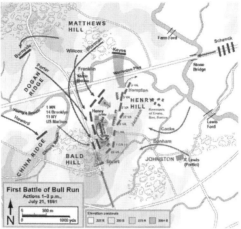

Image: Battle of Bull Run

Involved as all this was, it might have been simplified if it had been understood. It was not. Beauregard's attention was divided, and his aides were confused. His orders created confusion on Who should do What and by When he lost control of the widely spread brigades. A slow cannonade began, and enemy forces were advancing down Warrenton Pike toward Stone Bridge. Chaos shook the Confederate plan of action.

Confederate officers were baffled about what to do. The orders were overly detailed and vague at the same time- Such obscurities were paralyzing. Regardless of them, execution of the plan called for much staff work, prompt and complicated, which Beauregard's inexperienced staff, by no possibility, could perform. It seemed that nobody knew either the scope or recognized the conflict of orders at Beauregard's headquarters. Beauregard's elaborate plan of battle had been changed three times, with not one field general having a complete set of instructions.

Only the stubborn fighting of the first Southerners on the scene had saved the army from disaster. After fighting on the defensive for most of the day, the rebels rallied and were able to break the Union right flank, sending the Federals into a chaotic retreat towards Washington. The Confederate victory gave the South a surge of confidence and shocked many in the North, who realized the war would not be won as easily as they had hoped. Here is where the South and North diverged; Beauregard's performance was assessed, and he was quickly sacked. The South understood the importance of leadership and strategic planning. The North, as we will later learn, would take much longer to learn these lessons. [122]

The first civil war battle almost ended the war because Who has to do What and by When was poorly defined and understood. A poor planning approach caused chaos. The following sections of this chapter explain how leaders can remedy the problem.

CALCULATE YOUR UNDER ESTIMATION-RATIO (UER)

If you were to Google how to create more accurate time estimates, you'd likely see hundreds of pages returned for all sorts of sophisticated products, models, approaches, and frameworks. However, those who have worked in strategy-execution know that most "solutions" are just noise. In sharing a parallel with life, the best solutions are often free and straightforward, leading us to the Under-Estimation Ratio.

The idea of the UER is simple. For every instance where you communicate a time estimate to yourself or others, you need to apply a factor to multiply your initial or gut feeling for how long a task will take. If you find yourself constantly late or behind on your promises, the Under-Estimation Ratio will give you the time buffer you need to do the job well without feeling rushed or disappointing others. The best part of the Under-Estimation Ratio is that it's a practical tool that can be used at any time in just about every application imaginable.

Here's how it works:

1. The first step is to write down your gut feeling for how long something takes you to do.
2. Estimate a best-case, worst-case, and most likely scenario for task time and lay out the contributing factors in each.

3. Apply your gut estimate on by how much you typically underestimate the length of a task (a factor of 1.5-2x is common)
4. Ask others for their input to complete the same task.

For example, if your team needs to complete task A, you can combine your estimate and others' estimates to find the best estimate quickly. For task A, you estimate that it takes 1 hr to complete. Then, based on experience, knowing that work usually takes twice as long as initially predicted, you multiply the estimate by a factor of 2x. A second member of your team may estimate that the task should take 3 hrs, but they use a factor of 1.5x based on their experiences. Then, you weigh the two estimates together by averaging them out.

You: $1 \text{ hr} * 2 = 2 \text{ hrs}$
Team: $3 \text{ hrs} \times 1.5 = 4.5$
Final Estimate: (2 hrs + 4.5 hrs) /2 (number of estimates)
= 3.25 hrs to complete the task
Original Estimate w/o UER= (1 hr + 3 hrs)/2 = 2 hrs

The final estimate for task A becomes 3.25 hours. **Even though the calculation probably isn't exact, it doesn't matter- the point is to arrive at a solution that addresses your implicit bias to underestimate time.** Given the ambiguity of work and its often-changing nature, this calculation type will often serve as an accurate enough estimate for task and project completion time. As your team becomes more experienced in creating UER estimates, you can change the factor or alter the formula to suit your needs. However, the key is to use collaboration and a thought-out approach to reach an estimate, rather than just providing your gut feeling, which would have been 2 hrs. If you're unsure of where to start with your UER, think back to past projects or work that was similar in some way and use the actual completion time of that as your starting basis.

When determining the UER factor, some teams may be tempted to cheat the system and overestimate their factor to provide an additional safety buffer. However, if all parties added extra time to their estimates, the planning process would continue to fall apart by demonstrating poor communication.

To prevent overestimating, once all the time estimates are gathered, encourage your team to challenge the group's assessments.

Magically, the fluff will disappear.

The law of averages and social pressure will hone the numbers into a realistic forecast. Finally, the project total can be estimated and communicated. By going through this exercise at both the itemized detail level and high level of a project, teams can identify when strategy implementation targets are unrealistic.

MANAGING TIME

"If you say yes to everything, nothing will get done."
-Unknown

Without having a system or methodology to organize and complete our work, we often fall victim to inaction or, worse, busyness- which is where we spend a lot of time doing something, but nothing gets accomplished.

Most people begin their workday with at least eight hours available from start to finish. But when we look back before heading home, we cannot explain what got accomplished or where the time went. The problem is not that we are lazy or malicious with the use of our time. Instead, we easily fall victim to the fact that if we don't have a mindful system or consistent discipline in place, that time will begin to disappear into the void. A meeting here, a quick conversation there, emails, and then it's time to go home again- another day lost. To improve organizational efficacy in strategy-execution, all people must exhibit ownership over their time, priorities, and output.

The primary questions we should ask ourselves are:

1) How should we approach our work and priorities to maximize efficiency and effectiveness?

2) How do we create a large block of uninterrupted time in which we can focus intensely?

The key to effectively using your time at work is to understand where the time goes, understand what could change to reduce time spent on non-value-added activities, and build the discipline to your routine to safeguard against the time you do have.

FOCUS

"Things which matter most must never be at
the mercy of things which matter least."
-Johann Wolfgang von Goethe
"You don't get 100 percent results with
only 50 percent commitment."
- Anonymous
"The difference between successful people and
really successful people is that really successful
people say no to almost everything."
- Warren Buffett

Leaving time unguarded is like leaving the front door of your house open.

No, wait, it's much worse.

If someone entered your dwelling while you were away and stole your possessions, you could recover the value as your stuff would be insured. If you were home, you'd fight the thieves will all your strength and tenacity to protect your realm. You obviously don't want other people to walk away with the things you've worked hard to obtain and treasure.

Yet, with your time, your most precious asset, you leave it entirely unguarded.

Instead of fighting off intruders, you wave the interlopers in and allow them to take and take. You smile and wave as others place their burdens on you, borrowing and stealing time from you at will. What's wrong here? Why do we surrender ourselves to others' demands on our time and do what they want, when they want? Why do we allow someone else's top priority to become our top priority because of their poor planning?

Becoming more effective in strategy-execution needs to start with valuing and protecting our time.

At this very moment, take a quick mental count of how many people are capable of reaching and disrupting you? If I were to guess, the answer would probably be too many. As you try to relax and read this book, your ass will likely hang out in the wind waiting for the next call, text, email, or conversation to come by and smack it. Is it any wonder why you or the people around you struggle to execute when you can barely find time to do the essential tasks in a day effectively? As your attention is pulled in a million directions, how can you do quality work?

You simply can't.

If you allow yourself to exist in a state of perpetual distraction, your focus is weak, and your effectiveness is low. **It doesn't matter if you've mastered all the productivity hacks in the world; the faster you dig, the faster the world keeps flooding in.**

Image15- Digging

Put the shovel down.

Instead, time is protected and maximized by focusing relentlessly on getting one thing done at a time. Intentional bursts of focus will provide the most significant impact in the shortest amount of time. Effective and efficient execution means knowing with absolute clarity what things you should do to create the outcomes you want, what things you should say "NO" to, and then single-mindedly focusing on doing those things.

Focus, like strategy, requires clear trade-offs. Achieving focus requires removing distractions and prioritizing the critical elements of success.

Image 16- Critical Elements of Success

REMOVE DISTRACTIONS

Visualize the power of focus by reflecting on the effect of a magnifying glass on a leaf or piece of paper. When the glass is angled just right, the focused light will transform into a narrow yet powerful energy stream capable of setting the material on fire. Yet, without the magnifying glass, the sunlight is diffused and causes no effect on the other object- the energy serves only as a light source.

Image17- The Power of Focus

The same concept applies to how you concentrate your energy and focus at work. If you are thinking or working on a million things simultaneously, you will be ineffective everywhere. However, intense focus and eliminating distractions will make you infinitely more effective in achieving your goals.

To illustrate how damaging distractions are, Udemy released their Workplace Distraction Report—an extensive write-up on the distraction issue that confirmed that distractions are among the leading detractors of Getting Shit Done.

> "Noisy, interruption-prone offices make employees unmotivated, stressed, and frustrated. Employers could boost morale—and their bottom line— by giving people training for staying productive despite distractions." [34]

Not only do distractions hinder us from achieving our objectives, but they can also severely delay delivering the objectives that we do satisfy.

Far too many of us work in a seemingly endless stream of tasks, emails, notifications, and meetings throughout the day. Often multitasking in the process, we try and pursue the simultaneous completion of more and more every day. However, once the day is finished, we often have very little to show for our efforts other than being exhausted.

The problem is that we don't stop to think about what's going on and then change how we approach the work that we do. Despite being exhausted and ineffective the day before, we show up the very next day with the same game plan, ready for a mindless stream of tasks and distractions again.

Where did the time go? What happened?

The problem with time is that if we are not mindful of its allocation, we can get sucked into the vortex of what seems urgent. Distractions happen to be the worst offenders. These are the unwelcome intruders that interrupt you while you do the critical work and require you to divert your attention. With so much access to communication tools, it's not uncommon for someone's top priority to suddenly become our top priority just because they can reach us. At work, the emails, meeting invites, calls, texts, instant messages, birthday celebrations, and other impromptu conversations chip away at the time available to us.

If the work distractions aren't what gets us in trouble, our social lives are likely accomplices. I can almost guarantee that your cell phone is constantly beeping, buzzing, and chirping throughout the day. Oh, another funny cat picture- LOL- SMH- ROFL. You won't be surprised to learn that the average person has five active social media accounts and spends almost two hours on these networks every day. In an eight-hour workday, that can eat up nearly a quarter of your time! Even worse, our work environment's default parameters are not optimized to allow us to focus and get our work done. [23]

In trying to Get Shit Done on Time, we must take a stand and be more mindful of both the distractions from our personal and work lives. **Information overload is killing our brains.** The key to getting better results is doing a smaller quantity of tasks to produce higher-quality results. That requires a state of complete focus.

Consider the three questions below concerning how you approach work:

1. Are you set up for success with long stretches of uninterrupted time that allow you to slip into a state of maximum creativity and productivity?
2. Are you in an environment where distractions are at a minimum?
3. Do you know what you plan to accomplish in a specific day or timeframe, or do you throw your body into the surf to be churned by the waves of "urgent" emails, conversations, and meetings?

These questions answers are a definite no, no, & no for many of us people. Reading this sentence could be the first time that many are considering the importance of these factors. Fret not; there is hope on the matter.

One of the best books on purging distractions and maximizing focus and output is *Deep Work* by Cal Newport. Newport writes in-depth about why focus is such an essential asset in our professional and personal lives and what we can do to get more of it.

Whereas shallow work is the state of being distracted and working in interrupted bursts, Newport defines Deep Work as the:

> "Professional activities performed in a state of distraction-free concentration that pushes your cognitive capabilities to their limit. These efforts create new value, improve your skill, and are hard to replicate." [24]

Newport further goes on to explain:

> "To succeed, you have to produce the absolute best stuff you're capable of producing—a task that requires depth. The growing necessity of deep work is a crucial ability for anyone looking to move ahead in a globally competitive information economy... Deep work is so important that we might consider using business writer Eric Barker's phrasing as "the superpower of the 21st century." [24]

The thesis that Newport has defined for high-quality work produced is the following:

High-Quality Work Produced = (Time Spent) x (Intensity of Focus) [24]

To produce high-quality work consistently, we must allocate large blocks of time undistracted and focused. Unfortunately, the default for many of us is to have the distractions enabled, if not set to maximum volume.

Like any other resource that we'd treasure, the key to saving and maintaining our focus is to reduce and eliminate distractions from our environment actively. Both Cal Newport's books, *Deep Work* & *Digital Minimalism*, explore the issue of distractions and techniques to mitigate them and are highly recommended.

While there are various approaches and strategies, the best one you should choose to keep distractions at bay is, again... the one that works. What doesn't work is continuing to fall victim to distractions designed by companies to steal and keep our attention on their latest app or gadget. Avoiding distractions requires taking ownership of the tools and technologies used throughout the day in your personal and professional life.

The bottom line on distractions is that you will not get Shit Done or Done on Time if you can only focus 15 to 30 minutes at a time. **Each day we are gifted with time, and stealing it from us should be treated as a criminal act.** Create, experiment, and hone a system that allows you to take back ownership of your time to enhance your productivity.

THE 80/20 RULE

"Place all focus on the things that matter
most- and forget the rest."
-Unknown
"Out of every one hundred men, ten shouldn't even be there,
eighty are just targets, nine are the real fighters, and we are
lucky to have them, for they make the battle. Ah, but the
one, one is a warrior, and he will bring the others back."
- Heraclitus

The 80/20 rule or Pareto Principle is a fascinating and ever-present concept that defines much of our world. Whether you study business, science, or society, the Pareto Principle can be applied to all fields. The basic idea is that 20% of the inputs are responsible for 80% of the outputs. In business, 20% of our customers generate 80% of our profits; in the economy, 20% of people control 80% of the wealth, or 20% of employees generate 80% of a project's success in project management. The foundation of the Pareto Principle is rooted in the statistical and scientifically proven normal distribution of data.

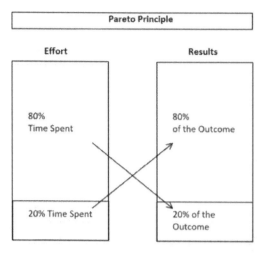

Image18- Pareto Principle

What the 80/20 rule means towards Getting Shit Done is that not all tasks are created equal, and all resources are limited. With this in mind, we must apply the available resources to the tasks or projects that will yield the most significant benefits. If we identify ten possible action courses, we need to identify the two that will generate substantial returns on time saved or costs reduced.

In a 2002 Harvard Business Review article, "Beware the Busy Manager," Heike Bruch and Sumantra Ghoshal suggested that only 10 percent of managers had the proper focus and energy to work on the stuff that matters. This means to leaders that The Pareto Principle should be a standard tool to become much more strategic with your time. You can't, and you shouldn't work on everything at the same time. You must work collaboratively with others to identify the 20% of things that matter to your organization. [53]

The 80/20 rule can be an eye-opening exercise to tease out what matters most by asking:
- What activity causes the most bottlenecks?
- Which customer causes the most time from customer service?

- Which activities do people spend most of their time working on?

Your ability to efficiently allocate time and resources can dramatically change the speed and impact you have in your organization. On the other side of the spectrum, you may find that many teams are currently ineffective because they spend far too long focused on low-value activities. Instead of working harder, focus primarily on the efforts that produce most of the results, and forgo the rest. That way, we have more time to focus on the most critical tasks. Stop saying "yes" to tasks that yield little or no result. To be most efficient with time, use the Pareto Principle to determine the 20% of activities to focus most or all of your time, effort, and resources on. 80% don't matter or can be handled by someone else on the value chain.

Perhaps Michael Porter may have said it best when he said, "The essence of strategy is choosing what not to do." The strategic question for leaders each day should be: If you're saying yes to this, what are you saying no to?

FLOW

In 1988, researcher Mihaly Csikszentmihalyi introduced the world to the concept of a state of ultra-focus that he called Flow. Whereas focus makes you fully productive, a flow state adds a multiplier effect to productivity. Csikszentmihalyi's research found that "Psychological Flow captures the positive mental state of being completely absorbed, focused, and involved in your activities at a certain point in time, as well as deriving enjoyment from being engaged in that activity."

Perhaps the Flow state, colloquially termed being 'in the zone,' is best described by one of the participants interviewed in the earliest stages of 'Flow research' with the following statement:

> "My mind isn't wandering. I am not thinking of something else. I am totally involved in what I am doing. My body feels good. I don't seem to hear anything. The world seems to be cut off from me. I am less aware of myself and my problems." [35]

Achieving focus and entering a flow state must involve eliminating anything that impedes us from dedicating 100% of our energy into a singular pursuit. **Being productive isn't working fast. It's working on what matters and doing that well.**

Focus – Distractions = Productivity= Excellence in Execution
Focus + Flow= Ultra productivity

A SENSE OF URGENCY

A Sense of Urgency is the feeling that there is a pressing need in an organization that requires everyone's immediate and focused attention to help overcome it.

The first obstacle in establishing a Sense of Urgency is ensuring every person in the organization assigns the same level of importance and prioritization to an objective. Effectively establishing a Sense of Urgency means that all involved clearly understand the shared problem and expectations. Once this happens, the whole organization can gear towards action and recognize that coordinated effort is the only means of survival.

However, keep in mind that the Sense of Urgency relates to strategy-execution efforts that are genuinely urgent/important and require a coordinated effort from multiple people and teams. With that comment, please note that cratering sales would be considered urgent, but a broken coffee machine would not.

�� **Sales= Urgent**

♉ ��**Coffee= Not Urgent**

The original pioneer on the Sense of Urgency, John Kotter, has this to say on the topic:

> "Far too often, managers think they have found the solution to this problem when they see lots of energetic activity: where people sometimes run from meeting to

meeting, preparing endless PowerPoint presentations; where people have agendas containing a long list of activities; where people seem willing to abandon the status quo; where people seem to have a great sense of urgency. But more often than not, this flurry of behavior is not driven by any underlying determination to move and win now. It's driven by pressures that create anxiety and anger. The frustrated boss screams, "execute." His employees scramble: sprinting, meeting, task-forcing, emailing — all of which create a howling wind of activity. But that's all it is, howling wind or, worse yet, a tornado that destroys much and builds nothing..."

The Sense of Urgency isn't excitable executives running around like 5-year-olds all hopped up from eating a whole bag of skittles. Go, go, go! Do, do, do! Stop, Go, Stop!

Instead, Kotter's article explains that the solution to the common complacency problem is to instill an organization-wide Sense of Urgency. Rather than chaos, a Sense of Urgency is a set of thoughts, feelings, and actions built around a purpose. Real urgency is valuable as it focuses the energy of many on critical issues versus scattershot agendas. The Sense of Urgency is built through a deep determination to win instead of fear of losing. [20]

The opposite of the Sense of Urgency that often dooms organizations is complacency. With complacency or false urgency, changes don't happen fast enough, smart enough, or efficiently enough.

From Kotter:

> "**Complacency is a feeling that a person has about his or her behavior, about what he or she needs to do or not do...**" **What makes complacency especially dangerous is that it is possible to see problems and yet be astonishingly complacent because you do not feel that the problems require changes in your actions.**"

A Sense of Urgency is demonstrated by a compulsive determination to do the right things in the right way to achieve strategic objectives at each organization level.

What the Sense of Urgency in motion looks like:
- Fast-moving decisions and initiatives that are focused on the critical issue.
- High levels of cooperation and teamwork on initiatives.
- A spirit of resilience—pushing to achieve more ambitious goals despite the obstacles.
- Measurable progress on objectives accomplished every day.
- Enthusiasm for purging low-value activities.

To demonstrate leadership in your organization in achieving a Sense of Urgency, focus on communicating with energy and passion. Speaking with power and purpose is vital towards inspiring others to act. As a leader, if you communicate with low energy, you can expect to have excuses back on the next deadline instead of results. People can tell whether someone is just echoing the "flavor of the month" change effort or whether they are working on something that they genuinely believe in-shoot for the latter.

Energy + Conviction + Purpose = Sense of Urgency

Keep in mind, though, that everything cannot be urgent. As the protagonist learned in the story of "The Boy Who Cried Wolf," declaring every issue urgent, large or small, neuters the effect altogether. Work with others to understand the genuine and urgent issues facing the business and then communicate well to ensure that each person knows **Who has to do What and by When**. Done right, the Sense of Urgency can give the people in your organization the superhuman energy and focus required to overcome almost any challenge.

If you're still skeptical whether the Sense of Urgency is yet another made-up management term, consider that when things seemed most desperate during World War II, the US and their allies embraced the Sense of Urgency to innovate with astonishing speed and intention.

As the second World War loomed, Britain noticed the Nazi military buildup and the increasing dominance of the Luftwaffe. As a response, in 1930, the British Air Ministry issued a challenge to the aircraft industry to upgrade the technology of their air force by formulating a new fighter that called for a machine capable of 250 mph and armed with four machine guns.

Although every British aircraft company studied the proposal, no changes resulted-The changes were regarded as impossible to fulfill. There was no threat.

However, once war became a reality, a change occurred. Britain would build more planes and better planes more sustainably and economically than their German adversaries. The Spitfire and Hurricane won the Battle of Britain and denied the enemy an opportunity to invade the island as a result. [146]

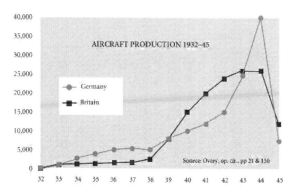

Image: The Art of Action

Without some of these innovations, the war might have ended differently or lasted longer. [48]

Jet engine

Penicillin

Synthetic rubber and oil

Pressurized cabins

Synthetic fiber

Aerosol Can

Freeze-dried coffee

Ballpoint pens

Nuclear energy

Enigma Machine

Radar

Real threats + Energized and focused people = Real results

THE EISENHOWER BOX

What is important is seldom urgent, and what is urgent is seldom important.
- Dwight Eisenhower

Yet another helpful tool for managing time is the Eisenhower Box.

The purpose of the Eisenhower box is to put a system in place to perform a triage assessment on the tasks at hand by breaking them down into four distinct groups which are:

1. **Urgent-Important:**
   - For the first group of Urgent-Important tasks, the action to take is to complete the job now.
   - This could be a question from your boss or customer where your input is required, and there will be repercussions for not acting.

2. **Not Urgent- Important:**
   - For the second group of Not Urgent tasks-Important, the action to take is to schedule a time to complete it with time blocking.
   - This could be a colleague's request to work on a presentation by the end of the month. You are required to act but can decide when (within limits).

3. Not Important- Urgent:

- For the third group of Not Important- Urgent tasks, the action is to delegate the tasks.
- This could be a request from a colleague for a report that was shared last month. You can ask them to locate and share the file. Action is required, but it can be done by someone else.

4. Not Important- Not Urgent:

- For the fourth group of Not Important- Not Urgent, the action is to eliminate it.
- These could be newsletter emails, a chain email on a distant topic, spam, etc.
- There is no penalty for non-action.

Every task you have falls into 1 of 4 quadrants, and we answer the questions of:

1. What should be completed immediately?

2. What can be completed in a few days?

3. What can be archived or deleted?

4. What can someone else do?

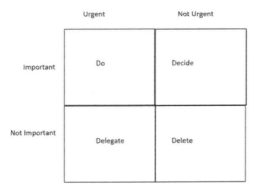

Image19- Eisenhower Box

The Eisenhower Box methodology forces you to decide what they will do for each task and then act.

For example, if there are twenty emails in your inbox, each

item can be quickly triaged and sorted out. The corresponding action or inaction can be planned, taken, or delegated. Fourteen emails might be deleted, one email might be urgent and require action, three emails might be scheduled for later in the week, and then the final two emails might be delegated to another person. A mindful system is much better than treating all twenty emails in the same way. For the emails that aren't important, note that ignoring them isn't an option, either.

This Eisenhower Box is a valuable tool to avoid falling victim to the trap of being overwhelmed with information overload. In the end, it doesn't matter so much as what system you use to manage time, so much that you choose a system. Choosing to use no system to manage your time turns you into a victim instead of an owner.

TAKEAWAYS

- We don't get stuff done because we have an inadequate system of planning and replanning.

- We don't get stuff done on time because we are too distracted.

- Commit to Being 100% present on critical work. Don't allow yourself to become distracted, and allow circumstances to dictate how your time is spent.

- Planning is essential, but the goal isn't to create a plan. The goal is to develop and sustain a clear, concise, and clear focus, effectively execute it, and do it repeatedly.

- Stop strategic planning. Commit to strategic management.

- Focus on the essential matters. As you begin each day, ask what important matters are being put aside for trivial matters that seem urgent. Focus on your essential contribution first, not around the edges of trivial matters.

- Stay un-distracted. Turn off all "push" notifications on your phone and computer.

- Managing time creates the freedom to work creatively by prioritizing and systemizing communication to increase the available time. Take control of time and focus. Review the tasks that must be completed and complete those that add to the organization's most significant impact. Guard your time like it is the most important asset you have.

REFLECTION

1. What tasks or work are you doing that can or should be delegated to someone else so that you have more time to focus on the big picture and keep the pieces aligned and moving?

2. Do you allow distractions to enter your world and steal your time? Review your phone and computer settings and set them so that you decide when to engage with them.

3. Are you clear in setting expectations with others and respecting their expectations?

4. Are you focusing on the 20% of things that matter or everything with the same level of prioritization?

5. Are you effectively motivating others by instilling a Sense of Urgency?

6. When plans or strategies are communicated, do you take the time to understand the assumptions and targets and then the available resources to determine if a strategy is feasible?

CHAPTER 3

Push Down the Power: Autonomy, Empowerment, and Decentralization

**"To have good soldiers, a nation must always be at war."
– Napoleon Bonaparte** [15]

There is never just one strategy.

The overall key to profitability is finding a unique strategy and fit among core activities facilitated by operational excellence. However, to make fit possible and close the strategy-execution gap, many other moving pieces must be considered.

THE BIG WHAT AND LITTLE WHATS

In addition to an overall direction supporting a primary strategy known as the Big What, a successful strategy also requires several secondary strategies that must be autonomously and simultaneously set and executed by people at all levels of the organization. The Little Whats gives people the time and practice they need to turn from amateurs to true professionals. These are known as the Little Whats.

The Big What= The primary strategy/vision
The Little Whats= Supporting competencies/execution

Think back to the last time you had attended a professional sporting event. As you sat in your seat and watched the pregame workout, did you see the home coach stroll onto the field, turn to face the fans in the stands, and then start selecting players for the match from the crowd?

"You with the painted chest, you with the beer helmet and cape, andddddd you with the full-body horse costume, come on down and suit up; it's game time, boys."

Image20- The Athlete

No?

Professional sports teams came across a novel idea a couple of decades ago: to play and win at the elite level, they need teams made up of professionals who live and breathe for the sport. Day in and day out, the professional athletes who make up sports teams hold themselves to absolute excellence standards. If they aren't better than they were the day before, that means that they are that much closer to being on the way out.

Better, faster, stronger is a way of life.

The strategy is clear to each professional on a team; win the next play, the next 15 minutes, the next game, and then the season. The competencies are built around teamwork and moving a ball around to score the most points and allow the least from the opposing teams. Professional athletes understand that showing up on game day is not enough to succeed. Before game day ever rolls around, an athlete has endured countless years filled with strength and agility workouts, training sessions, skirmishes, and game film study.

But wait... When we look at our organizations, why is the typical approach to finding and developing the big game's talent completely different?

Instead, organizations must change the way that they communicate shared team expectations. As technology and turbulent economic conditions require organizations to adjust on the fly to achieve their strategy, they need experienced and driven experts and professionals committed to demonstrating excellence in anything that touches them.

Too often, it's amateur-hour out here.

That leads us to The Little Whats. The Little Whats is all about setting expectations around continuously developing our execution muscles by improving the organization's work all the time. By demanding excellence and autonomy from each person in each function throughout the organization, the critical core competencies can be built, maintained, and improved.

The traditional strategy approach has been represented by a top-down hierarchical perspective of a single annual target. The mad scramble that takes place in the following twelve months is usually a big disappointment. And then we do it all over again.

Nilofer Merchant in the *New How* hit on this similar theme:
> "The pervasive idea that the high - level "where" of strategy is all that matters leaves many strategies incomplete. By establishing and maintaining a culture that stuffs the "how" under execution."

She notes that "executives unwittingly create a stubborn, persistent structural gap within the organizational entity that seriously undermines their ability to succeed." The statement explains that bucketing responsibilities incorrectly leads to the strategy-execution gap. [69]

If people aren't primed and ready to handle small challenges, they will be ill-equipped to handle the bigger ones. If people wait all year without working out or stretching, they won't be in any position to win a championship.

Instead, there's a better approach.

The Little Whats has two elements to it:

1. People should be empowered to do work within their zone of influence as efficiently, error-free, and cost-effective as possible and be rewarded for it.

2. Company leadership should have minimal/no decision-making power in how people accomplish their tasks in their areas of expertise.

The Little Whats builds trust throughout the organization to drive engagement, empowerment, and mastery in employees. As the people closest to the work identify obstacles, rather than saying, "That is not my problem," they should say, "Let's do something about it."

As professionals and teams self-organize, they will put themselves on a path toward setting objectives that look a lot like mini-strategies and then learning what they must do to reach the desired outcomes. People will discover and share new technology, tools, or frameworks that meet the organization's objectives with freedom and trust. The key is to direct their own learning experience, share knowledge, and craft a role they are proud to represent.

Alternatively, what kills the Little Whats is when an employee raises an issue, and policy dictates that all initiatives must go to the executive team, who then says, "No, I don't have time for that. Don't touch a thing." In this case, employees become disengaged and never develop the skills necessary to help carry out the Big What, or primary strategy, later on. The Little Whats does not rely on a hierarchy to ask permission to make the right changes. Instead, people work collaboratively with their team to recognize what needs to be done; and then they do it. The boss should have no say or very little decision-making authority over work tactics unless people are headed in the wrong direction

The Little Whats is continuous improvement and ownership with a license to kill.

Leadership who understands the Little Whats communicates, "Do whatever it takes to solve the problems around you to develop organizational competencies, and I'll do everything in my power to support you." Like the professional athletes found on sports teams, the Little Whats helps their employees become true professionals striving to reach peak performance.

The Little Whats provides the training field and practices necessary to handle the more significant obstacles, faster pace, and larger scale of the Big What when it comes around again.

A fully developed strategy creation process that includes both the Big What and Little Whats facilitates accomplished objectives and an engaged team. Pairing the Big What and Little Whats helps identify the critical interdependent tasks, identifies the weak spots, and champions making required changes; all of which are vital to obtaining buy-in and accountability.

Ultimately, employees are the ones who improve the processes and run the projects, programs, and initiatives required by the strategy. They must understand the strategy if they are to link their day-to-day operations with the overall objectives. Employees cannot implement a strategy they are not aware of, do not understand, or are excluded from.

To close the strategy-execution gap, getting the big things right means getting the small things right first.

DON'T DICTATE HOW

"The Road to Hell is Paved with Good Intentions."
-Unknown

"If someone has accepted responsibility, and agreed upon a goal, then we should get out of his or her way and let the individual do it. None of us should wait to be told what to do or how to do it. Micromanagement kills initiative, judgment, and creativity."

-David Maister [8]

"Ok, open the spreadsheet. Good. Click on the sheet to the far left. No, no, the other one. Ok. Go to cell A24 and look in the formula bar. Now write this in for the formula…"

Have you ever had something like the dialogue above happen to you? Most of us have, and it's profoundly insulting and degrading. When we work with co-workers or managers who feel that they must control How work is done by setting strict rules and processes, we can feel our initiative immediately drain away, our frustration grows, and progress grinds to a halt. Perhaps the worst situation is when someone thinks they have a better How in mind than you do, but their awareness and technical skills are light-years away from reality.

All of us can surely rattle off countless "dumb rules" or similar situations that we've encountered in the workplace. As the saying goes, "The Road to Hell is Paved with Good Intentions." Nobody creates rules that are dumb on purpose or out of maliciousness. Whoever created the rule must undoubtedly believe they are doing so for the benefit of the organization.

The problem is that rules send the message that you cannot be trusted to do the right thing by their nature. Rules are, well, rules — not to be broken. Rules, policies, and procedures are implemented to minimize risk (primarily financial loss), not maximize output and excellence in execution. **Because managers can't be everywhere and can't watch everyone, they decide to implement rules to protect against their definition of wasteful spending, inefficiencies, and low quality.**

Inevitably, though, rules disempower workers in the spirit of protecting against meager chances of risk or loss: innovation, creativity, and risk-taking plunge. Morale drops as there is no sense of ownership due to micromanagement.

From the HBR article, "Making Your Strategy Work on the Frontline," Nilofer Merchant, author of *The New How: Creating Business Solutions Through Collaborative Strategy*, had this to say on the subject:

> "Leaders often over-define the specifics of how the strategy should be executed," says Merchant. Leaders and managers can set the vision and targets, but they shouldn't dictate how employees achieve them. More specificity may make frontline employees' jobs more manageable, but it eliminates their need to think and diminishes their sense of ownership. "Let people figure out how to accomplish the goal best," says Merchant. Ask your frontline employees; how can we achieve our objectives? This question will likely uncover new approaches to execution that senior management hadn't thought of." [39]

Frankly, for organizations committed to becoming best-in-class in strategy execution, **there are no positive micromanagement aspects. Micromanagement is a telling sign of fear and immaturity in leaders**. Micromanagement behaviors are usually driven by overwhelmed or underperforming managers' insecurities, so they do whatever they can to keep employees under the illusion of control and cast themselves as an authority.

Sometimes this pattern stems from the manager's feeling of being the only one who knows how to get the job done right, making it necessary to provide detailed direction. Unfortunately, micromanagement often has the opposite effect of what managers intend. It reduces people's empowerment and motivation to get things done and reduces their ability to make decisions and take prompt action.

Micromanagement includes excessive reporting of progress, watching someone perform their job, requiring that employees ask permission to communicate with others, and otherwise acting as a bottleneck of information. It's the antithesis of Getting Shit Done. Even more, micromanagement has been cited many times as one of the leading causes of great employees quitting their jobs. It diminishes people's self-confidence, saps their initiative, and stifles their ability to think for themselves. **Micromanagement is a dangerous recipe for screwing things up. Micromanagers rarely know as much about what needs to be done or How it needs to be done as the people they're harassing do, the ones who do the work.**

Leading for execution is not about micromanaging, or being "hands-on," or disempowering people. Instead, it's about active involvement- doing the things leaders should be doing in the first place. Fortunately, there is a better way to make sure that Shit gets done- Commander's Intent. [3]

BUILD A STRONG COMMANDER'S INTENT

"As in war, so in life."
-Robert Greene

"Calm is contagious."
-US Navy Seals

"Just tell me what to do! How do I get the job done? I just don't understand."

Is there any worse combination of words in the universe? What comes to mind for you when you read the line above?

Weak? Helpless? Lost? Incompetent? Robot? Whatever responses you come up with, one sure thing is that it will not be flattering. The line reeks of desperation and helplessness from the person who utters it, and it invokes dread in those on the receiving end.

When leaders hear this line from someone in their organization, it is often very late in the game. The person pleading for step-by-step instructions had been previously deemed capable of handling their shit; instead, they're now whimpering like a toddler. Now, another person in the organization must stop what they are doing to hold this person's hand so that two people do one's job. Even worse, this is a sign of failed management.

There are no quick fixes for this sort of breakdown. Time, effort, and energy must be spent to assess whether the person can be rehabilitated or whether they must leave and then be replaced, which requires even more pressure on the scarce resources available—an ugly scenario for sure. Often, in building talent pools, autonomy isn't a trait that is screened for. Hiring managers ask about a candidate's favorite movie, which superhero power they'd choose, what school they went to, but they never get to the points that matter:

1. **Are you capable and willing to figure out how to complete a task or project without being told what to do?**

2. **Can you share multiple examples from your past and current roles in demonstrating mastery, drive, and above-average competency?**

If the answer is "yes," go to question two.
If "No," thanks for your time.

This approach might seem harsh, but the stakes are too high to play it any differently. It's better to be straightforward and honest with expectations than to become later embroiled in a mess, which becomes a lose-lose scenario for both parties.

When it comes to Execution, there are three personalities:

1. The one who waits for you to tell them What to do and How to do it.

2. The one who studies What needs to be done and How it should be done, memorizes it, and follows the steps, rules, and procedures.

3. The one who doesn't want or need a plan; they drive the culture, they set the pace in the Sense of Urgency, and they want all possible options open to them at all times.

Number three is what you're looking for.

As a leader, you want to build teams of people who move so fluidly and with such ease through obstacles that your biggest challenge becomes staying out of their way so that you don't slow them down. This is where Commander's Intent comes into the picture.

Commander's Intent describes how the commander envisions the battlefield at the mission's conclusion. It answers the question, "What does success look like?"

As you can imagine, in the heat of a battle, it becomes challenging for an officer to dictate to each soldier what they must do, where they need to go, and how they need to execute each action and objective. Instead, soldiers are directed and trained to understand the mission's intent, and they are empowered to take almost any path (within guidelines) necessary to reach the objective(s).

Commander's Intent fully recognizes the chaos, lack of complete information, changes in the enemy situation, and other relevant factors that may make a plan either entirely or partially obsolete when it is executed.

Success then depends on trained, confident, and engaged military personnel, or in our case, employees to fill in all the gaps in-between. Employees must understand the strategy and when they have to deviate to ensure the Commander's Intent is accomplished.

Commander's Intent is built around envisioning the end goal first.

DEFINE THE END GOAL

"In theory, there is no difference between theory and practice. But, in practice, there is."
-Jan L. A. van de Snepscheut

Similar to the concept of situational awareness, the military has found great value in developing people who can observe their surroundings and use their training to turn anything and everything into an advantage.

In his book, *Team of Teams*, retired four-star US Army General Stanley McChrystal, who oversaw Iraq's invasion in 2001-2003, explained his experiences leading a large and modern force in a complex urban war environment.

McChrystal initially assumed command of the Joint Special Operations Command (JSOC) Task Force and found a culture operating through silos, information hoarding, and lack of trust. Through trial and error, McCrystal found that the military's best way to succeed and reach its objectives was to define the end goal by facilitating a "shared consciousness." Among his team and partnering organizations, this strategy enabled decision-making to be performed at the lowest levels, which he calls empowered execution.

In the following quote from the book, McCrystal explains his methodology in this way:

"Shared consciousness demanded the adoption of extreme transparency throughout our force and with our partner forces. We needed transparency that provided every team with an unobstructed, constantly up-to-date view of the rest of the organization. The hierarchical command - and - control structure, where information flowed up, and decisions flowed down, made sense when the world moved at a slower pace." [41]

In an interview after his retirement, McChrystal explained that the traditional system of information flowing up the organization and decisions flowing back down was no longer sufficient. He said: "To defeat an enemy like Al Qaeda in Iraq, we had to beat them at their own game — the phrase it takes a network to defeat a network became our mantra." [41]

McChrystal wound up succeeding by making the end goal clear: defeat Al-Qaeda. Anything that anyone could offer in pursuit of this objective was welcomed and listened to. The military found that granting more freedom instead of new processes or management structures led to improved decision-making, making it much easier to hold people accountable. They created transparency through widespread information sharing and pushed decision-making down to the lowest levels.

Commander's Intent= Ownership= Accountability= Victory

Fortunately, many of us are not engaged in combat with our enemy (even though the competition sometimes makes it feel that way). However, the lessons developed from a military system can be broadly applied to modern business strategy and execution challenges.

Commander's Intent teaches us that the ultimate goal is to help people make good decisions. Ownership and accountability are core tenets that make for a happier & more agile workforce high in engagement and deadly in execution. Establishing Commander's Intent in your organization focuses on people and empowers them. Instead of using rules, Commanders Intent is communicated through guidelines. [19]

Guidelines are educational and broadcast the message of:

> **"Here's what we think is right in most circumstances but do what's in the best interest of the company. Do the right thing."**

An excerpt from the US Army's website concludes Commander's Intent very well:

> "Leaders should think about the end state and output of everything they do. Every action in command should have Commander's Intent behind it with an identified task, purpose, critical factors, and vision of the end state. Commanders and leaders at all levels to consider the end state and output first. You cannot give intent without knowing where you want to end up. Ultimately, leading through mission command not only sets conditions for a positive work environment but also allows others to grow and develop and drives the organization in a collective direction." [52]

Commander's Intent broadcasts this message: "We have problem X, and I'm trusting you to solve it." It doesn't matter, within means, which paths are explored or ultimately taken to solve a problem, so long as the problem is solved.

The best solution wins- period.

DECENTRALIZATION GETS SHIT DONE

"The greatest leader is not necessarily the one who does the greatest things. They are the one that gets the people to do the greatest things."
-Ronald Reagan

Rules and hierarchies are often put in place to mitigate the risk of facing alternative courses of action. While harmless as a concept, they are often disastrous in practice and result in having the opposite outcome desired. Each degree of rules and regulations increases the rigidity and inflexibility of an organization. Additional resources and structures are put into place just to support the previous level of structure.

Although there are several adverse outcomes, the worst effect is that a strict hierarchy or formalization level discourages new ways of doing things and reinforces the status quo. Workers feel as though their voices and opinions go unheard. An autocratic approach limits employees' control and decision-making freedom, resulting in less creativity and collaboration between employees and managers. Often, inward-looking management and the bureaucratic process can leave their people with little opportunity to flourish.

If you reflect on the example of Napoleon's victories shared later in this chapter, a core principle for the Grande Armée was, "If you see the enemy, start shooting." A French soldier would think, "easy enough," and start shooting. But for the soldiers in an opposing army, this scenario was so much more complicated. The enemy soldier would think, "Am I supposed to be here? What if we start shooting too soon, too late? What if we're outnumbered? Should I pull back or pull forward? Am I being flanked?"

The strict hierarchy imposed on the enemy soldiers dictated that neither the officers nor soldiers should handle the situation alone. Instead, the information had to flow upwards through several layers of the organization to the general, where he would make the call and then pass the information back on down through the channel. However, the problem is that the soldiers were likely long gone and fleeing for their lives by the time the information transfer was complete. A rigid, hierarchical process where decisions must go up the chain of command is not practical.

Hierarchies are ineffective when a decision-maker does not understand the current situation's context to make the best choice. The solution, of course, is decentralization. Rather than adding rules, authority levels, and signoffs, decentralization reduces and removes bottlenecks.

When determining who should have decision-making authority, consider two questions:

1. Who has visibility into what each person on your team does each day in their role? Task-by-task, minute-by-minute. Who has complete visibility into what they do, how they do it, the obstacles that they face, and the opportunities present?

2. Who has the most situational awareness and technical expertise on the productivity, organizational, and IT systems and tools available today?

As a quick example from history to illustrate the point, during the Battle of Britain, Fighter Command flying practices and official tactics made it easy for the Germans to down planes. The official formation consisted of a "Vic" of three planes flying in a tight V-shape. This formation forced two of the three pilots to concentrate on maintaining formation rather than the sky.

The Germans dubbed the vics as "Idiotenreihen" ("rows of idiots").

Initiative-taking was not just discouraged but forbidden. The 1938 directive for Fighter Command Attacks contains this sentence:
"Squadron Commanders are not to practice forms of attack other than those laid down unless they have been specially authorized by Headquarters, Fighter Command."

The order from HQ effectively meant that some degree of insubordination would be a requirement of survival. [146] Lives were lost because those who did the work could not define the most practical means of work.

More likely than not, the approach of trusting a few people to make all the decisions will lead to an over-reliance on stale technologies and processes that are familiar and already in place. Instead, trusting a larger group of people closest to the work to find the best solution allows more ideas to come to the table. It will enable more perspectives and the opportunity to weigh the pros and cons of each concept. The pressure will also be removed from the organization's leadership to have all the answers as people are trusted to put the best answers forward.

As each person is empowered to solve the problems closest to themselves, they develop mastery and excellence, which translates directly into the ability to execute on both the Little Whats and the Big What. **In most cases, it is the person closest to the work with the best and most timely information and is best suited to act.** They just need to be equipped with the tools, training, and guidance to identify the best solution to overcome each obstacle. Without having people on the ground who can overcome unforeseen obstacles, progress will drag to a grinding halt.

Decentralization makes strategy-execution possible.

NAPOLEON CONQUERS EUROPE

"If someone has accepted responsibility and agreed upon a goal, then we should get out of his or her way and let the individual do it. None of us should wait to be told what to do or how to do it. Micromanagement kills initiative, judgment, and creativity."
-David Maister [8]

A leaders' role is to lead and facilitate the discussion that pulls together the best information possible to set the strategy and coordinate the execution. They must rely on those closest to the actual work to be effective on both ends of the model.

Pushing decision-making authority to the lowest levels possible allows for speed and flexibility in executing a strategy. While it is easy to postulate such principles, it is essential to look back in time to see how our world has been changed by those who lived through these virtues.

Our next stop is 18th Century Europe.

Image21- Napoleon Crossing the Alps- Public domain. 1800 Jacques-Louis David

1789 to 1799 saw significant turmoil in Europe as a political upheaval wave embroiled the continent. Inspired by the US Revolution's success, the French people decided to take similar action against their government. King Louis XVI was the last king of France (1774–92), as both he and his wife, Marie Antoinette, were executed for treason by guillotine in 1793.

What began as a noble pursuit of liberty soon led to a bloody impasse in the country. In this period, known as "The Terror," heads rolled as political opponents sought to ostracize their foes and take power for themselves. Through this confusion, a series of weak governments came and went from power. Adding to the calamity, France's foes declared war on the republic to suppress anti-royalist ideas and expand their territory.

It was in this messy period of revolution and war where Napoleon Bonaparte rose to fame.

Napoleon, originally from Corsica, benefited from his family's aristocratic status, which allowed him to pursue a military education on the continent. As his training came to an end, the revolution broke out. During this time, Napoleon witnessed many of his peers and contemporaries forced to either flee the country in exile or face execution; and it is here that Napoleon sensed an opportunity. By being in the right place at the right time and now facing much less competition, Napoleon seized the opportunity to create a legacy, and that led France to a brief hegemony over the region.

Having first played a vital role in the French Revolution (1789–99), where he demonstrated military leadership protecting the new government from further upheaval, he was rewarded for his efforts and was named the Commander in Chief of the French Army in Italy. Through this initial campaign, Napoleon earned the acclaim and experience that would later see him serve as France's first consul (1799–1804) and later serve as France's first emperor (1804–14/15). [15]

Image22- Napoleon's Defense - El 13 Vendimiario,San Roque 1795
Litografía de Denis-Auguste Raffet (1804-1860). Public Domain

So, what happened? What did Napoleon do differently from opposing generals?

Napoleon succeeded because he formed a system of excellent communication based on decentralization. In battle after battle, Napoleon emerged victoriously, often defeating armies more than twice his size by pushing authority to make decisions to the lowest levels possible.

In the Napoleon biography, author Andrew Roberts describes the specific factors in Napoleon's military strategy that helped him rise above his competition.

Napoleon's forces benefited from:

1) The Corps System enabled troops to move and form up quickly.

2) Focusing large numbers of soldiers directly on his enemies' weaknesses.

3) Granting autonomy to all levels of generals and soldiers.

Before a battle, Napoleon did not know precisely where his enemy was, but he had a general idea in many battles. Napoleon split his force into smaller pieces to find the enemy and sent them into the opposing armies' direction. Napoleon would separate and maneuver his forces so that the enemy army would also break themselves into several pieces to pursue after him. Once Napoleon found an enemy position, he would reform and concentrate his army's power in the enemy's center to overwhelm and destroy his opponents.

The instruction given to every general and soldier was the same; when a French army met the enemy, soldiers were instructed to start shooting. As nearby friendly corps units heard the battle begin, they would change course and ride straight towards the sound of gunfire to align in mass against the opposing forces. The concentration of forces would break the enemy and send them fleeing from the field.

In contrast, Napoleon's enemies were organized with an outdated organizational system and a hierarchical chain of command structure that did not allow autotomy. If an enemy soldier observed the French forces approaching, the message had to be passed between several officers' layers to get to the general (often drunk). The general then decided what to do, and that information had to flow back down through officer layers to reach the army. While Napoleon's soldiers were focused on fighting and bringing reinforcements to the field, the opposing army was often frozen with indecision. The enemy regiment was already routing before a decision could come back.

Napoleon's communication strategy bore fruits to many successes; Prussia, Austria, and Russia all suffered staggering defeats against the French.

Lather- Rinse- Repeat.

It would take the better part of twenty years before Napoleons' enemies wised up to what was going on and then make the necessary reforms to mirror the French military system.

Since Napoleon's time, military forces worldwide have embraced the guiding principle that autonomy must belong to the lowest level person facing the problem. Napoleon was instrumental in setting a precedent in defining that the leaders' job is not to make decisions. Instead, it is to prepare their people to make the best decisions in a wide-ranging set of circumstances. The success of your units to adapt and overcome unknown challenges is how leaders are assessed.

In the book, Extreme Ownership, Ex-Seal Jocko Willink explains how the Navy Seals operates under the autonomy principle:

> "Leaders must delegate the planning process down the chain as much as possible to key subordinate leaders. Team leaders within the greater team and frontline, tactical-level leaders must have ownership of their overall plan and mission tasks. Team participation — even from

the most junior personnel — is critical in developing bold, innovative solutions to problem sets. Giving the frontline troops ownership of even a small piece of the plan gives them buy-in, helps them understand the reasons behind the plan and better enables them to believe in the mission, which translates to far more effective implementation and execution on the ground. [19]

In the Navy Seals, senior leaders supervise the entire planning process but are careful not to get bogged down in the details. They maintain a higher-level perspective to ensure compliance with strategic objectives. Leaders look to identify gaps or weaknesses in a plan. Next, senior leaders' role is to communicate the plan in a simple, clear, and concise format, so participants do not experience information overload. They understand that if frontline troops are unclear about the plan and are too intimidated to ask questions, the team's ability to execute the plan radically decreases. Thus, leaders must ask their troops questions, encourage interaction, and ensure their teams understand the plan. [19]

Delegating autonomy has become the basis of modern military philosophy. If it worked for Napoleon and works for the US Seals today, there's a pretty good chance that autonomy will also help you and your organization. What began as a military institution should be borrowed and applied anywhere possible in our lives and work situations.

WHY THE BOTTOM-UP APPROACH WORKS

"Every Rule takes away the opportunity to make a choice."
-Bill Erickson

With the bottom-up approach, managers communicate the overall strategic goals and milestones to their teams, and the individual team members then use their expertise to design the How. As team members find that they need to collaborate, bounce ideas off the wall, talk through challenges, or complete their tasks, that information and progress filter back up to the managers organically.

There are several key benefits to the bottom-up approach:

1. **Engaged employees:** Team members will feel more involved because they know their input makes a difference.

    b)   More **creativity** because employees have more space to bounce ideas off one another and solve problems collectively.

    c)   Improved **motivation** because employees have more control over their working day and company-wide decisions.

    d)   More **trust** as decisions, schedules, and budgets

are transparent. Those closest to the work have the authority to act and feel.

2. **Better scheduling:** Goals are formed around employees' requirements, which makes tasks more achievable and practical. Better collaboration and communication see that every employee participates in the decision-making process.

Delegating decision-making authority down to the people who face the challenges is essential and highly effective for several reasons.

1. Speed and flexibility help organizations stay on track.

2. Autonomy removes the complexity and demands an ownership mindset.

When people are granted autonomy, they feel empowered in their roles and responsible for their actions and their organization's success. Instead of roadblocks demoralizing the workforce, workers are energized by the opportunity to demonstrate their mastery in overcoming challenges. Autonomy leads to a feeling of higher engagement that helps address what people want most from their careers; a sense of purpose and meaning - they want to find work that they love and be rewarded for doing a good job.

Establishing an autonomous environment requires creating a space where your team feels "safe" communicating with you. In a work environment where trust and open communication exist, you will find fewer mistakes and misunderstandings, faster execution, and innovation. For the most part, you need some hierarchy because you don't want chaos, but you want just enough hierarchy — the minimal viable bureaucracy.

Even more encouraging, decades of research into professional engagement and effectiveness at work clearly show the correlation and effect of autonomy and an engaged workforce:

- Engaged employees report feeling focused and intensely involved in the work they do.
- They are enthusiastic and have a sense of urgency.
- Engaged behavior is persistent, proactive, and adaptive in ways that expand job roles as necessary. Engaged employees go beyond job descriptions in service delivery or innovation.

A recent poll published by Gallup in their annual report on employee engagement noted that as of 2019, worker engagement in the US is at a new record high. In explaining the improved performance, Gallup pointed out that organizations with **"high-development cultures educate managers on new ways of managing -- moving from a culture of "boss" to "coach" are leading the way forward.** Or, in translation, by giving people the autonomy to demonstrate ownership in how work is done, they are doing more of it and having a better time doing it. [22]

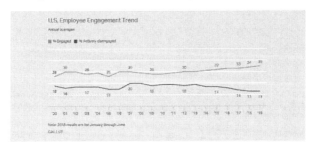

Image23- Employee Engagement

Both research and history have proven that the best organizations have a leadership philosophy that encourages their teams to solve problems locally rather than top-down commands. Best-in-class organizations focus their training and development programs on building local managers' and teams' capability to solve issues independently with an ownership and continuous improvement mindset.

However, a word of caution is that using the bottom-up

method prolongs the initial planning stage because you involve more people in the decision-making processes. When speed is critical, a combination of intuition and the facts available is required to decide the next move forward. **The key is to be on the lookout for bottlenecks, new and old, and be ruthless in removing them.**

Just keep in mind that finding the decentralization approach that fits your organization's Ways of Working is unique to you. Some organizations may find that their people have decreased output when faced with few rules or procedures to fall back on during the strategy execution. Organizations must resist becoming too formalized and rigid. They must also balance not becoming too informal and chaotic, as well.

KEEPING SCORE

"If a strategy is to be achieved, it must be publicly tracked, measured, and monitored. If you are trying to lose weight, you must get on the scales regularly."
-David Maister [8]

"What Gets Measured, Gets Done."
-Unknown

Think about the last time you watched a casual game of pickup basketball between friends in the park or a gym. The attitude is relaxed; people are joking around; people are half sprinting to make plays; people launch unlikely half-court shots; the amount of energy applied to each play varies wildly- it's fun.

Now, think about what happens to that same game and that same group of players when you add a live scoreboard to the match. Something switches "on" inside these players. Suddenly, the game is no longer a game but rather a test of their competitive spirit and skill. Each player tightens their game, collaboration increases, and each team strives at their best to win and reach their goal.

What made all the difference between the two games was that we started keeping score in the second scenario- that's the power of measuring our progress through goals. Naturally, humans are competitive creatures, and we are driven to compare ourselves to others and seek to improve what we do and how we do it.

Just as no world-class athlete would want to play a sport

without keeping score, metrics help world-class organizations know how well they're doing. **Without measuring progress, people have difficulty staying accountable.** It is impossible to measure the development of the strategy-execution without concrete objectives and milestones. Managing and improving strategy-execution then becomes extremely difficult, if not impossible. You keep score if you want to win.

Measuring progress towards outcomes helps us understand exactly where we are in terms of progress, and it also motivates us to do our best work, embrace growth, and then become better. If you want to get Shit Done and Get Shit Done on Time, you will need a system in place to measure and track outcomes and progress.

Key Performance Indicators (KPI)

In business, the measurements toward goals are generally known as KPIs or Key Performance Indicators. Ideally, these metrics should be the targets that individuals, teams, or organizations must achieve to reach their goals.

Companies enhance their process improvements and progress on strategy-execution by designing and deploying local operational dashboards. These dashboards are collections of key indicators that provide feedback on performance and enable executives, managers, and employees to drill deeper into the outputs and processes.

While sometimes a KPI will measure increases in sales, the number of new products launched, or time or cost savings in processes, the aim is to assess progress towards the What. Companies will use KPIs at multiple levels of the organization to evaluate their success at reaching strategic targets. High-level KPIs may focus on the business's overall performance, while low-level KPIs may focus on processes in departments such as sales, marketing, HR, support, and others.

However, for a KPI to be meaningful, several factors must be present:

1. The KPI needs to be well understood.
2. The KPI needs to be impacted by the group that it measures.
3. The KPI needs to be maintained and visible in a central location.

For example, if your annual bonus was tied to the ability to reduce your team's workload by 10% or 100 hours through automation, the chances are that you'd want to focus your energy on meeting this goal. However, if you didn't understand how the 100-hour target was calculated, or if you could not change the targeted processes, or that it was up to you to self-report the savings, then suddenly, this scenario would become an ineffective KPI.

If you don't understand your KPI, you will take no action towards it. If KPIs are outside of your realm, you will ignore them. If the organization does not have a centralized and systematic process for collecting the data behind the KPI and tracking its progress, you may be able to cheat the system and report that you saved 500 hours. The trick to set and manage KPIs is to ensure they are fair and challenging but not unrealistic.

A KPI is only as valuable as the action it inspires. Too often, organizations may be tempted to blindly adopt industry-recognized KPIs and wonder why KPI doesn't reflect their own business and fails to affect any positive change.

To identify the right KPIs to use, start by asking these questions:

- What is your desired outcome?
- Why does this outcome matter?
- How are you going to measure progress?

- Who is responsible for the business outcome?
- How will you know you've achieved your outcome?
- How often will you review progress towards the outcome?
- How can you influence the outcome?

The following section below will go into the details to set an optimal KPI that is SMART.

SMART

The key to designing a good KPI is to follow the SMART principle.

SMART stands for Specific, Measurable, Attainable, Relevant, Time-bound if you're unfamiliar with the acronym. In other words:

- Is your objective **S**pecific?
- Can you **M**easure progress towards that goal?
- Is the goal realistically **A**ttainable?
- How **R**elevant is the goal for your organization?
- What is the **T**ime-frame for achieving this goal?

Specific:

A KPI is a measurable way to highlight a particular factor that matters and focuses on its energy and resources. Alternatively, if an organization creates multiple weak KPIs, you will set a target that fails to address a business outcome. At best, you're working towards a goal that has no impact on your organization. At worst, it will result in your business wasting time, money, and other resources that would have best been directed elsewhere. A good KPI focuses on getting one thing right. Make sure you have a clear definition.

Measurable:

A KPI needs to be measurable and for the calculations behind it to be transparent and easily understood. A minimal amount of time and resources should be spent on tracking these results as an initiative. An organization should implement simple processes to measure critical success factors.

Example: Increase new product offerings by 10%.

The base is 100, and 10% is ten more. At year-end, it will be easy enough to count the individual new products successfully launched. Arriving at this measurement should be an objective exercise that is pain-free.

There is a quote from Regan that fits perfectly here: "Trust, but verify." If someone claims to have met a metric, walk through the validation of the results with them in detail. Ask, "Where can I witness the savings? Point them out for me." Every organization has seen a continuous improvement team with an Excel spreadsheet full of improvement projects displaying impressive yet entirely imaginary savings that can't be identified. Not in a general ledger account, not in a cost center, not in the P&L- these savings exist only in thin air.

Attainable:

A KPI target that is too high risks your team quitting before starting, while setting a target too low will be demoralizing. A good KPI should consider the team's skills and the available time to commit to reaching their goal.

Example: Increase new product offerings by 10% in 1 year.

30% could simply be impossible, but 2% is too easy.

While stretch goals can help people break old rules and do things better, they're worse than useless if they're unrealistic or if the people who must meet them aren't given a chance to debate beforehand and take ownership of them. Arbitrary deadlines negatively impact processes and cause people to panic about an impending deadline rather than concentrate on the work that needs to be accomplished. Often, managers randomly pick deadlines without knowing how long processes will take and destroy the opportunity to drive the team forward with metrics.

Relevant:

A KPI needs to be intimately connected with a critical business objective. A good KPI is not just another business objective but rather something integral to the organization's success. Setting a KPI to increase the number of internal processes documented would not be advisable as sales plummet due to increased competition.

Example: Increase new product offerings by 10% in the most profitable sales channel under competition pressure.

Measure what matters.

Time-Bound:

A KPI needs to have some sort of time limit set and agreed upon by participants. Just as a game has a point where the whistle blows and play stops, business metrics must have firm deadlines. The effect is that as different timelines come closer to the present, people will change the urgency and speed at which they work to meet the challenge.

Saying that we need to create 10% more new products (when you get around to it) just doesn't have the same impact as saying that we need to have 10% more new products by the end of Q3.

Example: Increase new product offerings by 10% by the end of the third quarter. Setting March as the goal would be demoralizing, while December may be too lenient since this team has experience launching new products under pressure.

If you don't measure it, you can't manage it- keeping score keeps progress on track. Great KPIs can be vital to achieving strategy-execution, just as mismanaged KPIs can demoralize an entire organization.

Great KPIs express something strategic about what your organization is trying to do. They are a way to create a scoreboard that the organization can rally behind. To remain engaged, the team should always know if they are winning or not. People play more seriously when they are keeping score. Without knowing the score, individuals will be distracted by the next thing that seems most urgent. **A great KPI essentially says, "If we can get these few things right, we will beat our competitors."**

There is no perfect KPI or set of KPIs; what works is what works.

On KPI's, Larry Bossidy famously stated:

> "When I see companies that don't execute, the chances are that they don't measure, don't reward, and don't promote people who know how to get things done." Simple, straightforward. And he's probably right. "You don't need a lot of complex theory or employee surveys... First, you tell people clearly what results you're looking for. Then you discuss how to get those results... Then you reward people for producing the results." [3]

When setting KPIs, include a balanced mix of forward-looking and backward-looking (leading and lagging) measures. Lagging measures tell us how we did, and leading measures tell us how we are doing. If you focus too heavily on lagging measures, we may be slow to react and respond to challenges that must be addressed quickly. If you focus too heavily on leading measures, you will not gauge your long-term performance. The key takeaway is that great KPIs must be more than just arbitrary numbers.

Tail-less Rat Metrics

If you want a memorable example of KPI's that produced the

opposite effect, Google the Hanoi Rat Massacre of 1902. Here, the French created a program intended to reduce the number of rats in the sewers below the city's French section.

Plan A created a bounty program with local contractors to kill and present whole rats to the administration office for payment. The poor native residents were eager to assist the French, and the bloodshed began swiftly. In the last week of April 1902, 7,985 rats were killed—and that was just the beginning. By the end of the month, the numbers were even more astounding. On May 30 alone, 15,041 rats met their end. In June, daily counts topped 10,000, and on June 21, the number was 20,112.

Eventually, the colonists realized that they failed to dent the rat population even with a small army of paid rat killers. And the French also recognized that counting and disposing of rat bodies was an unpleasant exercise.

So, the French proceeded to Plan B, offering any enterprising civilian the opportunity to get in on the hunt. A bounty was set —one cent per rat—and all you had to do to claim it was present a rat's tail to the municipal offices.

But then things got weird; citizens were spotting more rats than ever all-around town: alive and healthy, running around without their tails.

It turned out the rat hunters realized that amputating a live animal's tail was more profitable than killing it. A healthy rat, minus a tail, could breed and create many more rats with those valuable tails. Worse yet, there were also reports that some foreign rats from Vietnam were being smuggled into the city. The final straw for the program was that health inspectors discovered pop-up farming operations dedicated to breeding rats in the countryside on the outskirts of Hanoi. [56]

Rats proliferated in Hanoi's sewer system. INTERNET ARCHIVE/PUBLIC DOMAIN

Image24- Rat

Don't create KPIs that lead to tail-less rats.

Be sure that KPIs can tell you where to focus energy and resources to obtain the most significant benefit. If you expect excellence, it's up to you to set the standards for results and performance. Measure each task or goal and place it in a realistic timeline. Give people a clear target, and they'll work to reach it—and maybe even surpass it.

CONDUCT STATUS MEETINGS

The best way to ensure progress is being made and that people are meeting their targets is to perform regular check-ins at different organizations' levels. If time is not set aside and built into a routine, something else will fill the void. Structure and consistency with monitoring, assessing, and discussing progress and milestones keep execution on track.

The best status meetings are short and sweet.

For 10-15 minutes at the beginning of each day, gather the people you work with, ask what they're working on, what they expect to complete. Then, the following day, ask for a progress update on what was worked on. If the planned tasks were completed, note that down, and ask what is up next on today's schedule. If work was not completed, probe further to fully understand the root cause so that obstacles can be removed or additional resources assigned. This simple exercise will establish behaviors around good communication and accountability. When progress is expected and commitments are set forth, good things happen.

For more significant execution milestones, conduct premortem reviews during these discussions. Go through an exercise where you say, "We are now three months down the line- and we failed. What happened?"

As potential issues and problems are identified, find ways to acknowledge the pitfalls in the planning process. If failure is anticipated, the path can be adapted.

Takeaways

- The Little Whats involves people tying the Big What to their area of expertise.

- The Little Whats builds the core competencies and expertise to achieve the Big What.

- If departments, functions, and processes aren't optimized, fit between the Big What and Little What will not be found, and the strategy-execution gap will persist.

- Use the concept of Commander's Intent and decentralization to communicate the objectives and build cohesion.

- Concentrate on ways to get better and better. Work to close the gap between where you are and where you need and want to be. In that regard, achieving executional excellence is much like developing your core capabilities.

- Work in a concerted way to strategically upgrade the underlying skills, values, processes, and structures underlying capabilities that drive performance. That's the heart of where execution occurs, and that's how organizations excel.

- Set expectations that are SMART; Specific, Measurable, Attainable, Realistic, and Measurable.

- Focus people around one rule," Do the right thing." Then, give people the tools and support they need to identify and solve the problems. Give your people every opportunity and tool to meet those goals. Get out of their way. Focus on simplistic and common-sense approaches towards aligning others and measuring results. Good judgment is hard to define and harder still to acquire. Judgment can be improved with practice.

- Establish a strong Commander's Intent within the organization and a bottom-up hierarchy. Decentralization & empowerment are essential for helping others develop critical thinking skills and mastery. Hire the best people and empower them. Don't tell people what they can and can't do; tell them to do the right thing, and let them decide for themselves. If employees need a step-by-step explanation of the right thing, they're not the right person. Teach them how to be responsible and accountable for executing their own to develop a creative, diligent, and solution-oriented team because they don't need to wait for approval from you to implement when they're ready.

- Focus on realistic levels of errors and priorities. For example, the Pareto principle has proven that 20% of inputs control 80% of the outputs. Act on what matters.
- Getting things done through others is a fundamental leadership skill.

Reflection

Translate the strategy into the everyday.

- Is the strategy clearly communicated throughout the organization?

- Does each person understand what they must do each day to help the strategy succeed?

- Are there defined programs (for example, specific new technologies, new processes, or training programs) to further build the critical capabilities your organization needs to win with its strategy?

- Are ownership, accountability, and excellence a requirement for working at your organization? How is this level of mastery evaluated, measured, and improved upon?

- Has your organization taken steps to flatten the hierarchical management structure? Minimizing traditional organizational charts and special perks, like corner offices and fancy furniture, allows employees to feel more respected. If they feel equal, they will interact with leaders and become role models for better communication, recognition, and mentoring.

- Does your organization promote individuals based on initiative or tenure? Time spent in a role at an organization does not qualify you as an owner. Hiring, recognition, and promotion must foster a culture of focus on job results, commitment, and growth. This is the crucial leveler between the multiple age generations in the workplace.

CHAPTER 4

Ownership & Accountability

"How you do anything is how you do everything."

-Unknown

**"If people are not prepared to be held accountable
for what they do, it is unlikely that
they will achieve much."**

-David Maister [8]

**"If you can smile when things go wrong,
you have someone in mind to blame."**

-Unknown

Whose Job Is It, Anyway?

There are four people named Everybody, Somebody, Anybody, and Nobody who have been asked to take the lead in implementing strategy at their organization. In their pursuit to Get Shit Done, they must first define responsibility. The interaction goes a bit like this:

> There was an important job to be done, and Everybody was sure that Somebody would do it.

> Anybody could have done it, but Nobody did it.

> Somebody got angry about that because it was Everybody's job.

> Everybody thought Anybody could

do it, but Nobody realized that Everybody wouldn't do it.

It ended up that Everybody blamed Somebody when Nobody did what Anybody could have.

In the story, because no one took responsibility, nothing got accomplished. It works the same way if everyone is assigned an owner: because everyone owns it, no one owns it (too many cooks in the kitchen). In many organizations, companies, and teams, we see a situation like the one above play out every day.

Frustrating.

Even at the most basic level of getting work done, breakdowns in communication, expectations, and action happen continuously- they seem to be the norm rather than the exception. If you were to build a sturdy structure, you would start by building a solid base that can support an enterprise as it grows and shifts. The problem with too much of the existing practices around work in general or strategy execution today is that everyone is waiting for someone else to provide leadership and guidance. In building terms, the foundation is shaky.

To fix the circular logic and finger-pointing and finally solve the puzzle, each person needs to take ownership and work at a level of professionalism that maximizes groups' potential, not detracts.

If we are to understand how to Get Shit Done, it is crucial to first look back to history to understand the factors and driving forces that have led to our current situation.

PHYSICAL OWNERSHIP

A Short History

Ownership has been a pillar in the order of the world's economy and society for generations. And for a good reason. Ownership matters a great deal to those who possess the world's productive assets and wealth. It also matters to those who do not because ownership determines control in life. Control of things and assets has been used to obtain the lifestyle or comforts we want for ourselves and our families. Throughout history, power and wealth have been accumulated by controlling and exploiting physical assets as the means of production.

For thousands of years, humans have experimented with various forms of ownership in society to find a system that works. Slavery, mercantilism, communism, and feudal kingdoms have all come and gone. Each time, the definition of what is owned and who can own it has shifted to a more democratic base. With each iteration forward, we've tried to adjust the formula to create a more equitable, productive, and safe society. However, some flaws would eventually create an upheaval among the people with many of the early systems. The old owners and leaders would be expelled, and a new system would eventually be put into place.

Perhaps the most significant iteration in physical ownership was the Industrial Revolution that led humankind to its newest system, capitalism. The Industrial Revolution was first ignited by James Watt (1736–1819), a Scottish instrument-maker who, in 1776, designed an engine in which burning coal produced steam, which drove a piston assisted by a partial vacuum. This steam engine was then applied to manufacturing at the outset of the 19th century, and soon it was clear that using machines to spin the cotton thread on spindles and weave it into cloth on looms was practical and very productive. One steam engine could power many spindles and looms that previously took several human laborers on each. Costs decreased, efficiency increased, and innovation spread.

To scale the innovations, wealthy groups of investors provided the financial backing to build and operate these new and capital-intensive factories, while the working classes provided the labor. As the factories came online and produced more yield than ever with fewer resources, the rest of the world took notice, and pockets of investors in countries far and wide raced to compete.

In a relatively short period, industrialization spread to many other industries and countries. The driving idea was that economies of scale could be optimized, whereas costs could be fixed while an enterprise's profits were not. Once a certain fixed-cost threshold was met, the potential profits could be potentially unlimited. The system was attractive because capitalists could earn substantial returns on their assets and protect those returns through legal reassurances. On the other hand, workers now had access to a reliable and consistent stream of earnings and enhanced access to goods and services they could not previously afford. Increased production and lower costs for many items saw life at home and in the broader economy improve.

Over time, capitalism has continued to evolve and develop into a complex economic system driven by the idea that all property forms, such as land, factories, media, and transportation systems, are owned by private businesses and corporations. In a "free market" of competition, businesses compete with each other for market share.

For many in the working class, the availability of work provided by capitalism has been a boon. Previously, people would perhaps operate a family farm, pursue odd jobs, or learn a craft; good opportunities were too few and far between for many. Factories were attractive in that they provided consistent work at a steady wage.

From the Cambridge Journal of Regions, Economy, and Society, Volume 5, Issue 3, November 2012, Pages 307–324:

> "Capitalism and Ownership are historically and theoretically intertwined. Ownership stands at the crux of social science's conceptualizations of class and political-

economic theorizing about capitalism's nature. In class analysis, ownership was traditionally taken to mean ownership and control over the means of production, a position which separated the bourgeoisie from the proletariat, as it did feudal landowners and peasants, and slave-owners and slaves. This classical Marxist position undergirded the development of social sciences, providing a common framework for how scholars have theorized, on the one hand, capitalism as an economic system, and on the other hand, class as both a social and economic category." [6]

However, capitalism has drawn criticism. Critics of capitalism argue that it concentrates power in the hands of a minority capitalist class that exists by exploiting the majority working class and their labor; prioritizes profit over social good, natural resources, and the environment; and is an engine of inequality, corruption, and economic instabilities. Those with ownership rights to industries can and did conspire to keep out competition, collude on pricing, and cheat their workers by cutting corners on safety and wage protections. It seems that the rich have only become richer while the workers remained workers. Over time, the gap in terms of class wealth has only grown.

By 1900, for example, America was responsible for one-half of the world's manufacturing. Still, only 45% of American workers lived above the poverty line, while the top 10% owned more than three-fourths of the nation's wealth.

For monied capitalists, the new system was fantastic.

While it is true that workers who did not find industrial work appealing could pursue other pursuits such as self-employment through farming, many of these pursuits lacked the economies of scale to be profitable. In the end, you, as a worker, could choose either reliable industrial work with no control or ownership, or you could make your living as a sustenance farmer where you have complete control but little assurance of long-term viability. (In 1900, 41% of the workforce was employed in agriculture and supported 7 million farms. Whereas in 2000, 1.9% of the population were employed in agriculture and 2 million farms).

Image25- Greed- https://www.loc.gov/resource/cph.3g03108/, public domain

The Principles of Scientific Management

As the 19th and 20th centuries rolled by, the capitalistic system became more sophisticated and stratified in wealth and power. A few wealthy investors owned the market share of entire industries. Names such as John Rockefeller, Andrew Carnegie, J.P. Morgan, the DuPont's, and Henry Ford were industrial heavyweights.

To maintain control of their assets and further increase productivity, the study of management was initiated in 1911 by Frederick Winslow Taylor, whose classic, *The Principles of Scientific Management,* would enshrine a new way of thinking, organizing work, and treating workers.

Taylor's most famous example was his analysis of the productivity of a Dutchman called Henry Noll, whom he called Schmidt, loading pig iron from a field into a railroad car at the Bethlehem Steelworks. Taylor concluded that each loader could handle between 47 and 48 tons per day instead of the 12.5 tons they were averaging. Under Taylor's instruction, a man with a stopwatch stood next to Noll, telling him when to pick up a pig iron, when to walk, and when to rest, and gave Noll the incentive of being able to earn $1.85 a day instead of $1.15 if he did as he was told.

Schmidt complied in this experiment, and Taylor increased productivity in the short term. Businesspeople across the world rejoiced. For the next 50 years, Taylor and his disciples would advance and advocate this school of thinking and managing organizations.

Taylor's approach to management (Taylorism) rests on three premises:

1) In principle, it is possible to know all you must know to plan what to do.

2) Planners and doers should be separated.

3) "There is but one right way."

Taylor recommended the rigorous separation of planning and execution. "Thus, all the planning which under the old system was done by the workman," he wrote, "must of necessity be done by the management following the laws of science ... in most cases, one type of man is needed to plan and an entirely different type to execute the work." [54]

Taylor argued that flaws in each work process could be scientifically solved through improved management methods. Taylor believed that an empirical, data-driven approach to the design of work would yield significant productivity gains. The best way to increase labor productivity was to optimize how the work was done at the lowest level by professional managers.

To Taylor, workers were either too dumb or uninterested in maximizing their labor. The best solution was that a manager/planner would step in and dictate in painful detail what to do, how to do it, and when to do it. The manager's job was to design work so that it was systematic, task-based, and predictable. (Think of an assembly line worker, a cart pusher, or a meat processor. One worker wasn't too different from the next, and a replacement was readily available—a commodity.)

Describing his methods with pride, Taylor proclaimed that:

1. "The work of every workman is fully planned out by management at least one day in advance, and

2. Each man receives in most cases complete written instructions, describing in detail the task which he is to accomplish." [54]

The impact that Taylor had in the world of capitalism and physical ownership was enormous. His work helped solidify the idea that an enterprise is a machine controlled by a system of gears and inputs. Taylor was confident that careful engineering by skilled managers could predetermine the quality and quantity of the outputs.

As part of this machine, the workers now had an exact role; they were expected to work as automatons. Not only would workers not benefit materially from the fruits of production, but they also expected to surrender all free will as terms of employment. Employees could not own anything in a physical or psychological sense.

Image26- Automaton

In Taylor's system, workers were incentivized to follow orders and eventually hoped to be provided for in retirement with a pension. Ambitious workers could potentially rise to become managers or directors. But each of these people had a boss-the person who owned the physical enterprise. No matter how good someone was at their job, they could not start their competing firm. To the individual, working harder than the stated quota did not add more money to their pocket.

The world of physical ownership entrenched those in power so that wealth dictated who remained at the top of society. Workers could now afford comforts such as homes, cars and provide food for their families, but owning the means of production remained out of reach. While capitalism benefited much of the world and raised the standard of living, there was a clear cap to what the every-man could do with ambition, ability, and vision. For many, there was little advantage or incentive to working harder or differently.

The worker in an economy dominated by physical ownership thinks:

1) **"I'm here to work my schedule, clock out, and go home."**

2) **"What do I need to do not to get fired?"**

MENTAL OWNERSHIP

"There are two kinds of people in the world, those who make things happen and those who complain about what's happening."

-Unknown

A Short History

Taylor was so influential on Western management practices that his work has been partially credited with the enormous productivity gains of the 21st century. His book, The Principles of Scientific Management, was voted the most influential management book of the 20th century by the Academy of Management in 2001. Yes, for much of the last 110 years, organizations have been happily applying top-down command-oriented management and embracing his mandate to "know exactly what you want men to do, and then seeing that they do it in the best and cheapest way." For capitalists who valued physical property and absolute control of their enterprises, Taylor was a prophet.

In early capitalism and through much of the 20th century, Taylorism worked well enough; the factory owner told you what to do, how to do it, and when to do it- And you followed the orders. Work was more straightforward in many early industrial environments; less professional judgment was required to complete each task. Work could be measured using cut-and-dry metrics such as units produced and quotas met. If you weren't willing to comply, plenty of other people would happily take your job.

It was not until the 1980s that some writers suggested that Taylorism is an outdated idea. In management theory and business schools, modern business organizations were beginning to be viewed not as machines but as organisms that contained people with brains and hands and legs—not automatons.

Summarized, the shortcomings of Taylorism are the following:

1. Managers do not have the resources or technical understanding to dictate how work is done. At the same time, work complexity has increased. The less stable and dynamic the environment is, the more that specialist skills and expertise matter. The individual initiative-taking and problem-solving skills required to overcome these obstacles are discouraged.

2. The system dehumanizes work and disengages workforces. People value freedom, autonomy, and growth. Worker experimentation and decision-making lead to higher levels of knowledge and skill, and these activities are discouraged.

3. The surging ranks of middle managers created a barrier between an organization, its goals, and its means for achieving those goals (workers). Managers were the unilateral interface between owners and workers. Poor communication and misalignment occur more often.

In sum, Taylorism equated to compliance for money. Workers sold their time and presence for money but not their mind, soul, and commitment.

Clearly, Scientific Management has limitations. While managers found that they could compel workers to Get Shit Done in the short term, they failed to understand how to build a sustainable solution.

In our modern era, the nature and design of work have dramatically changed over the last one hundred plus years since Taylor. Computers are ubiquitous, the economy represents one of services instead of physical goods, globalization has accelerated, and work activities can occur anywhere (not just the office).

According to the law of accelerating returns, the pace of technological progress—especially information technology—speeds up exponentially over time because there is a joint force driving it forward. New technologies come and go, and we need people who can monitor and apply the most helpful technology to old problems.

The change doesn't stop there. To meet the growing demands of work, workers have become much more educated and much more skilled. Each year, a new record is set on the percentage of the population that earns at least a primary college education; advanced degrees are the norm for many. With the growth in education, new asset classes—knowledge and skills—have been owned and monetized. Once a luxury of the elite, college education has become much more common to support the changing economy.

From the Cambridge Journal of Regions, Economy, and Society, Volume 5, Issue 3, November 2012, Pages 307–324:

> "Ordinary people want financial security, opportunity, and liberty that come with owning assets. A homeowner has more security and hence more liberty than a renter. A person with a pension or a savings account can look forward more confidently to retirement than one who must keep working out of financial necessity. An individual who "owns" skills and educational qualifications is better bolstered against economic change and more able to get ahead financially than one who is unskilled. Throughout

American history, foreign observers have commented on the connection between the democratic self-confidence of Americans and the comparatively large proportion who owned homes, farms, or businesses, as well as the relatively high degree of education of the typical American." [6]

Today, workers are no longer seen as commodities in our new world but are heralded as a company's most valuable assets. As the economy has shifted from producing goods and things to producing services, the need for highly skilled and knowledgeable workers has increased. Work has fundamentally changed, so how we work needs to change as well. Complexity in organizational structures, changes in employment practices, the globalization of business, among other trends, all make incorporating autonomy in organizational practices increasingly critical. Organizations these days are under increasing pressure to achieve more, move faster, and adapt to change more quickly.

No longer does work involve pushing carts and acting as the machine but rather designing the work and controlling machines. Rather than telling people what they must do, companies and owners need to rely on the workers to tell them how to run the business and achieve their objectives.

Taylorism only leads to a significant lack of accountability in employees. Standing testament to the organizational fractures in management, in Gallup's State of the American Workplace report, only about one-third of employees feel like owners. Another 50 percent are "job renters," bringing only their hands but not their hearts to work. They show up every day, keep a low profile, and collect a paycheck. The remainder is actively disengaged and passively block or actively sabotage forward progress. Twenty-one percent of respondents stated that unaccountable employees make up 30 to 50 percent of their workforce.

Work has changed. Workers have changed. But the puzzling

aspect is that management of organizations and workers has remained... constant?

So, if Taylorism and Physical Ownership are in decline, the next question that comes is, well... what replaces them?

To maximize human potential, we need a system that can meet these requirements:

- We need a genuinely human management system, one that makes room for our bodies and spirits alongside our intellect and skills. A system that acknowledges the human needs for community, growth, security, engagement, and opportunity.

- Care and attention for what work feels and means to us, not just for what we can do at work and how—a system where we can be fully human, with all our contradictions and quirks.

- Management that halts the relentless pursuit of efficiency and alignment to appease shareholders.

It is precisely here that a system of Mental Ownership fills the void.

Ownership Definition

Mental Ownership is defined as the feeling that something is one's own even though they may or may not have legal ownership right to that object. It's all about leading from any position and in any direction. Ownership involves self-direction, self-motivation, a driving desire within oneself to get better. It exists in an excuse-free environment where individuals commit to mastering the fundamentals without being directed. Mental Ownership is about taking the initiative. It's an understanding that taking action is your responsibility, not someone else's.

"It can be felt toward physical targets such as homes

and cars, and toward non-physical targets, including one's ideas and work. This feeling of possessiveness encompasses multiple dimensions, including control, autonomy, and physical ownership. It results in the target (e.g., a team member's work) being considered an extension of the self." [55]

Simply put, Mental Ownership is that feeling that "this is mine." Mental Ownership is a feeling of having a stake in it due to commitment and contribution. Owners feel they have skin in the game and benefit from improved effort and results, rather than just getting blamed for problems.

Taking ownership of a project doesn't necessarily mean that you're managing a project. It means that you should care about the outcome to the extent that you would care if you were the organization's owner. You should feel obligated to the organization's results and act on items wherever and whenever required to achieve those results.

Mental Ownership is demonstrated in the following ways:

1. Taking the initiative to bring about positive results.

2. Not waiting for others to act and caring about the outcome as much as the company owner would.

3. Being accountable for your actions' results - that are of the highest quality and delivered promptly.

4. Showing others that you can always be trusted to do the right thing.

The recipe for creating an ecosystem where Mental Ownership thrives involves the following factors:

1) A sense of job control,

2) Essential knowledge of the job, and

3) Investment of self in the job and organization.

Work in a Mental Ownership system is not focused on the

short term but the long-term perspective. It holds the promise that by self-directing and producing higher results, we can increase our career trajectories, build trust, and gain increased exposure to opportunities. The Ownership Mentality manifests when individuals feel that they can be held accountable for the target of ownership and have the right to keep others accountable for their actions around it.

Mental Ownership is the state of mind where you feel fully in charge and do not provide excuses (or blame anyone else) for what needs to be done. It also means understanding, learning, and challenging rather than mindlessly following instructions.

Mental Ownership works because it combines the factors of employee engagement and ties them to outcomes. Suppose a worker can understand and willingly commit to the end goal of a task or the grand strategy and feels that they are part-owner of the outputs. In that case, they will ensure that their work and the people around them meet the highest quality and efficiency standards. Rather than begrudgingly complying with managers' wishes, Mental Ownership leads to teams that can self-organize and self-direct their efforts to produce the maximum output sustainably. As workers become more skilled, they will have the ability to share in the equity/profits and/or build equity in their personal brand.

Mental Ownership means you will deliver as promised, respecting any deadlines or budget constraints mandated to you. It also means you're forthcoming when, as sometimes happens, you couldn't deliver. Being accountable means that you are honest and proactive with your communication when you are ultimately unable to deliver what was promised.

By taking responsibility for failure and success, you demonstrate an acknowledgment of the impact you've had on teammates. In turn, Mental Ownership earns you the respect of your teammates, even if you could not deliver. As you read this, you can begin to see why accountability and trust are so closely linked.

The power in capitalism has shifted from a system that advantaged early capitalists where labor was a commodity to favor a system where highly skilled and motivated workers are in high demand and short supply. Failure to amass talent, not capital, can spell the end of an organization. Rather than continue to fight each other, Physical Owners and Mental Owners must create a mutually beneficial system that meets all needs.

If we win, you win. If I win, we win.

In Mental Ownership, workers have a say on what is worked on and how it is pursued. Workers are trusted partners to management- The What and How of strategy is trusted to execute.

Mental Ownership = autonomy + control + equity

Ownership Characteristics

The distinction between a Mental Owner and a work renter is not about the enterprise's job title or formal authority. It's about the mindset and approach to thinking about how work is done, doing the work to the best of your ability, and working with others to create high expectations and an accountability culture. Some common characteristics for each side as it pertains to work:

Owners:

- Always look to increase the value of the workplace and company.
- Willing to put aside short-term needs to tackle long-term problems and opportunities.
- Understand the concept of "sweat equity."
- Looking for others who can help increase the value of the workplace.
- We & Ours.

- Proactive.
- Life is a game of chess-more complex rules and relationships.
- Learns the skills to solve tomorrow's problems—Systematizes talent development.
- Finds new ways to do things.
- Owners refuse to accept failure. Can do attitude.
- They want to feel like they are making a difference.
- Accountable for the attitude and behaviors they bring to life and the workplace.

Renters:

- Some level of commitment but may also be looking for the next best thing.
- They draw hard lines of responsibility—my problem vs. our problem.
- Confirm their own beliefs by surrounding themselves with other renters.
- They are looking only at the short term, not the long term. An employee comes to work each weekday.
- Do what they are told, and nothing more (trained bears).
- Us vs. Them.
- Reactive.
- Life is a game of checkers- simple rules and relationships.
- Expects someone to pay for their training and tell them what skills to learn.
- Not accountable for the attitude and behaviors they bring to life and the workplace.

If you want to be a leader – think like an owner.

At all times, the one phrase that needs to ring in your head is the simple phrase, "I own this."

Your thought pattern should sound like this:

Because I own this, anything that I do is executed and

maintained at the highest levels.

> Because I own this, I will never submit to no. I will find the way around. Over, under, around, though- it makes no difference.

Because I own this, I am trusted and empowered to do the right thing at all times.

Ownership Impact

"You get leadership when you take ownership."

-Pat Summitt, head coach emeritus, University of Tennessee women's basketball team

The impact and outcomes of Mental Ownership are not new, farfetched, or academic theory. Compelling research and decades of experience show that employee ownership is a powerful tool that improves corporate performance – but only when companies have "ownership cultures" in which employees think and act like owners.

Here are some key research findings from: (Autonomy in the Workplace: An Essential Ingredient to Employee Engagement and Well-being in Every Culture 2011) [117]:

1. "Employees who underwent job enrichment showed increased work motivation, job satisfaction, and involvement, lower absenteeism, and turnover. A recent meta-analysis of over 250 publications showed that job characteristics explained between 24 and 34% of the variance in many work outcomes."

2. "Perceptions of job control, often considered a form of work autonomy, were associated with higher job satisfaction, commitment, involvement, performance, and motivation and lower physical symptoms, emotional distress, role stress, absenteeism, turnover intentions, and actual turnover."

3. "Increasing psychological ownership leads individuals to feel a greater sense of responsibility and concern for, and authority over, the target of ownership (Pierce et al. 2001; Brown et al. 2014). As such, individuals who feel more ownership are more willing to invest time and energy in a target such as their work, sacrifice themselves for it, or defend it from others (Van Dyne and Pierce 2004; Brown et al. 2014)."

Overall, the results are impressive and compelling. If you want your organization to Get Shit Done, Mental Ownership is a critical factor. When employees could participate in decision-making, they were more engaged, put more effort into their work, and felt less strain."

Mental Ownership is an ambitious but valuable tool that organizations must embrace to increase employee satisfaction and morale while improving their long-term profitability. The sense of ownership and its rewards can fulfill essential human motivations and needs even if it is not formal. Yet, with ownership comes certain expectations.

The development of Mental Ownership will lead to the desire to participate in decision-making and hold themselves and others accountable for success. In turn, Mental Ownership will require more inclusiveness and openness on the part of the organization. You will not attract and sustain happy and fulfilled employees while maintaining an iron grip on control. Management must be willing and open to share power and control with those below them.

Fostering a strong "ownership culture" also encourages employees to have a stake in the organization and its future. When this need is met with well-structured equity or profit-sharing plan, it can be an even more powerful driver of employee motivation, performance, and loyalty. Rather than shareholder stakeholders and workers being diametrically opposed, allowing them to become one-and-the-same removes tensions and indifference to outcomes.

A culture of personal accountability is alive and kicking when employees possess the freedom to make appropriate decisions and have the courage to take ownership. Ownership is the most powerful, most desired, and not surprisingly, least understood characteristic of a thriving work environment.

When employees take ownership of their work, they treat the business they are working for — and its state of well-being — as if it were their own. Employees make better decisions because they see the business as an extension of themselves. They also tend to be more driven and motivated, looking for creative ways to improve their work quality. The ownership mindset is infectious. The more powerful your culture of ownership becomes, the more successful your business will become.

People who don't take ownership are more likely to go through the motions and do the minimum required because the results don't matter. Unfortunately, this mindset is also infectious, and if left to fester, you will see large parts of your workforce rotting away.

The worker in an organization that embraces Mental Ownership says:

1) **"I'm here to add value and advance the business's mission."**

2) **"I bring my whole self to work each day."**

OWNERSHIP SUMMARY

In many parts of the world, ownership paired with the natural human motivation to succeed has been a driving force in raising millions worldwide out of poverty. Owning not just things but ideas redefines what ownership could be. Ownership of knowledge has allowed large numbers of people to become detached from entrenched systems where other people owned and safeguarded the means of production. Pure physical ownership has positively shaped our economy and world for decades, but changes in the world require adapting to stay competitive.

When individuals have control, we've learned that they suddenly care a great deal about maximizing output and minimizing costs and inefficiencies through innovation. By tying Mental Ownership to the goals of the enterprise, we create a powerful motivating force. Rather than telling people what to do and how to do it, we create a system where goals and shared and freedom to operate is granted. To achieve our means, we trust each other and collaborate to overcome challenges. The future of an organization's prosperity is placed directly into the individual's hands- both the input and outcomes are a shared responsibility.

Although the concept of ownership is most commonly applied to assets, the idea of ownership can equally, and with perhaps more significant effect, also refer to the experience of being psychologically tied to an idea, an identity, or an entity. Such feelings of ownership are fundamental to human life- humans are a collection of ideas and values that we embrace.

It would not be so far-fetched to say that Mental Ownership is one of the most undervalued assets readily available to harness. Just as with an arbitrage opportunity, if you have it and many others do not, you will be able to exploit the gap to your enormous benefit.

In today's business environment, it is no secret that an organization needs to continue to do more with less to stay alive. To not just survive but thrive, you need all employees to take full ownership and responsibility for themselves and their actions. You need every employee to be working towards delivering the vision and executing the organization's strategy.

Ownership=Control=Freedom

EXPECTATIONS OF EXCELLENCE

"Strategy cannot be what "most of us do, most of the time."

-David Maister [8]

Taking the first step and embracing Mental Ownership is critical to taking your career and your organization in the right direction. The second step, though, is to help spread the message of ownership and accountability to others. If only one person or a handful takes ownership of the work around them, they will be seen as a sort of amusing novelty. Worse, others will continue to shirk and put more responsibility on those willing to step up.

To counteract opposition and to spread the message and mentality of Ownership, an important concept is Expectations of Excellence. Expectations of Excellence can motivate others to operate at the highest productivity and professionalism levels. To help others, you must first set the tone and expectations for the people around you and be the change you want to see.

Expectations of Excellence means that you expect others to conform to the group's high standards. If promises are not kept, deadlines are missed, or waste is produced, it is the Mental Owner's responsibility to question these gaps. Rather than allow poor performance, we address it at each step to determine the root cause; then fix it. Instead of accepting weak explanations, we poke until the real holes are revealed.

As noted in *Execution: The Discipline of Getting Things Done* by Lawrence Bossidy and Ram Charan," **"In its most fundamental sense, execution is a systematic way of exposing reality and acting on it."** [3]

In setting Expectations of Excellence, no one can be out of scope. It doesn't matter who they are or what they do; your peers, subordinates, and bosses are all fair game. Owners understand that everyone needs to operate under the same principles if they want to move anything forward. You expect yourself to be the best version of yourself each day, and you expect the same from others by being an example.

Each day, work as we know it can consist of scores of people making thousands of decisions where no one person has total control over a project, an initiative, or an outcome. Since we cannot carefully monitor what each person does each day, we need to expect each person to think, do, and act with excellence. If each person were to act independently and, in their self-interest, and with their own set of principles and expectations, chaos would follow, and it usually does. The Mental Ownership culture builds a system that leads to the best decisions possible.

When the objectives of the execution effort fall short, the person responsible must be held accountable. Each person must know their goal in advance, have accepted it, and have the required skills and resources to achieve the objective with clear and measurable targets. If people miss fulfilling a commitment, it is, first, the leader's responsibility to look inwards and determine if they failed this person by not providing the proper clarity, training, or focus. After that obligation is fulfilled, it is up to the others to question themselves. Only when both roles are carried out to their fullest can execution happen. In working to understand and close the strategy-execution gap, the people who work towards a shared goal must all row in the proverbial boat together and in the same direction, or else, we spin in circles.

Organizations often hesitate to tackle the accountability problem due to a lack of clarity on what the person is accountable for in the first place. But, by holding everyone responsible for everything in their realm, we fix this issue- You are now your brother's keeper. Discussions around accountability can be straightforward and result in few potential conflicts because everyone knows what is expected and how we measure success.

A solid and sturdy organizational foundation is built when they are accountable to themselves and the person next to them. It is from this base that an organization can begin to work towards mastery in strategy-execution.

While excellence sounds glamorous, getting there requires a culture that holds execution above all. Create accountability in the system to clarify that others are responsible for taking ownership, taking responsibility, and taking charge- that's setting Expectations of Excellence.

EXTREME OWNERSHIP

"While it's true that someone can impede our actions, they can't impede our intentions and our attitudes, which have the power of being conditional and adaptable. The mind adapts and converts any obstacle to its action into a means of achieving it. That which impedes action is turned to advance action. The obstacle on the path becomes the way."

-MARCUS AURELIUS, MEDITATIONS, 5.20 [66]

"Accountability is something you choose to exhibit – it is not assigned to you. You are given responsibility, but you must take accountability."

-The Oz Principle [5]

There is ownership, and then there is an extra step above this, known as Extreme Ownership. **With ownership, if you observe a teammate make a mistake, they are at fault, and you are not responsible. However, with Extreme Ownership, what changes is that if you observe your teammate make a mistake, and you saw this occur but said and did nothing, then you're equally, if not more, responsible for the failure.** Because Extreme Ownership sets a high level of expectations for all involved, it serves as a dominant force in execution- lies, excuses, and missed promises are simply not acceptable.

Ownership:

Image27- Ownership

Extreme Ownership:

Image28- Extreme Ownership

The image below depicts ownership, not Extreme Ownership.

Image29- The Difference

The concept of Extreme Ownership has been popularized in recent years through the book with the same title by the Ex-US Navy Seal authors Jocko Willink and Leif Babin. In their book, *Extreme Ownership*, the writing duo documented how the U.S. special forces branch, the Navy Seals, operates so well under challenging, dangerous, and unpredictable circumstances. Even though the Seals have high expectations for physical fitness and mental durability, they clarify that teamwork and accountability are paramount; if they only look out for themselves, the operations will fail. Through years of training and carrying out missions, the Seals found that the way to succeed isn't by dictating what to do in every scenario. Rather, the Seals prepare their people to thrive in all situations using their judgment and self-organizing their leadership. By demanding that each person take ownership of all facets of the mission, leadership, obstacles, and successes, the Seals have built one of the world's most elite fighting forces. [19]

Extreme Ownership, as a concept, is unique because it works differently. We sometimes have a "hope for the best, wait for the worst" approach in ownership. We hope that the people around us are committed to their work and have high standards, but we never explicitly agree. Instead, **Extreme Ownership requires that each person guarantee a personal commitment to themselves and the others around them; if you say that you will do something, then you're going to do it**. With Extreme Ownership, accountability is fully embraced for success and failure, not just when things go well, and it's easy to have courage. While nothing ever succeeds 100% of the time, it is essential to show character and responsibility by owning up to the outcome and learning from it, whether good or bad.

Extreme ownership in action looks something like this:

1. The team assesses the mission's objectives and crafts the who, what, when, and how to handle them. There is no play-by-play tactics guidebook.

2. In communication, if a team member has not understood any part of the instructions, then the team leader cannot blame the other person. As a leader, it is their role to make sure that their team members fully understand the objectives, purpose, and detailed instructions.

3. If a subordinate doesn't understand their guidelines, they will quickly embrace responsibility and ask the leader for a more in-depth explanation rather than proceed with ambiguity.

Extreme Ownership works so well because all sides involved in execution commit to thinking and acting to their highest ability. A more straightforward way to phrase Extreme Ownership is this:

> **"If you mess up, you need to own the outcome, apologize, learn from it, and fix it. Even if you didn't mess it up, but something is still broken, then it's all the same- own it, apologize, learn from it, and fix it. If there is a problem or obstacle that you foresee, it's up to you to discuss it with others, obtain consensus, plot a path, and then move forward. "**
>
> **-Gabe Zubizarreta**

Extreme Ownership's exciting aspect is its broad application to our world outside of military operations. Signing up is easy: you must commit to Expectations of Excellence in everything you do.

Mastering responsibility is vital because we all know that strategies and projects constantly shift, grow, and transform —nothing ever ends as planned. However, you are set up to pivot as new information and facts come into light and expectations change successfully. It becomes your job as a leader with an ownership mentality to communicate with your team and managers to mitigate any chance of surprises. **If there is any level of surprise when a deadline comes and goes and the work still has not been completed, then you're not an owner; you're a renter.**

We all know that a professional reputation is difficult and time-consuming to build. Having an excellent reputation opens doors and opportunities and helps to build trust among colleagues. However, destroying a reputation is easy; it only takes one action and a few seconds to do. In earning a solid reputation, rarely is there any single grand deed performed. Instead, a reputation is the sum of a thousand small interactions —the things that people observe you do and say when you don't think that you're being watched. Extreme Ownership facilitates both protecting and extending your reputation—

when people see or think about you, they will only recall your level of commitment towards excellence in your life.

For you, it should be clear that Extreme Ownership starts here, today, and now. You must think about your life, work, and responsibilities with a different lens from this point on. By developing a systematic process of rigorously questioning and mastering the how's and what's in what you do, you will be able to take your life and career to a new level.

TAKE CONTROL
AND OWN IT.

ACCOUNTABILITY CHAINS

"True Freedom begins and ends with personal accountability."

-Dan Zadra

"Accountability: A personal choice to rise above one's circumstances and demonstrate the ownership necessary for achieving desired results —to See it, Own it, Solve it, and Do it."

- The Oz Principle [5]

The ancient Greek hoplite soldiers were among some of the most feared warriors in the ancient world, and for a good reason. As you may have seen, hoplites were popularized by the movie "300," which depicted their legendary victory at the battle of Thermopylae. At this battle in 480 BC, 300 brave Greek warriors from Sparta volunteered to move to the front to hold off the massive Persian army consisting of a much greater force estimated between 100,000 to 200,000 soldiers.

To buy time for their countrymen to prepare a defense against the coming Persian invasion, a small force of defenders chose to guard a narrow pass by the sea known as the Straits of Artemisium. History remembers these Greeks because they held off the entire Persian army for two days while causing heavy losses to their opponent and suffering few losses of their own. Only after the enemy found a goat path around the strait were the Persians able to defeat the Greeks.

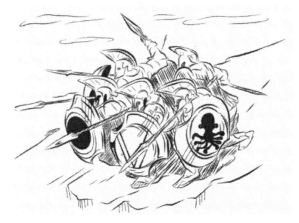

Image30- Phalanx

At a glance, the hoplite, armed with a shield, a spear, and a sword, often looked no different from their enemies' soldiers. However, **what made the Greek soldiers extraordinarily lethal was their degree of excellence, extreme ownership, and professionalism**. The signature defensive move the hoplites deployed in battle to devastating effect was the Phalanx Formation. Standing shoulder to shoulder, with shields interlocked, the Phalanx became a nearly impenetrable fortress to the men inside and deadly to those who would come up against it. The solid shield wall left no advantage to the attackers who would soon be pierced with a spear- all sides of the formation were fully protected yet lethal. If you study the formation, you'd see that the Phalanx's strength was not bound to one man or leader but rather the whole's coordinated effort. It would take only one man out of formation or one man whose strength faltered to spell doom for their comrades.

By recognizing both the opportunity and high stakes of the Phalanx formation, Greek soldiers thrived by putting their trust and life into the hands of the man to either side of them, thus forming an Accountability Chain that served as an unbreakable bond.

Although today, very few of us could see the need to deploy a Phalanx formation to combat our modern problems, we can still study it to understand how the Greeks were able to close the strategy-execution gaps that they faced. **In learning from the Greek hoplites, we can recognize strategy execution's futility if each person in an organization does not understand their individual and shared responsibility and commitment.** The Greek's Phalanx served as an Accountability Chain where each link (or man) in the shield wall was solid and sturdy so that the whole would never snap and fail under times of duress.

When strategy execution fails today, we can commonly attribute the disconnects to broken accountability chains. Something always happens at each stage of our work, where critical pieces of performance often get dropped, missed, or forgotten until the whole picture fails to materialize. We find it challenging to come together and execute or close the strategy gap if there is no strong sense of "we" because trust is never built.

As David Maister noted in his book, *Strategy and the Fat Smoker*:

> "While tools, systems, and organizational resources are wonderful aids for people who already want to execute, they will have little impact on people who don't want to use them. If the underlying problem is the culture or attitude, no processes, forms, and support will change things. Although you cannot change human nature, those in leadership roles (formal or informal) can help foster a better environment that enables others to operate at the highest responsibility level. The key is to set people up for success by clarifying expectations upfront. If your organization has a culture where no one cares, and no one takes ownership, the execution gap will persist." [8]

To build Accountability Chains in your organization, create a structure within your organization that resembles the Phalanx. Start by fostering a culture around a commonly held and strictly observed set of principles, where ownership and excellence are a given. When an individual masters ownership, then a team, and then an organization, execution begins to look like an impenetrable machine. **When a series of people and tasks are linked together, the whole's sum becomes greater than the individual components.**

If someone fails to uphold their commitment, their teammates will recognize this weakness and quickly address them. People should be upset when they fulfill their obligations, but others do not. However, the key is to keep in mind that **the most powerful promises are not coerced; they are voluntary.**

The accountability chain is built on implicit and explicit guarantees that foster coordination and execution across an organization. Just as a contract signed under duress is not binding in a court of law, the same goes for accountability. If promises are made under threat (although they may comply out of fear), most people will assume little personal responsibility for their actions. Unreliable promises cause leaders to waste too much time checking progress, exerting pressure, or duplicating work—the organizational efficiency and effectiveness suffer. By contrast, people feel deeply obliged to follow through on a promise if they exercised free will in making it.

Forced promises= coercion= compliance= $$$

Voluntary promises= commitment= ownership= $

The Accountability Chain works when promises are monitored and fulfilled in public to become more binding and, therefore, more desirable. When employees commit to promises out in the open, they can't conveniently forget what they said they would do by backing out of the commitment in front of their peers and bosses. Psychologists have found that most people strive to make good on declarations they've made in public. After all, their reputations for competence and trustworthiness are on the line. There's a quip that goes, "Get it in writing," which also works well here. [11]

Accountability means taking responsibility for an outcome. Where ownership is the initiative, accountability is the follow-through.

OWNERSHIP & ACCOUNTABILITY: CONCLUSION

The world's economy and management theory have shifted from unbridled capitalism and Taylorism to Mental Ownership and more equitable capitalism over the last one hundred plus years. In this shift, older organizations have been left struggling to adapt, compete, and thrive in this new environment as outdated management theories continue to hinder Strategy-Execution. Once abused by the power dynamics, workers now find their skills and abilities in high demand and their maximum potential seldom tapped.

A critical step in closing the strategy-execution gap requires a change in how organizations, teams, and individuals are managed and aligned. To do this, organizations must acknowledge the potential and capabilities that can be unlocked when those closest to the work are granted the autonomy, freedom, and control they require and desire. By allowing the workers to self-organize while keeping the firms' best interests in mind, individuals can innovate and participate with new engagement levels. By tying what people care about to work, people will be encouraged and rewarded for bringing their whole selves to work.

The Strategy-Execution competency is built on a foundation of Mental Ownership and accountability. Even though individuals may not have total authority in an organization, self-appointed leaders who can regularly assume ownership of tasks will distinguish themselves and put themselves on the optimal path to achieve their goals.

Granting employees greater authority and responsibility in performing their work goes a long way to building an ownership culture. Employees who feel empowered in their roles are more motivated to solve customer problems and develop innovative ideas for improving their business areas. Employees will feel more accountable for long-term organizational outcomes and be more likely to increase their equity stakes.

People resist coercion much more strenuously than they resist change. Each of us has free will at our core. People will choose to change more readily from the example set by our transformation than by any demand we make of them. **Organizations can either spend enormous amounts of time, money, and energy forcing compliance, which will be fought every step of the way. Or they can make a smaller but more meaningful investment into the culture to develop ownership.**

Remember that ownership begins squarely with you. You must understand that no matter the problem, obstacle, or issue is at hand or who had initially been responsible, you're now the proud owner of it. You're the new owner of the shit that no one else was doing before, the shit that someone else was supposed to do, or the shit that no one else wanted to do.

Once you do this, Mental Ownership becomes contagious.

Your success in work and life depends on how effectively you can master the factors around you to prevent and react to any circumstance so that the results reflect favorably on you. Ownership is the difference between being proactive versus reactive- you mentally and physically prepare for the things that can impact you. It means that you are strong enough to take a blow to the head and clever enough to duck away from a swinging flurry of fists.

Ultimately, no matter how bad, unfortunate, or ugly the circumstances are in your life, it's now your responsibility. You are responsible for owning your career, your fate, your actions, and the actions of the people that surround you. If you can see it, hear it, or smell it, it's yours. Accept that it doesn't matter who is responsible for the shitty environment and poor results that preceded your arrival. Because as of now, it is all your shit to deal with now.

You shape the world; it doesn't shape you.

Embracing the ownership mentality looks a bit like this:

If you have a:

- Bad boss, you own this. What a great chance to learn about working with difficult people, managing up, and communicating more effectively!

- Lousy job, you own this. What a great chance to improve a role, redefine the responsibilities, and demonstrate leadership!

- Flawed systems and data, you own this. What a great chance to learn new and valuable technical skills to address the problems and influence others to achieve better input and higher quality outputs!

- Inefficient processes, you own this. What a great chance to learn how the business works, fully document and define a future state, and then work together to fix the end system!

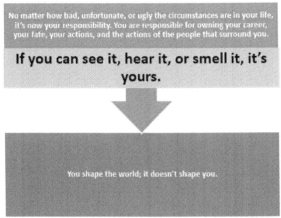

No matter how bad, unfortunate, or ugly the circumstances are in your life, it's now your responsibility. You are responsible for owning your career, your fate, your actions, and the actions of the people that surround you.

If you can see it, hear it, or smell it, it's yours.

You shape the world; it doesn't shape you.

- Inadequate education and training resources you own this. What a great chance to improve yourself by learning new skills and technologies on nights and weekends!

Image31- It's Yours

To avoid living in a world where problems are vaguely assigned to **Everybody, Somebody, Anybody, and Nobody,** YOU instead must commit to becoming the type of leader who takes responsibility for your own life and leadership results. If no one else rises to the occasion, guess what, the answer to the question of who is responsible becomes you. It's your ass doing whatever needs to get done as urgently as possible.

Only by fully embracing the ownership mindset can you take the first and most critical step in defining **Who will do What and by When**. The key now is not just to nod your head up and down and think, "Wow, cool idea," but instead to commit towards embracing ownership and mastering it and then encouraging as many people as you can to do the same. From this point forward, you will need the idea of taking ownership to begin to put the building block of execution in place.

Ultimately shared accountability comes down to the personal stake individuals have in the business." "How do you get them to change?" -→ "What is the transformation in me that is required."

Make no mistake about it; Excellence and Ownership are a choice- your choice.

TAKEAWAYS

- By becoming owners in outcomes, we are ready to remove any obstacle in our path to achieving the impossible. Ownership is to excuses as sunshine is to mold.

- The ability to fill the knowledge and execution gap is based on personal choice and discipline. All professionals can fill this gap if they decide to do better, but they must decide. Improvement is needed at all organizational levels for change to occur, top leadership, managers, and individuals. Ownership builds a collective mastery that is hard to duplicate.

- Despite how easy it is to assign blame and point fingers- we cannot blame the failure to execute on anyone else; our team, our leaders, and our organizations, but for ourselves. By taking ownership, we can begin to lift the fog around our failed initiatives and clearly see for the first time.

- When employees take ownership of their work, they treat the business they are working for — and its money — as if it were their own. They will make decisions thoughtfully, responsibly, and with more care. They will also be more driven, motivated, and have more initiative, seeking creative and innovative ways to improve and develop what they are doing, rather than going through the motions and fulfilling the minimum, and worse still, stagnating.

- Taking ownership tells others — "You can trust me to do

the right thing."

- When we think of accountability, we typically think of holding others accountable. But the most influential leaders and teammates are more focused on holding themselves accountable. By exhibiting ownership and accountability, the locus of control shifts from outside to inside. From practice to intentions. From strategic to personal. Accountability needs to be at all levels of the company.

- Ownership and accountability drive employee engagement. Employee engagement determines whether someone is genuinely committed to doing their best work and being part of an organization. An unengaged employee is tough to detect, re-engage, or replace with someone else if they decide to stay unengaged in place. In many organizations, unengaged employees can and do remain in place for years or decades while producing the minimum viable output- not enough to get fired- not enough to get promoted.

- Complaining is the voice of helplessness; Owners are accountable for reconstituting the world around them.

- Unless employees have realistic incentives to implement the strategy, they will not commit to it, and the implementation will fail.

REFLECTION

1. Who are you? Are you an owner or renter today? What could you change today to begin to exhibit the ownership mentality?

2. What excuse(s) do you commonly use to explain why work doesn't get done in your organization? What could be done to mitigate this?

3. Are you helping or hurting in establishing an environment that accepts excuses?

4. Where do you need to improve your technical skills?

5. Where do you need to improve your leadership skills?

6. What will you do to act on the above items?

7. Count the number of times you blamed Somebody else or an external circumstance and actively looked for how you could solve the problem. What do you need to change in your demeanor so that you can exhibit Extreme Ownership?

8. Is Accountability Explicit? Are expectations clear and promises honored?

9. What is your reputation? Are you seen as someone that drives people to be the best version of themselves?

10. Where can you start to build accountability chains in your work?

11. What can you improve on in terms of ownership and accountability? Where have you disappointed others, and what will you do to be sure it never happens again?

12. How many times have you thought, "that is not my job" in the past week or month? What were the results? What could you do to improve the outcomes next time?

13. What can you do to help shift the locus of control from outside to inside, from practice to intentions, from the strategic to personal?

14. How can you help people bring an emotional commitment to work to feel mutually accountable for results?

15. Is your organization doing its part to make the employees owners? Do you use stock and stock options to remove stakeholder conflicts of interest?

CHAPTER 5

Getting Shit Done by Communicating for Effectiveness

"Better to remain silent and be thought a fool than to speak out and remove all doubt."

-Abraham Lincoln

"Even a fool is thought wise if he keeps silent and discerning if he holds his tongue."

-Proverbs 17:28

Introduction

Communication aims to help organizational members understand the organization's strategy, why it is needed, its goals, and what must be done to succeed. Strategy communication often also involves communicating the vision, which is what the strategy aims to achieve. As strategy-execution is all about taking action and achieving results, communication is responsible for ensuring the Who, What, and When is apparent to each person throughout the organization. Not an easy task. The message needs to reach all places at all times and mean the same thing to all people.

Poor Communication

Communication is defined as the sending and receiving of information—a two-way street between involved parties. It's any form of sharing information with another person or group of people. When we interact with others in our lives, we can share information through various mediums: email, phone calls, video chat, meetings, face-to-face conversations, letters, faxes, pigeons, etc. The list is nearly endless—communication encompasses all the words, actions, and behaviors that prescribe how information and messages are transmitted. Communication involves not just what is said but how it is said and what is not said.

While the concept may seem simple enough, many professionals frequently fail when communicating with others because the intended message may not be interpreted the same way we had designed or intended. Thus, miscommunication or poor communication occurs. Poor communication is when information flow is asymmetrical: we say one thing, but another is heard and acted on.

Poor communication is a vital factor that must be addressed in discussing work delays or botched strategy-execution. So much of what we do in our roles depends on other people and their coordinated efforts. When we look to see with hindsight why failures occur, we can usually boil down the root cause because the receiving party did not fully understand what they needed to do, when they needed to do it, and even how they needed to do it. Furthermore, information receivers may have been unclear whether they needed to communicate with others to complete their work or know what was expected of them. **The fault may lie with either the message sender or the message receiver, but it doesn't matter: if one person is wrong, we're all wrong. Unless best practices are understood and adopted, miscommunication will keep occurring.**

To effectively implement a strategy/task/project, employees must understand what they are being asked to do and how they should support ongoing efforts—both before and during execution. Gartner's research has found that more than 65%

of employees lack an understanding of their role's integration with new initiatives due to poor communication. [1]

Sometimes people are genuine in their misunderstandings, and other times, people will use gaps in communications to defer responsibility. As the person taking ownership, you must take the lead to guide and shape these interactions into more profitable opportunities. A study by the Harris Group revealed that only 15% of individuals surveyed could identify their organization's most important priorities or goals because of poor communication. Since the frontline workers produce the bottom line, the problem is apparent. [11]

People are inherently good and want to do the right thing. When people are involved in collaborative efforts, they want to know the details of what they'll be working on: the who, what, when, how, and why of what is required and expected of them. People want to access this information to feel involved with the efforts and have an active and welcome voice in the discussion. **People who feel engaged are happier and more productive with their work; on the flip side, leaving people in the dark results in confusion and disengagement.**

As many careers now consist of knowledge work, the importance of building engagement through good communication is critical. It isn't easy to understand how productive someone is or isn't with their day. A problem no organization can survive is people who put on a happy face and pretend to work for their day's salary but instead use large chunks of their day to do other things or purposely work slowly. It can be difficult to measure someone's actual output or abilities; that is why winning their hearts and minds through engagement is so damned important. You want people to do their best work because it is in their best interests.

Excellent communication is how you win over hearts and minds so that each person is motivated and empowered to do the right thing at all times.

In an exercise to better understand the inefficiencies common in communication, let's start by thinking back to the last time you attended a planning meeting for a project. Like most, the planning meeting was not an effective use of the participants' time—a testament to why you're here today.

If I had to guess, here is how the meeting likely went down-- →

It all happened so fast: one day, out of the blue, as you were struggling to get other Shit done, you received an invitation just like the one below in your inbox.

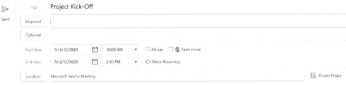

Image13- Meeting Disaster

As you grimaced and then double-clicked on the meeting notification, it instantly became apparent to you that multiple days' worth of your precious time was about to disappear into a black hole. As you glanced helplessly at the invitation, you noticed that the purpose (subject) for the meeting itself was a mystery—a general one or two words in the title and then nothing in the body to provide any context clues to help you unravel this mystery.

Further down on the invite, the lack of an attached agenda or description contrasted sharply to the abundance of attendees requisitioned. Who are these people, why are they here, what's the common thread?

Just when you thought that the worst was over, your face dropped as you noticed that the meeting called for a seemingly impossible block of time. Four and a half hours—who are these people?

$%^ !!!!!

As the organizer had placed all meeting invitees in the Required to Attend line of the evite, you, unfortunately, had no choice but to submit to their sick game. With resignation, you sheepishly clicked the "Accept" invite button. Then, adding further insult to injury, you had to review your calendar and reschedule every other meeting and bit of work you had set aside for that time after accepting the invitation.

The horror.

On the day of the meeting, you cautiously entered the room fully prepared to witness a disaster; and you were not disappointed. You sat back and grimaced as each predictable layer of disorganization unfolded:

- Each of the in-person attendees filed in several minutes after the official start time with a coffee and snack and then began making small talk with each other.
- On the phone to connect the off-site participants, each person took turns dialing in and announcing themselves with gargled voices, echo feedback, and static. The youngest person there buzzed through the room serving as an impromptu IT expert working on troubleshooting why the parties couldn't speak or hear each other correctly,
- On the big screen was a PowerPoint presentation overcrowded with text too small to read, which, of course, someone did read from. Word. By. Word.
- The highest-level manager hurriedly came into the room 15 minutes late from yet another meeting, so this meeting had to restart

from the beginning.

- The most extroverted person in the room made sure that they had something to say on the matter. Anything, something, just to be heard. Look at me!!!
- A Gantt chart detailing the specific action items and timeline was walked through as the room nodded in agreement. As the meeting leader explained that this project would be delivered on time and budget, setting a new precedent for the organization, not one voice dissented.
- When the meeting finally concluded its marathon session, one of the participants looked around the room to ask if anyone had taken notes and action items, and was met with blank stares and shrugs back.
- Then, everyone got up and left.
- As you left to return to your desk, you saw that the organizer had already set this meeting to a recurring time/date on each persons' calendar.

It's like a bad joke, right? We all know the punch line—that we are just setting ourselves up for yet another project that will deliver lackluster results and will never hit a deadline. While we are too busy trying to out busy each other, collectively, we forget to fill in the blanks for the one question that matters... **Who will Do What and by When**!

With such bizarre behaviors and a system of communicating depicted in the situation above manifesting itself in many organizations today, is it really any wonder why we struggle not just to Get Shit Done but also to Get Shit Done on Time?

Hopefully, you're tired of living like this and want to understand better the chaos that causes project delays and then learn the habits and structures required to improve the situation once and for all. Before you read onto the next section below, feel free to check out the video in the link below called "Conference Call in Real Life." The 22 million views speak volumes and strike a universal chord for most professionals: that the way that we attempt to get work done is so sad and maddening that it is actually funny.

It's like we are all actors rehearsing a comedy skit that was meant to be a drama.

Click here: https://www.youtube.com/watch?v=DYu_bGbZiiQ

If you don't have the e-book version, Google the title referenced above.

EXPLAIN THE WHY TO OBTAIN BUY-IN

The challenge with knowledge work is that it's almost effortless to look busy all the time. If someone had a dream to build a career pretending to look like they are productive but instead looked at cat pictures all day, it's entirely possible to do so.

If you had any doubt, consider the case of a story that came out in 2013, where it was discovered that an employee had outsourced his job to China. The employee was found to have done no work for years potentially, and the ruse was discovered only when the company became suspicious that its infrastructure was being hacked. The investigative team discovered that Bob shared his login credentials with a Chinese consulting firm for a fraction of his salary.

The investigative team even found that "Bob" kept a regular schedule of his activities in his office:

> 9:00 a.m. – Arrive and surf Reddit for a couple of hours. Watch cat videos.
>
> 11:30 a.m. – Take lunch.
>
> 1:00 p.m. – Ebay time.
>
> 2:00 – ish p.m Facebook updates – LinkedIn.
>
> 4:30 p.m. – End of day update email to management.
>
> 5:00 p.m. – Go home. [57]

Bob seemed to understand the Who, What, and When of his

work, but he missed the Why. Bob only saw the value in hitting his work quota and didn't see why the organization would instead employ someone to master these skills and competencies. Ol' Bob was there to punch a clock, turn in assignments, and had no interest in advancing the organization outside of these limited boundaries.

Just how many Bobs are out there in the world today may never be known. And Bob might be a bit of an extreme example. But worker disengagement is a far-reaching issue notoriously challenging to identify and remedy. There are still plenty of more accessible false productivity strategies for disengaged workers not quite ready to pull a full "Bob" yet. Anyone who does not believe in the work an organization does and/or doesn't want to participate can do some quick research online to learn how to appear busy.

Here's an example from the blog *Thought Catalog*:

    1. Always walk around the office with a sense of urgency.

    2. Always keep a stack of paper or binders in your hand while away from your desk.

    3. While at your desk, run the tape on your adding machine with random calculations (if applicable).

    4. Stare intently at your computer screen.

    5. Constantly write things on Post-it notes.

    6. Do the ol' shuffle-some-random-papers–on-your-desk routine.

    7. Always keep a coffee cup (empty or full) on your desk.

    8. Use your cell phone to call your desk phone. [58]

These sorts of behaviors are annoying to deal with for a well-performing organization but can become disastrous for an organization in crisis. Strategy-execution requires cohesion to facilitate an urgent change with a new strategy. Moreover, telling the difference between the output and commitment of a believer versus a non-believer can be a lengthy, challenging issue. An organization in crisis probably does not have the time, resources, or workforce to monitor each person.

That's the importance of obtaining buy-in by explaining the Why.

To ignore the Why in a change effort is to create an atmosphere with more questions than answers. Change naturally creates an information vacuum, and when the "why" is unknown, decisions can seem arbitrary and self-serving. When the "why" is known, it raises everyone's ability to align their actions. If you fail to satisfy people's craving for communication, rumors fill the void, leading to worst-case thinking, warped messages, and an overheated worry factor.

Communication is the tool to win people to your cause.

There is a big difference between understanding Who needs to do What and by When and trusting that others develop the internal drive to make it happen.

Not only must the content of strategy be communicated, but a strategy must also be clearly explained so that employees understand and believe in it. Employees should believe that the strategy is good for the organization and themselves. Explaining the reasons for a specific change to organizational members increases their commitment to that change.

To get someone committed to a plan and act on it, they must be a believer. They must believe that buying into a strategy will improve their situation and the organization they work at. They must believe that not acting is unacceptable and will include consequences. Anything in-between is a lost opportunity. Explaining the Why ensures that each person is pulling their full weight and encouraging the same from others.

To find out where your organization stands with buy-in from

the strategic communication efforts by assessing whether people understand the Why and believe in the mission, ask them. Facilitating a two-way communication flow is the best way to get your employees on board with the strategy and vision.

1. **Do they care?**

2. **Do employees internalize the ambitions of the organization into their values?**

THREE STEPS TO EFFECTIVE COMMUNICATION

Without strong leadership, proper project management tools, and healthy communication practices, we cannot solve our ongoing strategy and execution problems. The challenge with communication and poor communication is that no one intends to do bad work.

Instead, we tend to fall into comfortable behaviors. Over time, they become the norm or the organization's culture. We mimic others' actions and don't consider whether they are the right behaviors under the circumstances.

That's the bad news; we know we are failing at facilitating good communication, and the results of poor communication lead to Shit Not Getting Done, but what do we do about it?

As organizational leaders, we can step forward and help shape good communication by setting an example for others by learning about communication best practices. The three sections below cover the following main imperatives of communication, and each section also includes suggestions for what you can do to ensure these imperatives are met:

1. We must use clear, concise language in all communication.

2. We must use a process-centric approach to com-

munication that minimizes unnecessary back-and-forth.

3. We must choose our communication channels carefully.

CLEAR, CONCISE LANGUAGE

"I apologize for such a long letter - I didn't have time to write a short one."

-Mark Twain

"Brevity is the soul of whit."

-Shakespeare

Clear and concise language is a potent enabler of cohesion because it removes any chance of ambiguity. The more specifically expectations are defined, the faster it will be for others to wrap their minds around what they're supposed to be working toward. Without this clarity, others will often stumble around in the metaphorical dark, trying to divine what the leaders want instead of accomplishing it.

The challenge is that most strategy-execution scenarios are not as simple as marching in formation. At the organizational level, a strategy could involve hundreds or thousands of people worldwide in different business functions and segments coordinating to make a strategy a reality. However, clear and concise communication principles should never be altered or weakened as the magnitude of a challenge increases. Instead, keeping simplicity in a message becomes even more critical as the scale of the challenge rises.

Both the objective needs to be clear, and accountability needs to be clear.

In *The Implementation Challenge*, the author David Hussey commented that he had been frequently asked to assess a company's strategic plans in his career as a business consultant. However, he found that a typical pattern emerged over the years; after reading through these lengthy and comprehensive strategy documents, he surmised that most plans weren't worth the paper they were printed on. Many strategies were far too dense and confusing and served mainly to document the history of the organization. The actual plan often remained a mystery to him, and very few executives in the organization could explain what they wanted to do either.

Although Hussy's book was written in 1996, the same challenges are as present as ever. In boardrooms worldwide, the strategy is manifested in thick reports, overstuffed binders, and PowerPoint presentations explaining complex frameworks that few understand or do anything about. Organizations continue to bury what could be good ideas into layers of muck. What often begins as a clear idea warps and winds into a speech that leaves people more confused than ever.

To remedy this, Hussey also advocated that the best plans are simple plans and that they must be clear and concise: "A plan should be brief as possible, but must communicate the strategy. A verbose plan may be less clear than a concise one, particularly if it is also poorly structured. Experience shows that lengthy plans often have nothing to do with the decision process in the plan. What is there should be integrated." [25]

The strategic plan must be made as concrete and operational as possible. Executives down to each employee should know how the strategy influences their daily work.

To assess the state of your communication effectiveness, conduct a test of the people in an organization by asking them. Ask each person these questions:

1) **What are we doing?**

2) **Who is going to do What and by When?**

3) **How does your role support achieving the strategy?**

With the answers that you get back, score where you are and what is lacking.

From the questions, can each person articulate the strategy? Does each person fully comprehend what the strategy means? Do they believe the strategy is implementable at your company? Ask employees to describe the strategy and how they and their team fit in using their own words. Then listen. When both parties in the conversation are genuinely able to say they understand or that "it makes sense," clear and effective communication has been achieved.

Keep in mind that fuzzy explanations will produce fuzzy results, if anything at all.

If any of the questions are met with blank stares, then rework the message. Be mindful of reinforcing clarity.

PROCESS-CENTRIC COMMUNICATION

The second tool to deploy in becoming more effective at managing time is the idea of Process-Centric Communication.

In his book, *Deep Work*, author Cal Newport described the system he developed to respond to and write emails. By studying the inefficiencies in emails, Newport designed a new system that minimized the number of emails you will send and receive, which steal large amounts of time and take up energy and mental capacity.

Here's how it works:

A Process-Centric approach calls for you to put as much work back on the other person as possible by stating your expectations for each email you receive. You want to limit the number of volleys back and forth that will satisfy both participants.

For example, if someone were to send Newport a message asking if they could meet up one day for a networking event, they would receive the following response.

> "Process-Centric Response to Email # 1: "I'd love to grab a coffee. Let's meet at the Starbucks on campus. Below I listed two days next week when I'm free. For each day, I listed three times. If any of those days and time combinations work for you, let me know. I'll consider your reply confirmation for the meeting. If none of those dates and time combinations work, give me a call at the number

below, and we'll hash out a time that works.
Looking forward to it." [24]

Note that Newport did not respond to the sender's message with a simple response. Doing so would have created a stream of replies such as, "=) Sure, sounds great. I'm also available this week." A simple reply would have led to an exchange of many emails that would have been difficult to track. Ultimately, this exchange burdens the receiver when they have many concurrent exchanges coinciding. Things get missed, dropped, or crossed.

To make communication in the example above as efficient as possible, Newport identified the days he was available, the times he was available, the location and asked for only a single reply to the email.

The benefit of Newport's approach is that the number of emails (which are distracting) will decrease, and the time not spent emailing each other will increase, allowing him to do other, more valuable work. With a process-centric communication style, the sender commits to doing the work upfront by providing as much information as prudent to move the conversation forward.

In Newport's own words, the process-centric approach to communication works wonders because it:

> "reduces the time you spend in your inbox and reduces the brainpower you must expend when you do. Second, to steal terminology from David Allen, a good process-centric message immediately "closes the loop" concerning the project at hand. When a project is initiated by an email that you send or receive, it squats in your mental landscape — becoming something that's "on your plate" in the sense that it has been brought to your attention and eventually needs to be addressed. This method closes this open-loop as soon as it forms. By working

through the whole process, adding to your task lists and calendar any relevant commitments on your part, and bringing the other party up to speed, your mind can reclaim the mental real estate the project once demanded. Less mental clutter means more mental resources available for deep thinking." [24]

Deep work is focusing without distraction on a cognitively demanding task. Shallow work is non-cognitively demanding, logistical-style work, often performed while distracted.

Applying systems thinking and a process-centric communication process to all communications, including emails, is strategy-execution excellence in action. You can take the lessons from this section and begin applying them almost immediately. Review the emails and messages that you have sent and received and identify where efficiencies can be gained by applying process-centric precision to them.

NOT ALL COMMUNICATION IS EQUAL

Whenever someone wants to share a message with another person, there is a seemingly endless variety of channels they can choose from. However, each communication channel is not equal in terms of effectiveness or efficiency. Some communication channels are preferable to others for specific types of messages. Still, the key for the parties involved is to understand when and how to use each communication form.

Take a second to reflect on your experiences with communication:

- How many email chains have you been involved in that should have been a short in-person conversation?

- How many meetings should have been a phone call?

- How often does the message receiver incorrectly interpret your tone or intention?

- How often was another person unaware of a message because the email was lost or deleted?

As we consider our past experiences, we can note that technology can be either a blessing or a curse for getting the right message across to the right person. Poor communication often results from either the message sender choosing the incorrect channel or being sloppy in transmitting their message. The most common mistake that we humans make when communicating is to assume that either all communication is equal and/or discounting the cost-benefit relationship that goes into the decision.

Through our experiences, we come to learn that mindfulness is a must. In seeking to improve our communication efforts, leaders must individually and collectively be consciously aware of each message they send. When a message is transmitted, the channel used must be an intellectual exercise to maximize the message's chances of sticking through and driving action.

It doesn't take much for communication to go awry, so a wise precaution is to **always think before doing.**

Read through the following questions as examples of the necessary considerations for maximum effectiveness:

- Who is this message intended for?
- Which form of communication has the best cost/benefit relationship?
- Am I including unnecessary people or excluding critical people from this message?
- How important is the speed of the message?
- How important is the confidentiality of the message?
- Is there a chance that the message will not reach the receiver?
- Does this medium of communication support the level of detail in the message?
- Does this communication medium support the needs of all participants to have their voices heard?

Effectiveness in communication in Getting Shit Done and Getting Shit Done on Time means that you must be savvy and diligent in choosing which combination of communication techniques are to be deployed.

Read each of the items below to understand better when it is best to use email, phone calls, video chat, in-person conversations, or meetings in your communication.

Email

Benefits:
1. Fast, reach multiple people with the same message.
2. Able to structure complex ideas.
3. Able to attach supplementary files.

Cons:
1. Easy to ignore, nuances of the message (sarcasm, for example) can be misinterpreted.
2. Impersonal.
3. The message can be overlooked or deleted.

Use When:
1. Uniformity of communication and mass communication is necessary.
2. A chain of related messages is essential for context.
3. The same message needs to reach multiple people.
4. Urgency is not paramount.

Here are some specific guidelines that help increase the efficiency of communication via email:

- Avoid using email for any sensitive topics; always assume it will be forwarded.
- Assume that everyone in the company will read your emails.
- Make sure that the title of the email is either specific

- Avoid using email to discuss an issue in any depth.

Communicate factual information in writing. Most people only retain a small percentage of facts when communicated verbally- having a written record of those facts helps ensure that they don't get lost when making decisions. It doesn't mean that your message was received and correctly interpreted just because you sent an email.

Emails should be quickly scannable to the eye and should be readable in under 30 to 60 seconds. Summarize key points or action items for recipients in the body of your email. Share lengthy or dense information in attachments. If your message takes longer than 60 seconds, consider alternative paths.

Email is an excellent tool for "closing the loop" and defining Who does What and by When. As a business record, anyone in the communication can reference what was agreed upon.

The image below is a great example of closing all loose ends.

Image32- Closing the Loop

Phone call

Benefits:

1. Quickly share ideas and words.

2. Facilitate a personal connection with the other person.

3. The full attention of participants is required in the conversation.

Cons:

1. Call strength can vary; a limited number of participants before effectiveness decreases.

2. Lack of preparation possible for a conversation on either side.

3. Must remember critical points of the conversation or take notes throughout the session.

Use When:

1. Speed is critical.

2. Discretion and written records are not desired or required.

3. A focus on relationship building is an objective.

Video Call

Benefits:

1. Quickly share ideas and words.

2. Facilitate a personal connection with the other person: Voice plus facial expressions.

3. Able to share computer screens and collaborate. It's cheaper than the cost of travel.

4. Conversations can be recorded for the participants' benefit.

Cons:

1. Call strength can vary; a limited number of participants before effectiveness decreases.

2. It may require purchasing new tools.

3. People have to get used to it- newer technology.

Use When:

1. Collaborating with a team that is not in the same location.

2. A focus on relationship building is an objective.

3. Each person has access and comfort with the tool.

In-Person
Benefits:

1. Deeply personal. It allows for the reading of body language and emotions. Builds trust and transparency.

2. Full attention is required from participants.

3. Memorable experience.

4. Allows exploration and leads to conclusions.

Cons:

1. Slow.

2. It can be time-consuming. Conversations, as Machiavelli once quipped, are like Wars. That is, they "Begin when you will, but they do not end when you please."

3. Find an appropriate time. Sometimes the people required are not in the same place at the same time.

Use When:

1. The message requires relationship building; confidentiality is essential.

2. A focus on relationship building is an objective.

3. Time is not of concern.

4. Any communication that has high emotional content should be delivered in person.

Meeting
Benefits:

1. Able to communicate and collaborate with multiple people at the same time.

2. Opportunity to problem-solve together.

3. Able to build alignment on a topic.

Cons:

2. Time-consuming for multiple people.

3. Structure and planning in place are required for effectiveness.

4. The loudest people in the room may dominate the conversation.

5. Unless takeaways are written down after, decisions made in the meeting aren't recorded.

Use When:

1. Collaboration and attention are essential.

2. A discussion needs to occur from the perspective of multiple stakeholders.

3. A decision is required.

Because meetings are commonly attributed to being one of the highest sources of waste in any organization, it's appropriate to go into a bit more depth on what is required to organize, participate in, and run effective meetings.

While organizers set up meetings to communicate a message or idea, meetings become a source of complexity far too often. In contrast, after most meetings end, people walk out feeling confused or unclear about what happens next or without deciding on an issue.

To improve the quality of your meetings, keep these points in mind:

1. Clarify the purpose of the meeting and what needs to be accomplished. Set a goal-based agenda.
2. Send materials out at least a day ahead of the meeting. Include an agenda and any attachments (documents, slide decks).

3. Don't allow computer usage, except for the presenter and note-taker.

4. Request that phones be muted and put away, not on the table.

5. Get the right people (and only those people) in the room.

6. Designate a leader and facilitator.

7. Begin on time. Starting late or arriving late signals to others that your time is more valuable than theirs.

8. Manage the interactions.

9. Watch the time.

10. Spell out the next steps.

11. Send notes and action items right after the meeting.

The list above is just a starting point that will help you organize and execute meetings better. In developing Ways of Working, your organization can also define unique attributes that can add or subtract from the suggested guidelines. For example, some companies go so far as to advocate for standing meetings where participants cannot zone out, slip into a nap, or work on something more pressing for their time.

No matter what you choose to do, some sort of ground rules is essential. Just never lose sight of what works, works.

COMMUNICATION SUMMARY

The final point in this section of the chapter, Not All Communication is Equal, is to keep in mind that **good communication is conscious communication**. By considering the alternatives and then making the best choice based on the message and the participants involved, you will demonstrate an elevated leadership and ownership level. To reduce or eliminate costly work delays, it is always a good idea to follow up with any communication effort to be sure that recipients have:

1. Received the message.
2. Understood the message.
3. Can articulate back to you Who will Do What and by When.

By being as explicit and transparent as possible in your communication, you can prevent yourself and others from making assumptions. With experience, execution-minded leaders will improve their communication skills by learning their people and teams' preferences towards alternatives. For example, if you know that someone doesn't check their emails regularly, don't send them an urgent message through email; talk to them in person or by phone.

Excellent communication takes time to get right; the takeaway is to be a student from each interaction to maximize your effectiveness as a message receiver and a message sender. By better understanding the benefits and disadvantages of the most common communication forms, we can mitigate the risk of Shit Not Getting Done.

Takeaways

- Be clear, concise, and consistent with communication.

- If the Why is not communicated along with Who Will do What and by When, then the strategy-execution gap will persist.

- Focus on using communication to build alignment where everyone is focused on the same strategic outcomes, with a shared understanding of their roles, commitment, and accountability to deliver exceptional performance.

- Use process-centric communication to avoid excessive steps that consume resources and time.

- The right message needs to be delivered in the right way. Understand how to communicate each message to different audiences best.

- Offer the opportunity to ask people for specific examples of what support and additional information is required. And what they do not look like- it also holds them accountable for asking for what they need.

- Balance using all communication channels instead of those that are most comfortable to meet the audience's needs.

- Be accessible, speak often with your team about the challenges faced. Don't hide or discount the current reality of challenges and shortfalls.

- Be specific in communicating the vision and goals. Employees can't be owners if they don't understand the business targets and realities.

- Ask others for direct feedback on their understanding of the messages shared and ask for what can be improved or changed.

Reflection

- Do your communication habits inhibit or accelerate progress?

- Do you and those around you grasp the why? Is there a connection between tasks and workstreams to the strategy?

- Do people have more or fewer questions and concerns after you communicate?

- Does your organization clearly communicate the strategy, big picture, and current reality?

- Is your communication efficient? Do you communicate in ways to shift the burden of completing the communication back to the sender?

- Do you overuse acronyms and abbreviations that confuse others? Do you take the time to explain to others when they look confused?

- Are you mindful in communication? Do you carefully consider the best channel and use of everyone's time?

CHAPTER 6

Instill a Getting Shit Done Culture

"Our culture is very difficult to copy. You could copy our Billy bookcase or the retailing format or our warehouses, but how do you copy our culture?"
- Peter Agnefjäll, CEO of the INGKA Group at IKEA [29]

WAYS OF WORKING: ALIGNING CULTURE TO YOUR STRATEGY

It's essential to understand the intricacy and importance of culture on an organization and its ability to Get Shit Done and done on time. Organizational culture is a sort of dynamic and living "organism" that forms the heartbeat of progress. Culture is the collective result of accepted behaviors, interactions, and methodologies over time.

In his HBR article, "What Is Organizational Culture? And Why Should We Care?" Michael Watkins argued that "while there is universal agreement that (1) culture exists, and (2) that it plays a crucial role in shaping behavior in organizations, there is little consensus on what organizational culture is." He then offered the following quotes from industry leaders as an illustration of this lack of consensus:

1. "Culture is how organizations 'do things.'" — Robbie Katanga

2. "Organizational culture defines a jointly shared description of an organization from within." — Bruce Perron

3. "Organizational culture is the sum of values and rituals which serve as 'glue' to integrate the members of the organization." — Richard Perrin

4. "Culture is the organization's immune system."
— Michael Watkins

5. "An organization [is] a living culture... that can adapt to the reality as fast as possible." — Abdi Osman Jama [49]

John Kotter summarizes the culture issue succinctly:

"Change sticks when it becomes "the way we do things around here," when it seeps into the bloodstream of the corporate body. Until new behaviors are rooted in social norms and shared values, they are subject to degradation as soon as the pressure for change is removed." [70]

The takeaways on culture from the quotes and articles above are this:

- Culture and strategy entwined.
- You cannot build a culture in a recipe-like fashion.
- Culture is not fixed or static but instead dynamic and evolving.

Coupling culture with strategy is a complex and ongoing endeavor in shepherding influences, assessing outcomes, and adjusting the focus to build behavioral advantages that deliver winning results. Taking ownership of culture is critical to shaping the environment and expectations surrounding and influencing people each day.

Ways of Working does just that.

Bushido

The ancient Japanese samurai thrived for hundreds of years (1603-1867) guided by their code, Bushido, which meant "Way of the Warrior." Bushido was significant because it served as a widely accepted framework to define the samurai warriors' moral and behavioral code. There were established norms for each aspect of life, whether love, battle, or business. Honoring these norms, listed below, earned each person honor, translating into the success and level of power and authority over others. It became the cultural currency that could help you obtain influence, investments, or lovers. [13]

1) **Jin:** Benevolence toward humanity; Universal love; compassion.

2) **Makoto:** Utter sincerity; truthfulness.

3) **Chugi:** Devotion and Loyalty.

4) **Meiyo:** Honor and glory.

5) **Yu:** Valor; bravery, tinged with heroism.

6) **Rei:** Proper behavior; courtesy.

7) **Gi:** The right decision, taken with equanimity; Rectitude. [14]

Today, the Japanese Bushido code still exists in their culture's roots, but not in the same form. It has grown and been adapted to fit the needs of modern Japanese society and the economy. Bushido today is represented more because every person intuitively knows the role they play in the collective harmony in Japan. There is no "me," only the "we" - there is a conscious knowing that whatever one does affects the whole. Even a lowly worker with a menial job takes extraordinary pride in their work. They perform their responsibility to the best of their ability because they realize their output will somehow affect everyone else.

Many foreigners who visit the country are surprised that the trains in even the busiest cities run precisely. The streets are clean and orderly. The people are polite and respectful. All because of a collaborative culture. All because of Bushido, which is core to their Ways of Working.

Image33- Bushido

Think of Ways of Working as a sort of warrior's code for professionals.

Haitian Revolution

A second and fascinating example from history whose success was attributed to Ways of Working was the Haitian slave revolt led by Toussaint Louverture.

Image34- Toussaint Louverture- Public domain, https://en.wikipedia.org/

Amazingly, the French colony of Haiti would be the only example in history where a slave rebellion succeeded in gaining autonomy from their colonial masters. Throughout Louverture's campaign, there were many instances where he displayed high levels of military and professional conduct towards friends and foe alike. Always taking the high road when revenge was such an easy option, Louverture set a powerful example by building a culture distinguished by honor and professionalism, which was a critical element that led to their eventual success. Louverture became successful because of his fantastic ability to understand his people and build a culture around their natural strengths.

In his book, *What You Do is Who You Are*, Ben Horowitz described the sophistication and insights that Louverture had into the importance of an organization's culture. First, Louverture selected five hundred carefully chosen men and drilled and trained them religiously. He taught them discipline, command, and the art of war. Louverture elevated his fighters' natural instincts to make the army hyper-effective.

> "The first was the songs the slaves sang at their midnight celebrations of voodoo. Louverture was a devout Catholic who would later outlaw voodoo—but he was also a pragmatist who used the tools at hand. So, he converted this simple, memorable vocal template into an advanced communications technology. His soldiers would place themselves in the woods surrounding the enemy, scattered in clumps. They would begin their voodoo songs—which were incomprehensible to the European troops—and when they reached a certain verse, it was the signal to attack in concert. " [4]

The success of Louverture and the Haitian Revolution is attributed to how he took the best parts of the Haitian culture and turned what may have been a disadvantage into an advantage. He brought in Western military professionalism yet kept voodoo to build morale and terrify his opponents. He clearly defined what would be accepted, what would not and never wavered. He forgave honorable foes and executed dishonest officers. As you've read above, Louverture also understood the importance of excellent communication practices.

People don't readily adopt new cultural norms, and they simply can't absorb an entirely new system all at once. Louverture succeeded by adapting preexisting cultural strengths to significant effect. **The traditional song tactic meant that each soldier knew precisely Who needed to do What and by When in battle.** No ambiguity.

Interestingly, this struggle, which saw 50,000 French soldiers' deaths, became one of the leading causes of Napoleon Bonaparte eventually losing power in Europe and the US doubling in size with the Louisiana purchase from his beleaguered government. A sign of how just one man with a clear vision and a mastery of cultural practices can truly change the world. [15]

Ways of Working: Summary

As we reflect on both examples of the Japanese and Haitians, we can understand that Ways of Working is vital because it helps an organization always remember that we must build alignment between culture and strategy.

By setting an example, leaders, both past and present, can become guiding forces in aligning culture and strategy elements. Although it may take months or years, it is worth pursuing because old ways of doing things and incumbent attitudes can become a stubborn obstacle to successful strategy development and execution. Ways of working, supported by leaders and managers' total commitment, can rapidly accelerate the pace of change. By advocating Ways of Working, you will demonstrate ownership and leadership skills that will not go unnoticed.

The strength of adopting Ways of Working is that each organization can set a unique code that conforms with its existing culture and desired results. It doesn't matter so much what the code says, so long as you have one.

Once the organization's leadership decides the code, building Ways of Working into the organization involves tapping influential individuals with or without leadership titles to embrace these principles in their daily life. The next step is to reinforce the shared values by recognizing and rewarding those who set exemplary examples. Others will follow once it becomes evident that the organization is moving in a new direction, where rewards are shared based not just on what we do but how we do it. Change then happens one interaction, one project, and one day at a time.

Ways of Working is all about driving cultural change by bringing forward consciousness in communication. It is a thoughtful approach to reshape the organization's culture around principles that bring out the best in each person. When each person is held to high standards, the whole becomes greater than the parts' sum. The people around you should never have any doubt that you will honor your word and commitment.

AMAZON

"We are stubborn on the vision. We are flexible on details."

-Jeff Bezos

The third example of an organization that has thrived through Ways of Working is Amazon. Amazon's commercial success and ever-rising stock price appreciation serve as a testament to the power of having a strong communication culture that embraces execution best practices. There are two specific aspects of the Amazon work culture that blend to help their organization complete projects and innovate with stunning success.

1. The Memo Approach
2. The Two-Pizza Rule

Image35- Amazon

Memo Approach

The Memo Approach to Amazon meetings dictates the rules for how meetings are organized and executed. Every meeting at Amazon begins the same way- all attendees spend the first twenty or thirty minutes of the meeting quietly reading a memo that has been prepared in advance by the organizer. The memo is written as a professional thesis on an idea or proposal, backed by supporting ideas and evidence. The act of preparing a memo is an important and thoughtful step in setting clear communication expectations. The views of the organizer must go through several iterations before their ideas are shared with others. By writing a professional thesis on a topic, an idea must be fully understood, contemplated, revised, and rewritten until each point and idea is crystal clear to all in attendance. The effect of putting a belief in the format resembles the process of placing a gemstone into a polishing device.

Bezos prizes the Memo Approach because "full sentences are harder to write. They have verbs. The paragraphs have topic sentences. There is no way to write a six-page, narratively structured memo and not have clear thinking." The memo approach works because it requires a higher level of communication, critical thinking, and answering the questions around Who Will Do What and By When beforehand. [16]

Even more, at Amazon, the memo format is not an optional alternative to PowerPoint. Amazon has explicitly outlawed PowerPoint from the communication playbook, which is quite powerful since most organizations today run on slide-sharing software. The memo works as an antidote towards our inclination towards poor planning and execution.

Image36- PowerPoint

To write a persuasive memo, the organizer must have a personal conviction around the idea and possess the discipline to assemble a well-thought-out dissertation. Before the meeting ever starts, the organizer has likely spent hours or days thinking through the idea's various angles, arguments, and counterarguments to structure their ideas clearly to others. The basic premise is that it's challenging to bullshit your way through this exercise. If you're going to hold a meeting at Amazon, you will be sure that the idea merits yourself and other participants' resources and energy. We've all been in a meeting where some big bag of air talks and talks with really nothing to say; that doesn't happen at Amazon.

From "What Might Amazon's Six-Page Narrative Structure Look like:"

[The six-page narratives are structured] like a dissertation defense:

1) The context or question
2) Approaches to answer the question – by whom, by which method, and their conclusions
3) How is your attempt at answering the question different or the same from previous approaches
4) Now what? What's in it for the customer and

the company? How does the answer to the question enable innovation on behalf of the customer? [16]

The memo is a vital part of Amazon's Ways of Working code.

For organizations looking to adopt a similar approach towards meeting, companies and teams don't have to mirror the same rules and strategies that Amazon does to communicate effectively. However, leaders must keep in mind that they must find a system that works to bring out the best in their unique culture and safeguards against ineffectiveness.

Two-Pizza Rule

The second principle of communicating effectively at Amazon is their Two-Pizza Rule. This rule dictates that meeting attendees should be compact enough so two pizzas could feed the entire room. A meeting that fits these parameters can be four people, it could be 10, but it will never be 20.

The Two-Pizza Rule seeks to eliminate the impact of Death by Committee. The term Death by Committee describes the slow, painful death of an idea, initiative, or project from the bureaucratic process's stifling effects. Too often, a good idea suffers a painful and slow death by suffocation from too much well-intentioned attention.

Meetings with too many participants have a peculiar habit of warping towards a solution to reach a consensus. To illustrate this point, a common saying that illustrates this type of joint dysfunction is that "A camel is a horse designed by a committee." A committee compromises and comprises to get the job done to move on to the next thing. As you can notice, quality is compromised.

Image37- Committee Design

The Two-Pizza rule ingrains discipline into Amazon's Ways of Working to ensure that the meeting organizer is conscious of who is in attendance and has a compelling reason for being there. Each person must have an exact role to fill in the meeting, which keeps the conversation on topic and ensures engagement and a fruitful discussion. Each person in attendance is aware that they have a clear purpose and value the joint effort. [17]

Amazon understands this formula well. So, let's borrow it: **Fewer people= Only the people needed to add information or decide= Higher Engagement = Excellent Communication**

The key for Amazon has been that they understood the pains in communication and were proactive in fixing the problems by building an influential communication culture. For Amazon, to ensure that their Shit Gets Done and Done on Time, they developed Ways of Working that drove accountability, robust analytics, and efficiency. Excellence in communication at Amazon is the norm- each person and the team must demonstrate high ownership levels to spell out Who will do What clearly and by When.

GETTING SHIT DONE CULTURE

"No one diet idea is free of flaws or drawbacks. The best diet for you is the one you will stick to."

-David Maister [8]

"Culture eats strategy for breakfast."

-Peter Drucker

To Get Shit Done, you need a high productivity culture, autonomy and empowerment, ownership and accountability, and effective communication—all covered in the previous chapters. It would be best if you also had a culture in which people can question assumptions, encourage candor, and embrace conflict.

DON'T ASSUME ANYTHING

"The minute we begin to think we have all the answers, we forget the questions."

-Madeleine L'Engle

In the ownership chapter's opening story, nothing was achieved because Everybody, Somebody, Anybody, and Nobody all assumed that someone else was responsible for taking ownership of the work.

That's the problem with assumptions. If underlying assumptions are not challenged, understood, or the limitations identified, those responsible for execution will not bridge the gap between dreams and reality. When communication does not clearly state the Who, What, and When, we guess to fill in the blanks.

Don't assume others instinctively know what to do and when to do it, or even what you expect from them. Before people can take responsibility for their work, they require clear communication. The more you communicate, the better you communicate, the better the results are likely to be.

To combat assumptions, keep these points in mind:

1) Clarify strategy

Clarify high-level strategy statements, separating and organizing goals, objectives, initiatives, aspirations, and strategies.

Create a transparent model that helps the organization understand the current strategies and differentiate them from operational improvements.

Then, communicate the milestones and explain what "good looks like" and what "done" looks like. Be careful not to assume that each person knows where the organization is headed and what each person knows what they need to do day-to-day to facilitate it towards happening. You must make sure that your audience can clearly explain what is required to guarantee the results or reactions you want.

2) Assess capabilities

Capabilities encapsulate the organization's ability to act through its people, processes, and technologies. In chapter one, Getting Shit Done, we learned that Fit is a combination of a strategy and an organization's capabilities. Assuming what an organization is capable of or good at invalidates the strategy instantly.

No matter how large or small, every organization requires a core set of capabilities to successfully execute its business model or mission. To embark on strategy-execution without developing business capabilities asks people to do something new without providing the tools needed to succeed. Instead, document, discuss and share the capabilities and strengths of the organization.

Once you've gathered your understanding, summarize what you think they have heard and ask them to confirm or disconfirm your perspective. We all have filters and mental models that cause us to hear things differently. Take time to clarify so misunderstandings don't occur.

Don't assume that people have the skills, knowledge, or capabilities required. Ask and assess. Don't assume the technologies and core competencies are in place to support change.

If you're not sure, ask. If you don't ask, you assume.

ENCOURAGE CANDOR

"Truth over harmony"
-Bossidy, Larry. Execution [3]

In *Execution*, Bossidy espoused that "Candor helps wipe out the silent lies and pocket vetoes, and it prevents the stalled initiatives and reworks that drain energy." Even more, Bossidy did not just acknowledge that we need to use more candor. Still, he called for businesspeople to embrace the use of "Intense Candor," which he summarizes as "a balance of optimism and motivation with realism, whereas the goal is to bring out the positive and the negative."

In other words, candor is being clear and concise with the truth.

The goal for communication in any strategy-execution effort should be that we expect and emphasize telling the truth despite not always being desirable versus accepting or only celebrating a pretty lie. People are quick to observe how good and bad news is received by their peers, leaders, and organization. It doesn't take long for the truth to seem like an ugly thing that should be glossed over or swept under the proverbial rug. Perhaps, one of the worst things for people to feel is uncomfortable discussing problems and expressing their honest opinions. The damage can be immediate, and long-term as two different versions of the truth exist.

While ignorance is said to be blissful, the truth can be painful. The truth and expressing what we think is the truth open us to vulnerability and others' judgment. Calling out the truth and bringing the facts to the table can be uncomfortable at first, but this will become easier and more natural over time. **Even though the information may be disappointing or uncomfortable, the value of getting to the truth and quickly cannot be overstated.**

Beyond our efforts to set the right example, candor facilitates developing ownership skills in our teams by providing them a positive work environment, personal and professional growth opportunities, and regular and direct feedback. Aim to foster the building of a culture that celebrates not just honesty but radical candor so that people know the truth is the norm, even when it's difficult or awkward. The truth is the truth- anything else is an enemy of the truth. Don't fear candor. Done right; it can be empowering and liberating.

There shouldn't be any guesswork or "read between the lines" innuendos in your communication. Teams want to work with a leader who they can trust. Candor and honesty build that trust.

Candor in Action:

1. "We had spoken last week, and you agreed to complete the project plan by today. What happened? What can I do better to help you meet your goal?"

2. Candor is demonstrated when those closest to the work say that a plan is not realistic based on what they see and know.

3. Candor also involves the leadership of an organization acknowledging that a skills gap exists in key competencies to achieve Fit and that investment and training are required.

A few tips to keep in mind with candor are to keep humility at the forefront of the process. Always remember these points from Dale Carnegie when dealing with others:

- "Show respect for the other person's opinions. Never say, "You're wrong."

- "If you are wrong, admit it quickly and emphatically."

- "Let the other person save face."

- "Praise in public, criticize in private."[118]

EMBRACE CONFLICT

"Being open, putting your problems on the table, and being transparent requires taking a risk. Change requires risk."

-Unknown

When candor is embraced, the opportunity will be presented for different perspectives and opinions to clash. Inevitably conflict will enter the picture. Conflict is a good and healthy sign of progress. Conflict is necessary to understand one version of the truth and understand another party's arguments and viewpoints. At the same time, conflict can also be dangerous if not managed well. Tempers flare, feelings are hurt, trust is lost.

Like most things, there is a right way and a wrong way to go about conflict. While you might be thinking WWE Smackdown is the best way to let Shirley from accounts payable know to stop using your coffee mug, that probably won't play out too well long term. While the instant gratification of bringing a chair down on someone's back in the breakroom may feel good, it won't solve the underlying problems or keep you employed long enough to discuss them.

Image38-*"My coffee cup!"*

Not only should we expect that in a healthy working environment, that conflict will occur but that we should embrace conflict. If teams do not encounter pushback or disagreement with others, they probably are not pushing hard enough to drive beneficial change and progress in the organization. As an organization goes through change, be prepared for when different groups of people have different expectations or competencies that should be exhibited and mastered.

Before setting people loose, there should be training or at least discussions on conflict management best practices so that when the parties involved do wind up in a disagreement, they are well-equipped to manage it themselves. Aim to get people to resolve issues independently through a process that improves—or at least does not damage—their relationships. The key is to train employees to understand the signs of conflict and then have the wherewithal to know the difference between good conflict and lousy conflict- and how to deal with each.

It's ok to disagree, but how we offer up disagreement matters more than any particular position. Never blame, accuse, yell, or humiliate. Instead, respect one another's dignity and identify precisely where our disagreements are- between our facts, opinions, feelings, or needs. Fight fairly and deal with tension above board; embrace good fellowship afterward. Unpreparedness may allow difficult situations and conversations to boil over past tipping points where feelings are hurt and unprofessional conduct may occur.

Perhaps the best way to engage in constructive conflict is to be ready for when disagreements can and will pop up. The first step towards handling conflict is to BREATHE. Deep breaths allow more oxygen to get our brains and cool a situation down. In through the nose- hold it- out through the mouth. Humans tend to either go into a "flight or fight" mode when tempers rise. Deep breathes and perhaps a long walk will give everyone involved the time and opportunity to cool down so that a conversation can happen.

Image39- Conflict

To not let a disagreement fester into personal animosity, look to hold a discussion close to the time of disagreement- The same or next day is a good idea.

Reach out and set an agreed time and location next to discuss the situation with both sides calmly and directly. Each side of a disagreement should gather any data or information you need before the meeting. For conflict management, it's a good practice to focus on "I" statements. "I understand this issue as... I see it this way... the way I'm reading the market signals is..." "You" statements make a conflict unnecessarily personal. Charged You statement like: "You're an idiot...You have no idea what you're doing... You're a liar," take the conversation no-where.

Focus the conversations on measurable performance or ob-servable conduct. As the goal is to understand the current situation and the factors that are contributing to it, keep it a collegial discussion: "Ray, your location has missed its goal by 30 percent each of the past two months. Let's talk about what's happening and why to develop a solid understanding of the situation."

Beware, though, the trap of agreeing to disagree. This cop-out from conflict leaves a fundamental understanding of unsaid and is used to protect ourselves or limit our awareness. The goal with your conversations should be to share what you see, why you see it that way, how you feel, what you believe to be accurate, and what you think is crucial for them to under-stand.

Rather than fear conflict, we must foster the culture and ex-pectation that clashes between parties are an excellent thing to have- this means that ideas and healthy perspectives are present. It means that people care enough to speak out and challenge each other. By providing a platform for each side to understand the other better, we can open the door to develop-ing creative solutions and innovative trade-offs among com-peting objectives and priorities.

The main benefits of embracing conflict are that it leads to bet-ter work outcomes, enhanced opportunities to learn and grow, and improved relationships. [45]

Better work outcomes

When coworkers feel that it is ok to challenge and push one another to find a better approach to problems continually, creative friction will likely lead to new and better solutions that each person would not have discovered individually. Fostering an environment where the combination of the best ideas win will lead to a more collaborative and competitive environment where what worked yesterday may not work today.

Opportunities to learn and grow

Growth is about accepting that we may not be correct or have all the answers. As uncomfortable as it may feel when someone challenges your ideas, it's an opportunity to learn and develop your skills and strengths. By listening and incorporating feedback from other people working to solve the same problems, you will gain experiences, discover new ideas and tools, and keep evolving as a professional.

Improved relationships

The third and final point emphasizing the benefits of good conflict is that by working through conflict together, you and your team will begin to feel closer to the people around you and better understand what matters to them and how they prefer to work. Not only will you develop a more robust professional relationship, but you will also likely learn more about their personal lives, which will make future conversations easier to engage in and influence easier to develop. By fostering a culture where it is expected and ok to have "good" fights, you will set an important precedent that the organization is serious about getting work done and doing it in a way that everyone will ultimately feel good about.

ALIGNMENT

"You are what you do, not what you say you'll do."

-C.G. Jung

"Align, at every level, everywhere, all the time."

-Jacques Pijl

If you don't have alignment, you cannot and should not move forward. Closing the strategy-execution gap will remain a fantasy.

Do not pass Go.

Do not collect $200.

Go straight to jail.

Alignment is a state of cohesion where everyone is focused on the same strategic outcomes with a shared understanding of their roles, commitment, and accountability to deliver exceptional performance.

Misalignment, then, is to attempt to execute first without coordinating. An innovative strategy might be identified. Core competencies might be identified. But not linking them together will not create success. Failure is sure to follow when people cannot translate the strategy from high-level ambition to specific actions the organization must take to make that ambition a reality.

In essence, misalignment means that you have a few people who understand the strategy and execution plan and many more who don't. Using a sports metaphor, imagine the result of a game where each player doesn't know their position, the score, or which goal the ball needs to go through—a recipe for chaos.

If the people required to implement the strategy don't know the plan or what they should be doing, how can they help? While they may have the best intentions, different interpretations of the goals do not maximize the resources available. Each person needs to understand their role in what needs to be done and where it is headed.

Alignment: Who will do What by When and Why.

Alignment: The strategy is known, the competencies are in place, and there is Fit.

At this point, you should understand that creating alignment is not a once-off task; it requires constant communication and coordination from the leaders. Two points keep the alignment in order; 1. feedback and 2. communication repetition.

As we learned in just the previous section, feedback is key to ensuring that each person has heard and understood the required plan and actions. By obtaining feedback, it should be apparent whether people are on the same page or not. If you're not there, plowing forward with a change initiative can turn anything into a complete mess. Create alignment by allowing others to participate in the decisions and path forward and allow them to critique action plans. Allow people to ask questions to determine what the strategy means at their level. The higher the level of upfront collaboration, the stronger the eventual alignment will be. Ask. Listen. Learn. Repeat.

Image40- Alignment

Higher levels of alignment can be built through communication repetition. The Project Management Institute summarizes the importance of being constant and consistent in strategy and execution communication in this way:

> "Communication is an essential process in our day-to-day life, and the entire world revolves around it. However, how important this communication is in project management, we can say that this is "Project—Life Blood" as everything in a project is based on how efficiently we perform this. Communication is an essential tool in the field of project management. It is gaining importance every day and is the center of all management processes. The success of a project largely depends on the efficiency of its communication network. It starts working from day one of the venture and continues for the project's entire life span. It provides regular updates to notify the status of the project as well as its performance capacity. But surprisingly, it has been found that most projects experience a breakdown in communications. It has been said that 90% of a project manager's time is spent communicating what is going to be

done." [44]

As PMI is one of the top professional associations for project managers worldwide, we should undoubtedly embrace their enthusiasm for the subject. Until all fully understand the message, communication isn't complete. Effective communication is critical alignment and towards achieving success.

Leaders must repeatedly communicate the strategy at all levels as message saturation increases everyone's overall reception, recall, and agreement within an organization. Just as in this book, key ideas have been identified and repeated in each of the following sections. To say something once and expect it to be identified as a core theme would be stupid. Instead, communication involves identifying the core message and then intentionally weaving the idea through everything else.

However, keep in mind that too much of a good thing can be offputting. Repeating the same message will lead to a message that is eventually tuned out and ignored. When repeating the strategy, it is wise to find new and exciting ways to communicate differently to keep it relevant. Share stories of employees' journeys and learning experiences, share small wins and share some of the challenges they face. Employees respond more positively when they hear about the strategy differently instead of repeatedly hearing the same message.

As HBR notes, keep the communication focus on the critical points that reflect the Pareto Principle shared previously. "It's difficult to convey every nuance of a strategic plan throughout a large corporation. Ensuring that most employees are clear about their roles in achieving the most critical 80% of the plan is usually more important than communicating the remaining 20% to everyone." [59]

The strategy-execution gap remains persistent because people can't support and align with what they don't understand. Without bringing an organization together through excellent communication, very few can answer Who needs to do What and by When and Why. A strategy that only lives in executives' minds will die there, too.

Despite the many things that a great leader must do, perhaps communicating to build alignment is the most essential piece that is crucial to connecting the moving pieces strategy-execution. The leader(s) or owner(s) must be the keystone that makes sure that each person is fully aligned and optimized to contribute. It is not enough to just say it, but it must be believed and said well. While no one can predict the future, we can create the future through excellent communication practices.

The strategy's content must be clearly communicated, and it must also be clearly explained in a way that everyone understands and supports. Communication is key to winning the hearts and minds of the people to facilitate change. Communication translates strategy into operational terms and aligns the organization to the strategy.

Stephen Covey had an excellent quote that fits perfectly here to end this section:

> "Organizations are perfectly aligned to get the results they get. Think about that. If you are not getting the results you want, it is due to a misalignment somewhere in the organization, and no pushing, pulling, demanding, or insisting will change a misalignment."

KEEP IT SIMPLE, STUPID- KISS

"There is no greatness where there is not simplicity, goodness, and truth."
- Leo Tolstoy

"Simplicity is the ultimate sophistication."
-Leonardo da Vinci

"Life is really simple, but we insist on making it complicated."
- Confucius

The final barrier to high productivity and successful time management is complexity. The challenge with simplicity is that we must always be vigilant to instill and protect it. If we lose focus or ignore it, complexity creeps in, almost unseen. Through many iterations and pervasions, tasks and responsibilities can become unnecessarily complicated and time-wasting.

Large organizations are, by nature, complex. Usually, there are many product lines, services, sales teams, supply chain teams, production workers, management layers, support functions to keep the different groups coordinated, and the list goes on. An HBR article, "Simplicity-Minded Management," summarized the current state of affairs on complexity well:

"Well-intended responses to new business challenges

—globalization, emerging technologies, and regulations like Sarbanes-Oxley, to name a few—have left us with companies that are increasingly ungovernable, unwieldy, and underperforming. In many, more energy is devoted to navigating the labyrinth than achieving results. Accountability is unclear, decision rights are muddy, and data are sliced and diced time and again, frequently with no clear idea of how the information will be used." [37]

Despite many books and articles having been written on the subject, the issue remains an ever-present challenge. Ron Arsheknas, the author of *Simply Effective*, had this to say on the matter as it relates to managers and organizations:

"Chances are, like most managers, you're creating complexity without realizing it because all styles of management can and do cause complexity; they just do it in different ways. Fighting through complexity and creating a more straightforward organization is hard work. The floods of complexity- economic, social, technological, and psychological- continue unabated. And it is human nature to unintentionally and unconsciously exacerbate and amplify complexity. If it were easy, every organization would be simple." [40]

A second author, Lisa Bodell, would also impact the subject with *Why Simple Wins*. Bodell's book advocated identifying the mindset and actions required to keep complexity at bay.

In our age of complexity, simplicity is one of the most powerful ways to add value and stand above all the mediocrity and complacency. First, **simplification can't just be a one-time, spring-cleaning kind of event. The impulse to embrace work that is minimal, understandable, repeatable, and accessible needs to be cultivated, ingrained, and deepened over time**. Simplification needs to be a habit and a way of looking at the challenges we face every day. It needs to be part of every moment and every decision, woven firmly into the business culture and defining the ethos of each and every employee. Many companies fail at simplification because they don't integrate it deeply enough into the organization. They don't simplify the work that everyone does, in turn making simplicity a defining part of the culture." [42]

These sources drive home the point that if we can't explain why something is done, it likely increases costs, complexity and requires additional resources to maintain. Instead, we must take ownership of the problem and simplify the work. Simplicity means thinking of everything in organizational design as a dynamic, ongoing, and living process instead of a one-time exercise. **In other words, simplicity is the art of maximizing the amount of work not done.** Simplicity involves distilling workflows, conversations, meetings, and execution down to its most basic and workable level. On the other hand, complexity is a greasy cockroach- Smash it, spray it, trap it, exterminate it. Just like the loathsome pest, if you see one prominent example of waste, that means that many more unseen instances abound behind the walls.

Regarding strategy-execution, the simpler the vision and strategy are, the easier it is for organizational members to understand and execute. A clear and attractive vision increases the confidence of employees in the successful outcome of the change initiative. Reducing complexity is not just a matter of making it easier to get things done. Building simplicity into business processes has the added benefit of turning a function into a core competency and long-term competitive advantage — not by solving every business problem — but by increasing your capacity to address issues quickly and effectively.

To achieve simplicity, you cannot expect others to take simplification seriously unless you model a commitment to it yourself. Unless you think about your own patterns and ways to shift them toward simplicity, you may discover later that you unconsciously sabotage the effort. **Simplicity is everyone's responsibility, not someone else's problem.** The ownership mentality is critical so that each person feels the duty to keep their work, communication, and processes as simple, efficient, and practical as possible.

Be the first to demonstrate leadership of a simplification strategy for your organization. Eliminate complexity and create space for more meaningful pursuits by starting with your work's parts; you can control and expand from there.
Here is what simplicity looks like in action:

- Question and remove multiple levels of middle management.
- Map out processes and identify redundant work or roles.
- Reduce the number of product offerings to customers.
- Remove product features that increase costs that customers don't value.
- Mindful process design and execution. What are the fewest, most practical steps possible to achieve our target?
- Reduce the number of non-profitable or low-volume customers. Identify which 20% generate 80% of the profits and when 20% generate 80% of service costs.
- Streamline business processes (planning, budgeting, analysis).
- Facilitate collaboration across organizational boundaries. Create a system where people can self-serve their own needs and requests.

Surround yourself with simplifiers rather than complicators.

Enable people to reach the core of an opportunity or threat, understand the drivers, discuss options, and take the action you need in the way you need it. By minimizing complexity and bureaucracy, you can explore ideas, prioritize work, ensure accountability, and focus on delivering value through your strategic initiatives.

Keep it simple, stupid.

TAKEAWAYS

- Creating the right organizational infrastructure is what allows companies to excel in their markets. Building and sustaining advantages is not just about winning today but building an engine for growth that will last long into the future.

- Culture is an important component of strategy-execution that defines the organizational values and how people work together and communicate. Culture is ever-changing, and building it must be a mindful exercise to get good habits to stick.

- If underlying assumptions are not challenged, understood, or the limitations identified, those responsible for execution will not bridge the gap between dreams and reality.

- Embrace conflict and candor to build alignment, resolve issues, and increase the level of trust and transparency. Take issues head-on, especially the uncomfortable ones. Confront reality, not the person. Don't bury your head in the sand.

- Alignment between a strategy and core capabilities is critical to closing the strategy-execution gap. Strategy-execution is not a "one and done" effort. It grows from the compound effect of decisions, investments, and actions over time.

- Small actions by lots of people will result in a significant change.

- $1^{365} = 1$
- $1.01^{365} = 37.7!$

REFLECTION

- Does the culture of your organization inhibit or enhance the organization? Can you answer: What Must Our Culture Look Like to Win?

- What can you do to influence the culture in the right direction?

- Does misalignment exist because of assumptions, a lack of candor, and an aversion to conflict? If so, how can you change your behavior and influence that of others to improve the situation?

- Does your organization provide employee feedback and coaching in real-time? Can you describe specific behaviors that must change and provide your actual examples so the team member can "step into" the past scenarios?

- Are you setting a positive example to influence the culture?

- Do you look for ways to simplify everything? Do you encourage others to do the same?

INTERMISSION

So far in this book, we have become aware that there is a serious and persistent problem between setting a strategy and making it happen (execution). We learned that either, Shit Doesn't Get Done or Done on Time because of a pervasive lack of ownership and accountability at both the leadership and individual contributor levels of an organization. Someone always thinks that someone else is responsible for making something happen.

In Part II, we explored the dimensions of autonomy, empowerment, decentralization, ownership and accountability, communication best practices, and culture's impact in closing the strategy-execution gap. We also learned that continuous improvement is critical to maintaining an organization's Fit between the strategy and operational capabilities. Wrapping up this section, we now understand that excellent communication is vital to share the message with the whole organization and maintain the Sense of Urgency throughout.

Part III (You are here) is all about understanding and developing the leadership skills necessary to ensure that people at all levels of an organization have the mindset, capabilities, and drive to create a best-in-class organization. Leadership isn't something that only the people at the top of an organization must possess, but each person at each level of a structure. We understand that **Leaders are not born but are developed through a disciplined structure of personal development, growth, and learning**. This chapter is the first to examine what is required to become this leader and inspire others to lead by learning. The subsequent two chapters build on this material in Thinking and then Executing like a leader.

The first step in becoming a great leader is awareness and education- as the saying goes, we must first crawl to walk to run. Over time, an individual's persistent, focused, and applied efforts can and will generate outstanding performance. There is a quote attributed to Abraham Lincoln, which goes: "Give me six hours to chop down a tree, and I will spend the first four sharpening the ax." To execute well today, you must have prepared (and learned) and sharpened your ax yesterday.

As Kotter noted in his HBR article, *Leading Change: Why Transformation Efforts Fail*,

> "A paralyzed senior management often comes from having too many managers and not enough leaders. Management's mandate is to minimize risk and to keep the current system operating. Change, by definition, requires creating a new system, which in turn always demands leadership. Phase one in a renewal process typically goes nowhere until enough real leaders are promoted or hired into senior-level jobs." [70]

It's 100% true. Leadership, at all levels, is a focus area that requires a great deal of attention. As Warren Bennis once said, "Managers are people who do things right, and leaders are people who do the right thing."

PART I

PART II

PART III

CHAPTER 7

Getting Shit Done by Learning Like a Leader

"Career momentum can do a lot of the work for you and, indeed, carry you a long way. However, it is only when you add force to this that you create enhanced capability and extra achievement."

-David Maister [8]

"Nothing good ever happens to the slowest gazelle."

-Unknown

"The roots of knowledge are bitter, but its fruits are sweet."

-Aristotle

Once upon a time, in a land far, far away, career paths and employee education were safe, predictable, and worry-free. In exchange for loyalty and lifelong employment, the deal was that you surrendered autonomy. Thus, being an employee meant that you followed the rules, came in, did your job, and let the big wigs at the top of the hierarchy make the decisions and set the direction. What to do, how to do it, and when to do it would all be prescribed for you. If and when you became the boss, then you'd get to tell others what to do and how to do it.

When it came to employee development, the company also told you what to learn and what skills you needed to maintain. To facilitate this, the expenses were paid for, and the training took place on company time. So long as you joined a large organization, your career progression, development, and education would all be taken care of by someone else. As many industries used to be heavily regulated and safe from foreign competition, most business models stayed consistent and resilient from upheaval. Training classes, conferences, professional memberships, and advanced degrees were all par for the course over a long, long career. There was less to learn and more resources and time available to learn it in a simpler time.

However, things have changed over the last few decades—a lot.

The world has seen a sharp increase in the pace and scale of emerging global competition and, at the same time, a drastic acceleration in technology. To first survive, then thrive, incumbent organizations have adapted to become flatter, faster, and, as a result, more turbulent than ever before. The change in business models saw the old social contract between organizations and employees began to erode when downsizing became a way of life, and costs and headcounts were slashed to survive. **These changes have meant that a job is no longer guaranteed for life AND no longer were employees seen as an investment or as value to be maximized but rather a cost to be minimized.**

Previously, employees would stay with one organization for most of their careers. It made sense for the employer to invest heavily in employee education and development- there would be a return on the investment. The company would invest in an employee and expect a return over several years of improved performance. Simultaneously, the employee would not expect an immediate pay increase but may receive closer consideration for promotions. However, employee training became another discretionary expense with the new structure where management's attitude has become, "Why invest in them if they're just going to leave?" The puzzle, though, is that while companies have become more reluctant to pay for employee training, professional work has also become more specialized, and skills require constant upkeep. To illustrate the scope of the challenge, in a survey of executives by PWC this year (2020), eighty percent of CEOs now believe the need for new skills is their most significant business challenge. [64]

On the one hand, automation and new competition threaten many existing jobs- A study published by the Organization for Economic Co-operation and Development in 2018 estimated that 46 percent of all jobs have at least a 50 percent chance of being lost or considerably changed. Many older, long-established employees are discovering their skills, and jobs are becoming obsolete. At the same time, many young graduates find themselves unemployed and unemployable as college programs are disconnected from in-demand job skills. The industrialized world faces a severe skills crisis as there is a severe shortage of qualified talent for the new digital economy. In short, companies are looking for employees who have the talent, skills, and training to get shit done. [63]

This research reflects the bright side to the skills dilemma- the risk/reward scale has shifted in favor of employees. In today's environment, employees who take learning and their skills seriously can see an immediate and ongoing increase in salary and career progression. Demand for highly-skilled employees has increased, and competition (supply) has decreased since staying relevant now requires more effort and attention than it did before. The rewards are immense for those who can get learning right and make it part of their value offering.

The challenge is to get learning right. For many people, getting shit done begins with learning how to learn. Many of us have already found that learning isn't intuitive or as easy as we hope, and we sometimes find that what we think we may know may not be true at all. Learning is a skill that takes time to master, and in that vein, there is a right way to do it and a wrong way to do it.

This chapter will answer the following questions: How can we make learning part of the daily workflow? How do we develop and maintain new skills? How much time and effort is required to learn a new skill? Can we continue to learn as we get older, or is there a limit to what can be learned?

In this world, each employee is now responsible for themselves and must take ownership of their education and career to remain relevant. In this chapter, you'll learn the do's and don'ts of learning and developing the habits, practices, and methodology to mastering new skills and knowledge.

DUNNING-KRUGER EFFECT

"The only true wisdom is in knowing you know nothing."

– Socrates

**"If I don't know what I don't know, I think I know. If
I don't know what I know, I think I don't know."**

-R. D. Laing

Without fail, at almost every large family holiday get-together, there always seems to be that one aunt or uncle who takes the initiative to "educate" others around the dinner table on the hot issue of the day. Unafraid to speak freely on their feelings towards a particular matter or subject, throughout the meal, your relative will spout off at the mouth on a topic (most likely politics, religion, or both) with great confidence. While possessing the assurance of someone sharing the secrets to life itself, this relative will explain why his or her opinion is right, and everyone else's opinion is stupid, uninformed, or just plain wrong. Even though it is evident to everyone else (who are now visibly uncomfortable) in the room that the relative has no idea what he or she is talking about, that doesn't prevent this mouthy relative from continuing to talk on and on and on.

While at a family dinner, this sort of behavior can be downright painful or awkward to bear witness to. However, this sort of thing occurs even in business environments where the effect can be toxic. People who are ignorant of their shortcomings will simultaneously believe their ability is superior to others and will act only on their intuition.

So, what's going on here? Why do different people see, understand, and interpret the same information differently? If we are to learn about learning, we must first understand why the wires sometimes get crossed and misconstrued.

The scenario may seem familiar to most people because it is a real and researched condition known as the Dunning-Kruger effect. If you have not heard of it before, the Dunning-Kruger effect is a form of cognitive impairment bias in which people believe that they are more intelligent and more capable than they are. Essentially, **low ability people do not possess the awareness to recognize their incompetence.** This combination of poor self-awareness and low cognitive ability leads people to overestimate their capabilities.

The effect was coined in 1999 by researchers David Dunning and Justin Kruger. In their research, the two social psychologists performed a series of investigations and documented how people would consistently overrate their skills and underrate others' skills. Dunning and Kruger called this meta-ignorance, or ignorance of ignorance, leading to individuals overestimating their abilities.

The findings were summarized below:

> "People who scored in the lowest percentiles on tests of grammar, humor, and logic also tended to dramatically overestimate how well they had performed (their actual test scores placed them in the 12th percentile, but they estimated that their performance placed them in the 62nd percentile)." [119]

Low awareness + low cognitive ability= overestimation of capabilities

To further validate the Dunning-Kruger effect, we can see that Larry Bossidy came across these same ideas in his book, *Execution*. From his many years of experience as an executive consultant and CEO, Bossidy observed the same Dunning-Kruger phenomena and prescribed advice to combat the condition:

1) "Good leaders surround themselves with people smarter than themselves. So, when they encounter a problem, they don't have to whine, cast blame, or feel like victims. They know they'll be able to fix it." If you're the smartest person in the room, you're in the wrong room. If you look around the poker table and you can't see the sucker, you're it.

2) "Self-mastery: When you know yourself, you can master yourself. You can keep your ego in check, take responsibility for your behavior, adapt to change, embrace new ideas, and adhere to your standards of integrity and honesty under all conditions. Self-mastery is the key to true self-confidence. "[3] Take ownership of everything within your domain.

From research and anecdotal evidence, what is clear is that aside from increasing your skills, value, and influence within the organization, self-awareness is critical. Leaders who embrace self-awareness set the right example for others to follow. By acknowledging the Dunning-Kruger effect, they exhibit humbleness, which radiates authenticity and positivity instead of masking weakness or insecurity. Leaders who can consistently execute will acknowledge they don't know everything and openly own up to this around others.

The key is self-awareness and maintaining a system to check yourself.

If you recall back to the chapter of How Shit Gets Done, there was no magic formula or sure-fire tool provided to solve every problem. Instead, the How was highly fluid and dependent on the people facing the problem to self-identify the best solution by working collaboratively. By sharing knowledge between yourself and others, you can identify the best possible solutions, which can then be vetted to find the solution.

To raise self-awareness in yourself, seek to become actively curious, and encourage debate to bring up opposite views and learn from others. Armed with knowledge and inner security, you will develop your methodology for dealing with the unknown and linking what you know and don't know regarding the actions that must be taken.

The first step is to acknowledge that you are probably less self-aware than you think in seeking the answers. Doors open to new possibilities when we accept that no one knows all the answers all the time. Great leaders set themselves apart by accepting that training and learning is a journey with no end, nor do they embrace the fallacy that they are the smartest person in the room. Instead, great leaders are humble in accepting that they don't know more than they know, and they listen to others regardless of age, level of education, experience, or tenure.

Awareness is thinking, "What am I missing?" and not, "I know I'm right."

GRIT & PERSEVERANCE

"Nothing in the world can take the place of persistence. Talent will not; nothing is more common than unsuccessful men with talent. Genius will not; unrewarded genius is almost a proverb. Education will not; the world is full of educated derelicts. Persistence and determination alone are omnipotent."

-U.S. President Calvin Coolidge

"Success is the ability to move from failure to failure without loss of enthusiasm."

- Winston Churchill

Writer and director Woody Allen was once asked about his advice for aspiring creative professionals. Woody Allen replied with this reflection; "My observation was that once a person actually completed a play or a novel, then he was well on his way to getting it produced or published, as opposed to a vast majority of people who tell me their ambition is to write, but strikes out on the very first level and indeed never write the play or book. "

The message is simple (and as old as time); far too many people don't put words into action. There are plenty of organizations, executives, and teams with strategies and goals but cannot execute their plans. **Talk is cheap... but showing up, knowing which action to take, and taking action is a real differentiator in the business world.**

The challenge, though, is that mastering execution is a bit like remembering to eat right or to exercise regularly, we all know that we should be doing it, but it is too easy to fall back to what we know and what is comfortable. While we know what is good for us, we still struggle to be mindful enough to build up the mental armor that keeps poor habits at bay when we're exhausted. The gym memberships go unused, we eat more sweets than vegetables, and then we pack on the pounds.

What often happens with strategy-execution is that once people realize how long a journey will take or the amount of perseverance required to implement a strategy, efforts typically wane. What gives? Why can some people say that they will do something, and some people fall short somewhere in-between? Which factors determine why some people are consistently successful in the face of adversity? Even then, can perseverance be learned, or are we born with these traits?

The good news is that the answers to all these questions can be found in the concept of grit.

The idea of grit became mainstream in 2016 when author and researcher Angela Duckworth wrote her book with the same title, *Grit: The Power of Passion and Perseverance.* In her research, Duckworth studied multiple diverse teams, including West Point cadets, and identified the phenomenon where highly resilient people can, over time, hone natural talents into considerable skills to help them overcome adversity and hardships. [120]

The challenge that has perplexed observers for years is that at West Point, for example, nearly all candidates appeared equally capable of enduring the challenges faced on paper. The Cadets at West Point enter the program as outstanding athletes with excellent grades and team-leading experience... and yet only a portion of the students go on to complete the program each year. Duckworth's research studied the traits and characteristics and found the key to explain why certain people are outliers who consistently defy the odds. Surveys, interviews, and testing found that the students who would stick through the arduous training were those who had grit, which Duckworth defined as "demonstrated passion and perseverance for long-term goals."

Grit begins with having an" ultimate concern"–a goal you care about so much that it organizes and gives meaning to almost everything you do. Grit is about sticking through tough times and obstacles and maintaining the same top-level goal for a very long time.

Gritty people then overcome, adapt, and learn until that goal is reached. Gritty people hold steadfast to their goals even when obstacles are presented, mistakes are made, or progress grinds to a halt. When there is a will, gritty people find a way. Grit boils down to three words: perseverance, tenacity, and doggedness.

The good news for everyone is that grit is not an inherited trait but can be learned and developed. As Duckworth explored the topic, she developed the following formula to explain how skill is developed over time:

TALENT X EFFORT = SKILL

From the equation, we can understand that skill is a combination of talent and effort. Without effort, your skill is nothing more than what could have been done but wasn't.

$1 \times 0 = 0$

On the same note, effort without a baseline of talent is also ineffective.

$0 \times 1 = 0$

The key is effort; without effort, your talent is nothing more than unmet potential. Tremendous effort can compensate for modest skill, just as immense skill can compensate for modest effort, but not if the basis of either factor is zero. Grit comes into play and impacts effort when it manifests in focus. Focus allows individuals to apply effort for long durations through obstacles and over distractions. Only with a sustained effort does that talent become skill—quick bursts of effort for short periods are ineffective. In even fewer words: Duckworth had this to say, "If you work hard, you'll be rewarded. If you don't, you won't." [120]

Developing grit and sticking with the habits, discipline, and fortitude makes it possible to get good enough to make things happen. Strategy-execution requires grit to persevere through setbacks and resilience to remain persistent through difficult times. The emotional fortitude that comes from developing grit makes one unafraid of the technical hurdles that inevitably arise on the path to reaching their targets.

To assess your baseline of Grittiness, Duckworth has developed a free assessment on her site: **http:// angeladuckworth.com/grit-scale/**

To become grittier, set a goal and Pursue Deliberate Practice (become good enough to make execution possible).

DELIBERATE PRACTICE

"Strategy is a system of expedients. It is more than science; it is the application of knowledge to practical life, the evolution of an original guiding idea under constantly changing circumstances, the art of taking action under the pressure of the most difficult conditions."

-Helmuth von Moltke, 1871 [72]

Like Angela Duckworth, author Malcolm Gladwell was also curious about the factors that lead high-performing individuals to astronomical levels of success. They got amazing shit done; how did they do it? Gladwell's research in pursuit of an answer led to his book, *Outliers*, which explored the factors that led certain people to become extraordinary and identify a correlation between achievement and the amount of time people spent to hone their skills to expert levels.

You may be more familiar with Gladwell and his work due to his 10,000 hour-rule popularity, which was touted as a universal benchmark for the time required to become good at something. The promise of Gladwell's 10,000 rule led to its popularity by emphasizing that by hitting a clear threshold for hours of practice, that anyone and everyone could become an expert at anything. Golf, chess, art, business- the application was lauded as equally applicable. [71]

However, like many things that seem too good to be true, research has since debunked Gladwell's claims. Just spending 10,000 hours pursuing a goal does not make you an expert.

Playing 10,000 hours of tennis in the park with your friends won't get you to Wimbledon, just as 10,000 hours of watching Jeopardy won't make you the next Ken Jennings.

However, there is one thing that Malcolm Gladwell did get right and is worth further study. Without a doubt, it takes many years of effort to reach a level of expertise in any field. But while the time spent practicing is necessary to improve a skill, it is far from the only factor determining positive outcomes- what matters far more is how that time is spent. All practice isn't equal; someone repeating the same basic exercises over and over won't make them an expert over time.

Duckworth's work challenged the 10,000-hour rule for developing expertise and addressed this theory's weaknesses to make it more actionable for professionals. We now know that **deliberate or high-quality practice — not just practice alone — can make the difference in whether someone continues to improve or plateaus**. As Duckworth has noted, "It's possible to stay on the plateau if you're not practicing as experts do." Deliberate practice, which begins with a stretch goal, is applying complete focus on attaining that goal, obtaining feedback, and then reflecting on that feedback and refining one's practice as needed. If you wanted to get better at tennis, for example, you wouldn't play the same casual Saturday game with your friend. Instead, you would hire a coach, focus intensely on drills that improve each part of your game, you would play opponents of increasing skill, and you would continue to get feedback on where you need more practice. [120]

With the research from Duckworth and the adaptation of Gladwell's work, we can better understand that expertise is attainable for more than a small handful of gifted people. The takeaway is that by deliberately practicing a skill for long periods, mastery can be attained.

Summarized are the features of deliberate practice:

1) Deliberate practice is a highly structured activity,

the goal of which is to improve performance.

2)   Specific tasks are identified to overcome weaknesses. Performance is monitored to provide clues for ways to improve it further.

3)   Deliberate practice requires effort and is not inherently enjoyable.

4)   Individuals are motivated to practice because practice improves performance.

5)   Deliberate practice and output need to be measured over time to assess growth.

The good news from these findings is that you can improve your skills by identifying the aspects of execution or ownership where you are lacking and put a plan in motion to apply deliberate training. The time range may vary for different people, but what cannot vary is the persistence is sticking after the goal until it has been reached.

To reach our goals, we must first change our lifestyle and daily habits to see changes (and results) later. We must build and maintain new habits and not yield to all the old familiar temptations. There should be no excuse for not sharpening your current skills or looking to develop your hidden talents.

In your pursuit of knowledge and increased skills, keep in mind that practice must be balanced as it is deliberate. Rather than focusing on reaching some benchmark like 10,000 hours and cramming it into the shortest period possible, reflect on the words of the philosopher Seneca,

> "The mind must be given relaxation— it will rise improved and sharper after a good break. Just as rich fields must not be forced— for they will quickly lose their fertility if never given a break— so constant work on the anvil will fracture the force of the mind. But it regains its powers if it is set free and relaxed for a while. Constant

work gives rise to a certain kind of dullness and feebleness in the rational soul."

ON TRANQUILITY OF MIND, 17.5 [66]

Learning like a Leader means that you are balanced and deliberate in all that you pursue.

TWO TYPES OF INTELLIGENCE

"You are either improving or getting worse."

-Unknown

We've all heard someone explain away learning a new skill or technology by using the ole' standby, "you can't teach an old dog a new trick." The problem with this type of thinking is that it is not valid. While no two people are identical, most people do not have clear separations between what they can achieve or not.

Yes, while some people are born with a higher IQ than others, the advantage is not as enormous over time as we might assume. As we have learned previously in this chapter, that skill is a product of talent and effort combined; we can understand that applying deliberate practice and sticking with goals by developing grit can shorten this gap.

TALENT X EFFORT
= SKILL

To learn and to improve our skills and knowledge, there are two pieces to the whole picture that must be understood that will illustrate that these concepts are not a pseudo-business-psychology concepts.

FLUID INTELLIGENCE + CRYSTALIZED INTELLIGENCE= TOTAL INTELLIGENCE

Our total intelligence is not a fixed score but rather something that can be improved over time. Intelligence is not just one but two separate elements. Intelligence is the power of both types of intelligence combined- fluid intelligence and crystallized intelligence. Although we are born with a certain amount of intelligence and potential, we can study, learn, and grow our intelligence over time. People become smart!

In his book *"Intelligence: Its Structure, Growth, and Action,"* Raymond Cattell referred to the ability to reason as fluid intelligence because it "has the 'fluid' quality of being directable to almost any problem. He referred to knowledge acquisition as crystallized intelligence because it "is invested in the particular areas of crystallized skills which can be upset individually without affecting the others."

Cattell challenged the idea of the generalized intelligence factor (known as g), which contends that intelligence is a single construct. Instead, Cattell contended that there are two independent intelligence factors: fluid and crystallized intelligence. [121]

Fluid Intelligence

> **"Education is the kindling of a flame,**
> **not the filling of a vessel."**
>
> **– Socrates**
>
> **"The measure of intelligence is the ability to change. "**
>
> **-Einstein**
>
> **"It's not what you know, it's how fast you can learn."**
>
> **- Liz Wiseman**

Fluid intelligence can be understood as your essential analytical capacity- your raw processing power. Fluid intelligence refers to the ability to take in information and reason and think flexibly. Fluid intelligence involves thinking and reasoning abstractly and solving problems and is considered independent of learning, experience, and education. We are all born with fluid intelligence, which increases through adolescence and early adulthood. Fluid intelligence begins to decline gradually beginning in your 30's. [121]

Fluid intelligence is described as the "general ability to think abstractly, reason, identify patterns, solve problems, and discern relationships." It depends mainly on one's native ability and is not obtained or acquired through education, training, or even experience and exposure to various environmental factors.

Fluid intelligence is used when solving puzzles, answering riddles, or developing strategies to solve a particular problem. If you are someone who is "street smart," that's a way of saying that you have high fluid intelligence. One way to identify this type of intelligence is its flexibility and how adaptive it is. It can be applied or used in different ways, depending on the situation.

1. Capacity to reason

2. Ability to learn new things

3. Abstract thinking and problem-solving abilities

Crystallized Intelligence

"Knowledge is having the right answer. Intelligence is asking the right questions."

-Unknown

"The illiterate of the 21st century will not be those who cannot read and write but those who cannot learn, unlearn, and relearn."

- ALVIN TOFFLER

The second intelligence curve, which social psychologists call the crystallized intelligence curve inversely, goes up through your 30's 40's, 50's and beyond well into advanced age. Crystallized intelligence is what you learn from experiences, reading, school, and relationships. Crystallized intelligence refers to the accumulation of knowledge, facts, and skills acquired throughout life- this is the tribal wisdom highly valued across the world. As we age and accumulate new knowledge and understanding, our crystallized intelligence becomes stronger. [121]

Crystallized intelligence is the opposite of fluid intelligence because it is about accumulating knowledge and skills obtained through education, learning, and experience. While fluid intelligence remains the same throughout a person's life, crystallized intelligence can increase. Crystallized intelligence is your pre-existing knowledge: facts, skills, and information you learned in school or from experience.

An example often cited as crystallized intelligence is vocabulary. As you go to school every year, your vocabulary knowledge increases. We all begin with a basic grasp of the English language, but we build on what we know each year. We use old words in new ways and learn more, adding a more dynamic and creative use of words to express ourselves. Only by becoming more familiar with new words does our vocabulary increase.

1. Based on facts
2. Increases with age
3. Prior learning and experiences

So, how does this apply to the strategy-execution gap and Learning Like a Leader?

We must be aware of both types of intelligence in regards to the strategy-execution. We are often presented with challenges and must answer the question: What do we do, How do we do it? Who does it? When do we do it? Fully answering all of these questions requires fluid intelligence and crystallized intelligence.

To reach our maximum potential, we must embrace education in all forms as a never-ending yet rewarding exercise. We can no longer believe that we are as good as we will ever be, but rather that we are only a fraction of our true potential.

Our new understanding of intelligence helps us accept and advocate that everyone has the potential and ability to learn and grow in their personal lives and careers.

MOST TRAINING IS USELESS

"It is, after all, the dab of grit that seeps into an oysters shell that makes a pearl, not pearl making seminars with other oysters."

-Stephen King

"Businesses often use training as a surrogate for the hard work of true skill development."

-Bill Peper, facilitator within General Motors' Standards for Excellence process

"Training is too often used as an inexpensive way to look like you're doing something if you're a manager. As typically done, it requires little time and little personal change."

-Ted Harro

As we learned earlier, the most effective approach to learning new skills as individuals is to apply deliberate practice to training and develop grit to set, reach, and reset our goals to get better as we go along in our careers. By studying the Dunning-Kruger Effect, we have learned to be more self-aware of our inclination to assume that we know more than we do and continuously challenge our understanding of the world. In the last section, we learned that intelligence is not fixed, and growth has no limit to what can be mastered or achieved.

In all, it's fair to say that much of this chapter has been about independent study. Yes, we can improve ourselves and encourage others to learn on their own time, but what about organized group education? How's that going along?

And, of course, here is where we come upon another paradox. When learning involves more than an individual effort and takes place in a corporate setting, we take something fulfilling and valuable, squeeze the life out of it, and transform it into this unholy abomination we recognize as training.

When most people hear the word training today, the blood runs out of their faces, and their body slumps as if the life has just been sucker-punched. Training connotes an experience that is a painful, time-consuming, and utterly useless exercise by most accounts, pretending to take employee development seriously. As soon as more than one person is added to an educational exercise, all the rules and best practices go right out the window. Not only is most training in today's companies ineffective, but the purpose, timing, and content of training are flawed by design.

We've all been through the gamut of training workshops, online courses, and lectures that give training a bad name. Most training has turned into a box-checking exercise rather than a genuine development activity. Only a tiny fraction of formal training is ever put into practice, and as a result, most of the business training is a waste of money and time for everyone involved. Because most training, courses, and conferences are organized as stand-alone events, they are deemed irrelevant because they are disconnected from the work done and the problems at hand.

While we attend the sessions as a prerequisite to keeping our jobs, many of us have developed our own tips and tricks to get through the sessions as quickly as possible. We'll patiently listen and half-tune out the instructors, then go through the motions to complete the courses and guess our way through any sort of assessment at the end. Once we see a window of opportunity to escape, we'll quickly run back to our offices so that we can finally get back to doing our jobs.

Year after year, it's the same charade that we torture ourselves and the other people we work with. Frustrating and ineffective puts the situation lightly.

More than anecdotal evidence or perceptions, there's a great HBR article titled, "Where Companies Go Wrong with Learning and Development," which brings to light the hard evidence of the training plight:

1. "75% of 1,500 managers surveyed from across 50 organizations were dissatisfied with their company's Learning & Development (L&D) function;
2. 70% of employees report that they don't have mastery of the skills needed to do their jobs;
3. Only 12% of employees apply new skills learned in L&D programs to their jobs; and
4. Only 25% of respondents to a recent McKinsey survey believe that training measurably improved performance. " [63]

The source of the training problem has been cited on all sorts of issues, whether lack of managerial clarity, uninterested learners, or outdated training practices.

Suppose you've had experience attending corporate training. In that case, you will have noticed that most training is designed from a top-down hierarchy and is initiated by someone at the executive or director level who thinks: "The people need these skills, and we'll hire someone to teach it to them." The people who come in to do the training are so detached from the organization that they don't know how to connect the message to the organization's priorities or the work done each day. Or if the course is video-based, the training is so generic that the message tries to reach everyone, but in doing so, reaches no one.

Rarely (or just about never) has someone come back from a three-hour marathon workshop and immediately applied what they have just half-listened to. When employees don't use the skills they've learned after training, knowledge decay sets in quickly.

To illustrate this point, German psychologist Hermann Ebbinghaus pioneered experimental studies of memory in the late 19th Century, culminating with his discovery of "The Forgetting Curve." He found that if new information isn't applied, we'll forget about 75% of it after just six days. New skills must be practiced and applied. [63]

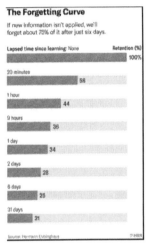

Image41- The Forgetting Curve

If we were to step back, reflect, and think about the skills that we have learned throughout our lives and careers, we would find that the most impactful learning occurs when facing an immediate and pressing problem. An obstacle that halts progress causes us to apply all of our focus and energy to conduct our research, test the idea, and apply it.

The root cause of this core problem with training — that training is rarely applied — comes from training designed and dictated by people other than those who do the work.

Like most other practices, the best training is most helpful when it comes from a decentralized process. Decentralization strikes again. When one person comes across an idea, a tool, or technology that helps them do their job with more significant results in less time, they should be so excited that they can't wait to share that information with others.

Even though someone may not be a professional trainer, **what matters is what is being shared and whether or not it can be applied to real business problems**. Training done by an organization's people results in much higher acceptance and application rates. As Bossidy commented in execution, "80% of learning should take place outside the classroom. Every leader and supervisor needs to be a teacher; classroom learning should be about giving them the tools they need." [3]

To maximize the training's effectiveness, the training should be conducted by the teams and groups that work together regularly so that the training can be action- and decision-oriented and collective commitments can be established. If the training applies to what the team is working on, good ideas and practices can be discussed in detail and then tested. A team member would share the information they discovered and the application and gauge interest to see if others would like to learn how to solve similar problems. Then, training would occur—no fancy PowerPoints or speeches but real problems and real solutions in real-time.

When people understand and "own" the importance of a topic, they recognize the topic's purpose, meaning, value, and role in their careers; thus, they often seek out and find resources. **Any person who has found a good idea and has applied it to their work should be the trainer for others.**

Rather than adding distractions to other people's busy schedules, training should be structured and carried out in a way that helps others improve the quality or efficiency of what they are doing today. Training should be scheduled on topics that can be applied straightaway.

The key is to assess the effectiveness of training offered in your organization by asking the following questions:

1) What behaviors must change to convince people that new skills, abilities, and capabilities are required?

2) Are the right people performing the training?

3) How will the impact of the training be measured? Who will perform the follow-ups?

4) What must happen before and after the training sessions occur to bring about change?

Today's dynamic business environment calls for organizations and their people to adapt to changing circumstances and always be learning rapidly. Excellent training requires allowing people closest to the work to experience new ideas, discuss them, test them, and implement them. With the proper preparation and follow-up, training can be compelling. And even better, decentralized training can be organized and executed in much less time and with much less cost than the traditional methodology.

Furthermore, as technology continues to grow and organizations face new challenges at a furious pace of change, we need to arm ourselves with the information necessary to adapt to our circumstances. What may have worked or used to work to solve a particular problem may no longer be applicable. We used to live with the issues because we could not find a solution that may now be solvable. As we learned in How Shit Gets done, there is no clear-cut recipe for overcoming obstacles. We need to commit to becoming the best versions of ourselves to set ourselves up for sustained success.

Without all this in mind, training will be (and usually is) a wasted opportunity.

TAKEAWAYS

1. The Dunning-Kruger Effect- ignorance of one's ignorance.

- We are not as good as we think we are—we frequently overestimate our ability and underestimate others' abilities.

- There is room to improve.

- We must practice self-awareness by embracing humility and critical thinking. Businesses and individuals who challenge their assumptions will, at worst, come away better equipped to improve themselves and their processes.

- "We are blind to our blindness." -Daniel Kahneman

- "To transform an organization, you either have to change the people . . . or change the people."

-Strategic Execution

2. Grit

- "No" isn't an option.

- talent x effort = skill

- All challenges can be overcome.

- Adversity is a friend, not an enemy.

- Grit begins with having an" ultimate concern"– a goal you care about so much that it organizes and gives meaning to almost everything you do. Grit is about sticking through tough times and obstacles and maintaining the same top-level goal for a very long time.

3. Deliberate Practice

- We only improve with a focused practice that stretches our capabilities.

- We must regularly assess our skills and improve both strengths and weaknesses.

- Knowledge + skill is what are required to bridge the gap between strategy and execution. (Knowledge + Skill = Capabilities)

Learning is a powerful and valuable practice that maximizes our potential and the value that we add to our professional and personal lives. Learning delivers fulfillment through new experiences, new ideas, better working methods, and increased satisfaction levels. Learning and enlightenment are genuinely part of what makes life a joy.

By incrementally adding knowledge each day, over time, anyone can become a leader by learning to overcome obstacles and deliver results through strategy execution consistently. This will lead to additional responsibility, higher compensation, and reaching career goals. If you want to stay mentally strong, despite your career's slow growth, focus on the things you can control; your thoughts, feelings, and behavior. Keep a positive attitude and focus on your effort.

What separates great leaders from everyone else is that they have a unique ability never to stop learning. They are incredibly flexible and quick to adapt to changing conditions, and they master the skills that help them become influential leaders. They are excited about the possibility of learning a new skill or tool because they don't compare themselves to others- they compete against who they were yesterday.

REFLECTION

1)   Ask Yourself This Question Every Day: Ask yourself, "Did I sharpen my skills today?" Your skills might involve technical skills related to your job, or they might refer to your listening skills if you're looking to improve your communication. What new skills or knowledge have you been building on?

2)   How will you measure and track your progress to reach higher levels of masters for yourself and your team?

3)   How well do you empower your organization's members to own and solve problems, distribute decision-making lower in the organizational structure, and gain from their collective knowledge?

4)   How effective is your organization in establishing the capacity to manage reasonable risk by trying new things, prototyping, testing, and learning?

5)   How well does your team and organization share what you've learned with other parts of the organization?

6)   Is a learning mindset a nice to have or a must-have at your organization? Has this led to positive results or dissatisfaction?

7)   Are people encouraged to take on new challenges that require perseverance and determination to

complete?

8) Is training at your organization led by skilled insiders or outsourced to outsiders? Who decides what skills and technologies will be trained on- the people or management?

CHAPTER 8

Getting Shit Done by Thinking Like a Leader

"Improvise, adapt, overcome."

- Green Berets

"Grant me the serenity
to accept the things I cannot change,
the courage to change the things I can,
and the wisdom to know the difference."
- Serenity prayer

"Theory without practice is pointless; practice
without theory is mindless."

- Andrew MacLennan

INTRODUCTION

Characterizing what a leader is and how a leader thinks can be a daunting exercise. Take a minute, go to your web browser, and Google the term "leader" or "leadership mindset," and read through some of the results. As you scroll down the page and click on the different articles, you will find no lack of creativity or quantity in the leadership behaviors, characteristics, and actions identified by different people and organizations. How different people address the leadership question will likely depend on each person's perspectives, experiences, and intended audience. Everyone has his or her own little spin on the idea.

To make the definition of leadership even more challenging, consider that the exercise above only covers the context of general leadership. When you now add in the requirements of defining what leadership is in a strategy-execution context, the list of characteristics only grows larger and more intricate.

If we were to step back and think about what's been covered so far in this book, you'd note we've learned that a leader is a master or aspiring master possessing both soft and hard skills. To bridge the strategy-execution gap, a leader is also responsible for aligning the organization's main strategy, "The Big What," to all "The Little What's" that define the daily life in the organization by integrating The How.

As Bossidy noted on the disparity between strategy and execution,

> "Setting strategy is elegant. It's a clean and sophisticated process of collecting and analyzing data, generating insights, and identifying smart paths forward. When

strategy is finished, there's a PowerPoint deck, board meetings, and high-fives. Execution, on the other hand, is putting on boots and trudging through the mud. Execution involves everything that comes next and is a "systematic way of exposing reality and acting on it." [3]

Because they are so different, strategy and execution require different types of thinking. Strategic thinking is long-term thinking, usually in the context of 3-5 years out. Execution thinking is action-oriented thinking, focused on the present or near future. Thinking like a leader requires the ability to do both with equal skill. Leadership thinking isn't just about doing one thing right; it's doing many things and many different types of things, and often at the same time. As shades of grey color our environment, do you have the mental bandwidth, perspective, and experience necessary to overcome the hurdles? Can you apply the spirit of the GSD body of knowledge to tackle each scenario appropriately?

Yes, it's fantastic to have a great leader's situational awareness and learning habits, but your overall impact will be limited if you aren't ready to step up and think differently.

To close the strategy-execution gap and build operational and professional excellence in our organizations, we must act differently and think differently.

CHESS, NOT CHECKERS

"Chess is like looking across an ocean. Checkers is like looking down a well."

- Dr. Marion F. Tinsley

"Winning in this game is all a matter of understanding how to capitalize on the strengths of each piece and timing their moves just right."

- Bobby Fisher

"Everybody Has a Plan Until They Get Punched in the Mouth."

- Mike Tyson

Most of us begin in our leadership journey by utilizing a management approach with striking similarities to the game of checkers. Checkers is a fun, highly reactionary game often played at a frantic pace. The rules are clear and easy to learn. The available strategies employed in this leadership style are limited, if not rudimentary: jump over enough opposing pieces while losing fewer of your own, to reach the opposite starting point on the board.

In checkers, all the pieces are uniform and move in the same way; they are interchangeable. All the pieces are identical at first and exhibit the same behavior until they are "Kinged." Only then can pieces receive additional dimensions to their movements. As a player, you must plan and coordinate each piece's movements, but all pieces move at the same pace, on parallel paths. Checkers is akin to having a limited toolset and a black and white view of the world and problem-solving approach. Early in our careers, we are free to move quickly and have fun along the way.

Leadership today can better be compared to chess, a game in which strategy matters—a game in which individual pieces have unique abilities that drive unique contributions. The saying goes, "it is easy to learn but takes a lifetime to master." Chess is deceptively deep and requires heightened focus and intuition to win. Each of the six types of pieces moves differently in chess, and you can't play if you don't understand each piece's unique value and vulnerabilities.

Chess champions and great leaders reach high success levels due to their lifelong study of the game- masters train themselves to recognize the many and various play patterns. No chess player has ever walked into a professional-level tournament off the streets with little to no training and won. Chess mastery involves years of study, practice, and coaching for each player. Similarly, to build an execution mindset, you must be willing and able to commit to the same discipline in increasing your awareness through deliberate practice.

By understanding how to play each game and use each piece against each opponent, you will have a broader and more dynamic set of tools available to you. When you take a harder look, the difference is that checkers is a game about following the rules, while chess is about knowing how to apply the rules in different contexts best.

Perhaps the most remarkable difference between chess and checkers is how the players prepare for matches. Checkers players show up, and whatever happens, happens. Chess players study the game and are never done learning.

Strategy-Execution in Chess
Strategy Thinking in terms of chess is approaching problems

with the mindset of: "What is the fewest number of moves required to win?"

In chess, the most important thing is simple: protect the king. If you protect your king and check the opposing king, you win. So, in playing the game, each move revolves around doing everything you can to protect your king while taking out the other king.

When the chess game begins, the best chess players have their strategy set. They have a plan for winning the game, capturing the opponent's king in the fewest moves possible without losing their king first. Now comes the Execution part.

One of the first execution lessons from chess is to remember what is important. It doesn't matter if you captured more of your opponent's pieces, whether you've taken their highly valued queen or anything else but whether you have "checked" their king into submission.

As a leader participating in strategy-execution, you must know what is most essential and shield it with everything you have. It's easy to get distracted during the game and chase the wrong things. Like chess players, good strategy-execution thinkers also realize that a single loss on the board does not necessarily lead to total failure—losing a piece is not the end of the game unless the king is lost. If you make an error or lose a person on your team, that's okay- It is not the end, but you must look at what you have remaining to continue the game. You must be able to adapt, redefine, and execute on your path to victory. There is a nearly infinite set of paths towards achieving your goal.

Chess- Develop a Strategy but Prepare to Adapt

In chess and life, you can have a strategy, but an unexpected move or circumstance can and will often force you to adjust your plan.

Chess players are known for their ability to quickly iterate between alternatives in their minds and play out the probabilities and reactions to each set of actions. Each action or process is viewed from multiple perspectives: If A, then B, or C. If B, then D, or F. Chess players learn to see the game holistically and understand that they are playing not just a strategic game but a mental game, as well.

Before, we learned that "plans are useless, but planning is everything"; that applies here because the game of chess depends on your opponent. If your opponent does not react to the initial strategy intended, you must adapt on the fly. Winning strategies are not memorized start-to-finish choreography but rather practical and proven patterns. Chess players learn to recognize patterns of pieces that turn into success.

Leaders who bridge the strategy-execution gap think and act like master chess players: they can see the whole game—the sequence of all probable steps and actions, not merely the next piece to move. In every game, the player must react to their opponent's moves and strategy to their strategy. What could have been the plan might quickly change depending on the opposing strategy in play? Rarely do master chess players get surprised by losing because they forgot to move a piece or fell into a simple trap. Instead, chess players prepare themselves for play by accepting that the best strategy is not the one they started with but will win. Chess champions see opportunities or weaknesses in their opponents; they must then work to lay a trap for their opponent to walk into. It's subtle until it's not.

Lessons from the Chess Board

Both chess and strategy-execution are similar because there must be a flexible strategy and an understanding of the intricate players and roles. In chess, the objective is to capture or "check" the opponent's king. While there are hundreds of answers to this riddle, the right solution that wins that game comes from studying your current opponent and making the right decisions under the present circumstances.

In this chapter, we'll explore in more detail the lessons in thinking like a leader that we can draw from chess, which includes:

Be Decisive. The best chess players have a strategy set for capturing the opponent's king, but the play doesn't begin until they make their move. In professional chess matches, there is even a timer. It doesn't matter how brilliant you are; you have to ACT.

Be Proactive. Chess is not checkers. You are always thinking three, five, maybe even ten or more moves ahead (if you're a chess master).

Be Prepared. The best chess players are masters of the game. They've learned all the moves. They've done their homework or know from experience the strategies and playing styles of their opponents. They can execute because they come prepared.

Be Focused. Chess masters stay focused on the battle they've chosen. If an opponent's move suddenly makes one of the opponent's chess pieces vulnerable, the chess master will not be distracted from his strategy. Think like a leader, choose your battles carefully, and then stay focused on that battle no matter what tempting detours or distractions may appear.

Be Innovative. Chess masters win with strategies and moves that their opponents never envisioned or expected. But they also play within the norms and rules of the game. Groundbreaking chess masters are mavericks, not heretics.

BE DECISIVE

"You're allowed to fail; you're not allowed to not try."

- David Maister

"Done is better than perfect."

- Cheryl Sandberg

"Not making a choice is still a choice."

- Unknown

The strategy-execution mindset is about making the best decision possible with the available facts and information and committing to action. It's having the knowledge, grit, and skills to assess a situation, collaborate, plan, and then move forward. Execution is a process of considering alternative paths to achieve a clear goal and then taking action. You either do, or you don't.

If we wanted to boil this down to even fewer words, we could say that closing the strategy-execution gap depends on decisiveness.

Strategy-Execution thinking isn't a lengthy process of considering your options, deliberating, thinking, discussing, pursuing one option, pulling back, deliberating further, and then doing nothing. This is the typical reaction to challenges in organizations. Responsibility is diffused, and nothing is decided, and because nothing is decided, nothing happens. When decisions are denied or deferred, the organization as a whole takes note- engagement plummets, and then productivity plummets. Once a challenge becomes a crisis, scenario upon scenario pile upon each other with no one doing what is required to address each one.

Just like a ticking time bomb, deferring action can cause the problem to blow up at an inopportune time... and cause severe damage. The problem with indecision is that it starts with the small things and graduates to the more critical challenges and difficulties. Even worse, indecisiveness can be perceived as doing something to others who aren't carefully observant.

Strategy-Execution = Decisiveness

Take Ownership

As we learned before, leadership is tied to ownership. A decision demonstrates ownership in acknowledging that we are responsible. Instead of hiding from outcomes, decisive leaders instead look for and embrace challenges as opportunities.

Indecisiveness is a dangerous trait in weak leaders because rather than face a challenging scenario, they hide from it or delegate it away. Rather than say the right thing, which may cause a confrontation and debate, they remain silent.

Thinking like a leader is having the mindset and critical eye to determine when "I am the best person to decide." In other words, decisiveness is a must-have trait in leaders because it puts ownership and accountability back into the hands of the people who have the best vantage point and resources required to make an impact.

Indecisiveness signals to others in the organization that your strategy as a leader is hope—hope that someone else knows what to do and will, by some chance, know that they must do it. You hope that someone else will step in to solve your problems. When you fail to act, you fail to display leadership. Momentum is lost. Enthusiasm is lost. Confidence is lost. If you don't make a decision or make a change, then your strategy is hope. You should say it loud and proud to those around you to eliminate any confusion about your value proposition to the organization.

Thinking Like a Leader > hope

Be Collaborative—Up to a Point

To think like a leader and take ownership and accountability does not mean that you make every decision without input or help from others.

Great leaders can quickly and fluidly assess a situation by pulling together people to help think through each path and understand who must agree, who should have inputs, who has ultimate responsibility for making the decision, and crucially, who is accountable for follow-through. By having a process to iterate through these steps quickly, smoother coordination and quicker response times follow.

While multiple people can contribute ideas and suggestions on what should be done, there should be a single decision-maker who is the single point of accountability. This person must bring the decision to closure and commit the organization to act on it. Whoever does wind up making the final decision should have sound business judgment, a grasp of the relevant trade-offs, a bias for action, and a keen awareness of the organization that will execute the decision. Always be ready to answer "Who needs to do What and by When" in each scenario.

Decisiveness is about gathering the relevant information based on activity drivers, building assumptions for the unknowns using the best information available at the time, and then pulling the trigger. The objective shouldn't be consensus, but buy-in after the decision is made.

In working to reach a decision, collaboration is essential, deliberation is vital, but there needs to be a cutoff point where people move forward in a coordinated effort. A strong leader intuitively knows where this point lies.

Talk <> Action

Good Is Good Enough
Often, good is good enough to make a smart decision.

To think like a leader, we recognize which factors matter to performance and which don't. While we must accept some ambiguity, we should seek to minimize it as much as we can, as quickly as we can. Indecisiveness is sometimes caused by a perfectionist mentality where we focus an incredible amount of time and resources chasing the things that don't matter. Execution and decisiveness are about identifying the 20% of factors that drive 80% of the results.

Thinking Like a Leader > Overthinking

The appealing aspect of strategy-execution thinking is that even if (and when) you make the wrong decision, you will have the opportunity to learn from it. Once the smoke settles, you can step back and examine the pattern of thoughts and actions that led to your faulty conclusion. You can chart out your state of mind in considering the factors and explain your actions so that next time a decision is required, you will better understand what should or should not have been done.

With each new challenge, you can adapt your approach and improve over time. The faster that you can arrive at a decision, the faster you can execute. The better you get and the faster you can adapt from wins and losses, the better your chances of delivering superior skyrockets in the long run. Every time you execute, you can learn what works and what doesn't work- and, importantly, why.

Making good decisions and executing them quickly are the hallmarks of high-performing organizations. **As the saying goes, a good decision executed quickly beats a brilliant decision implemented slowly.**

REACTIVE OR PROACTIVE

"Failure to prepare means preparing to fail."

- Unknown

**"I am not a product of my circumstances.
I am a product of my decisions."**

- DR. STEPHEN R. COVEY

In *The Seven Habits of Highly Effective People*, being proactive is the first habit that needs to be mastered. And rightly so. The paradigm of being reactive versus proactive touches all aspects of life. Whether it is in education, your community, or your job, outcomes are more favorable when you demonstrate ownership of your life and your condition to make the most of it. [123]

Being proactive means that you're prepared to act.

Being reactive means that you're ready to blame.

Reactive people don't act; they're acted upon.

Of the characteristics included in strategy-execution, being proactive is critical because it is so closely tied to the concept of ownership. For example, if you aren't mindful of how work is best conducted in business, you may leave a web of resource-consuming madness behind you. If you aren't proactive in your education and skills, you'll be unprepared to meet new challenges or keep up with old ones.

Proactivity is powerful because it requires an individual to accept responsibility for his/her situation (no matter how dire) and take the initiative to make things better. Successful leaders embrace proactiveness and go above and beyond when delivering ideas and time to a project. The next time you or someone on your team thinks you've done enough, do just a little bit more to ensure that Shit Gets Done and done right. Always think about "what if" rather than "what is" to become more proactive.

Thinking proactively is more than being prepared; it is a posture you take towards the world. Instead of letting conditions and circumstances shape decisions, proactive leaders allow their values, experiences, and perspective to determine the choices they make. Proactive people act on their world rather than being acted upon. Even though they aren't sure what to expect, they know how to handle themselves when life shows up.

Proactive leaders become comfortable with ambiguity as they learn always to anticipate what could and may happen. Being ready and hoping for the best but expecting the worst will make you more effective and skilled in reacting to and handling the unforeseen. If you fail to plan, you plan to fail.

Proactive leadership thinking focuses on eliminating problems before they have a chance to appear, while reactive thinking is based on responding to events after they have happened. The difference between these two mindsets is the perspective each one provides in assessing actions and events.

Reactive leaders suffer and strain as they let their circumstances and conditions control them. They don't see the gap between the circumstances and outcomes and might inadvertently believe that one determines the other. If the weather is foul, a reactive leader will be in a foul mood, too. If someone is short with them, they are short with others. When reactive leaders get negative feedback, they become defensive and bitter. Reactive leaders see the world as not their problem and have detached themselves from any form of ownership.

Thinking proactively matters a great deal, not in just leading or participating in strategy-execution but in staying relevant and employable. As New York Times columnist and bestselling author Thomas Friedman wrote, "Employers are all looking for the same kind of people — people who have not only the critical thinking skills to do the value-adding jobs that technology can't, but also people who can invent, adapt, and reinvent their jobs every day, in a market that changes faster than ever."

Some reactive thinking phrases to look out for:

1. There's nothing I can do.
2. They make me so mad.
3. They won't allow that.
4. I have to do that.
5. I can't do that.
6. If only I could.

Whenever you catch yourself using one of these reactive phrases, replace it with a proactive one:

- Let's look at our alternatives.
- I can choose a different approach.
- I control how I respond to this.
- I choose.
- I prefer.
- I will.

Be clear and systematic. Take ownership. Think proactively.

LUCKY OR PREPARED

"Anyone can get lucky; not everyone can persevere."

- The Daily Stoic

"Luck is what happens when preparation meets opportunity."

- Seneca

"There are facts and opportunities and realities, and how you respond to them determines whether you succeed or fail. Luck becomes a convenient excuse when things don't go your way and a rationale for staying comfortable while you wait for luck to determine your fate. You can't become excellent at execution if you're willing to gamble everything on the unknown. "

- Grover, Tim S. Relentless: From Good to Great to Unstoppable

"I believe that people make their own luck by great preparation and good strategy."

- Jack Canfield

When General Dwight D. Eisenhower wrote to his wife on the eve of the invasion of Normandy, he told her, "Everything we could think of has been done, the troops are fit, everybody is doing his best. The answer is in the lap of the gods."

Powerful, right? The leader in charge of perhaps the most powerful army the world had ever assembled, on the eve of the most expertly organized and planned invasion the world will hopefully ever know, was humble enough to know that he could not control the outcome. Instead, Eisenhower did everything in his power to be ready for whatever challenge arose the next day. [66]

Eisenhower was a great general because he understood the importance and distinction between being prepared versus being lucky. Being prepared means that you have considered the possible, you've considered the improbable, and you're considered the impossible. You've put together a plan and have trained for each scenario. Luck is picking one of the three possible scenarios and throwing everything into just one basket.

However, the challenge is that being prepared instead of lucky requires a lot of work and leadership. It involves training for events that are likely not going to happen but being ready if they do. It involves anticipating the unknown through contingency plans. Leadership thinking is hoping that plans work out and that people know what they have to do and by when, but still planning for what we can't possibly know. We become luckier by training ourselves and the people around us to handle unforeseen circumstances.

It's important not to confuse risk aversion with luck. If we take no chances, then our odds of not being wrong go down by 100%. Instead, leaders who exhibit the strategy-execution mindset identify the scenarios with a high payoff and more than likely odds of succeeding. Preparation, then, addresses the circumstances that could later be prescribed as bad luck. Preparation is responsible for what outsiders might observe as "good luck." A professional poker player betting on a strong hand does not have the same odds as an addict playing scratch-off lotto tickets in a convenience store. Both take risks, but only one takes action, precautions, and a strategy to command ownership of the outcomes.

Here's the litmus test: If good fortune comes your way and

you're surprised, then you're lucky.

BATTLES WIN WARS

"The talent of the strategist is to identify the decisive point and to concentrate everything on it, removing forces from secondary fronts and ignoring lesser objectives."

- Carl von Clausewitz

Sun Tzu's "Art of War" implored readers to be mindful in the pursuit of opportunities. To think like a leader, recognize that not all opportunities are equal, and some opportunities should never be pursued:

> "It is said that if you know your enemies and know yourself, you will not be imperiled in a hundred battles; if you do not know your enemies but do know yourself, you will win one and lose one; if you do not know your enemies nor yourself, you will be imperiled in every single battle." [43]

You will find that wherever you work and whatever you do, there will always be more opportunities than resources enough to engage with each one. While many tempting battles or business opportunities are available to choose from, we must be capable and willing to identify the most critical opportunities to win, producing the highest output. Those that produce the highest output are those fights that take place on the critical path to achieving an organization's strategy.

From Art of War:

> "The main strategy in war is to define the desired outcome and specific goal; the tactics in war deals with current tasks and problems. The chances to win are

high; if the commander has made strong preliminary calculations, he wins even before the battle starts. If the commander does not think and reason and refers depreciatingly to the enemy, he will surely become his prisoner." [43]

Here, it is worth pointing out that awareness and decisiveness go hand in hand in warfare and strategy-execution. People who think like leaders are hyper-aligned and laser-focused on the highest-impact actions that drive the organization's most important outcomes. They study the opportunities available, rally and commit the resources, and say "yes" to the critical battles and "no" to the distractions. They pick the battles that set the stage to give themselves every benefit possible and their detractors every obstacle.

When choosing your battles, always take the time to organize, create a plan, and connect what you're considering to the organization's strategy. Sometimes, it is tempting to commit heavily towards early battles meaningless in the war (strategy). If you are too quick to jump into action and tend to start a project without a well-organized plan of attack, resources and energy will get bogged down.

Because we have limited time and energy, we must learn to pick our battles. Some battles are not worth fighting if we can find a way around them. Some battles will never be won, and we should not even try to fight them if we want to stay alive. And some battles are not ours to fight. The battles worth fighting for are the ones that consume the fewest resources, take the least amount of time, and produce the most significant results. Your goal is to win the war by successfully reaching the end objective or achieving the company strategy and ignoring the rest.

Thinking like a leader is knowing what is within our control and what is not, rather than fighting an unwinnable battle. You can't take on every problem at work. Each person, no matter who there are, only has a finite amount of political capital. If you make a huge fuss over something silly, you may not be able to get your way when it's something really important. Even if you're confident that the issues you want to tackle are critical, your reputation may suffer if you take them all on at once.

Ask yourself if you would rather be right or be effective. You can be right sometimes, but you sabotage yourself by going after the wrong challenge, at the wrong time, with the wrong resources, and in the wrong way.

ATTACK THE FLANKS

"Attack him where he is unprepared; appear where you are not expected."

-Sun Tzu

A natural transition to follow up on the concept of picking the right battles to win the war or achieve a strategy is to continue with Sun Tzu and his teachings. In the Art of War, Sun Tzu is credited with the military maxim of attacking the flanks with the words, "Attack him where he is unprepared, appear where you are not expected."

For thousands of years, military leaders have acknowledged the power of attacking the flanks of their enemies. Often, by successfully executing a flanking strategy, past military generals have overcome disadvantages in both troop numbers and weaponry.

If you can imagine, in war, an enemy that is about to be attacked will have a good idea where their enemy's main force is, and with that information, they will build up defenses in one general direction. The attacking force then has its own choices to make. They can run straight into the front of the enemy's defenses, take heavy losses and possibly lose the fight. The attacking force can survey the enemy defenses and maneuver around one side or more that appears weak and press their greater numbers. Rather than just theory, this strategy has been used to shape the world we live in, both current and ancient.

To understand the power behind pursuing the enemy's flanks, consider the battle of Cannae in 216 BC during the Second

Punic Wars.

At Cannae, Hannibal of Carthage led his forces to perhaps one of the most significant military victories of all time when he defeated the numerically superior army of the Roman Republic on their domain. In this fight, the Romans fielded 80,000 soldiers and 6,000 cavalry while Hannibal fielded just 40,000 infantry and 10,000 cavalry. Hannibal assessed the situation, recognized his forces' unique strengths, and built a strategy around it.

First, Hannibal deployed his superior cavalry to neutralize the enemy's numerical advantage and increase his forces' flexibility. Then, he set his weakest troops in the middle of his battle line with his seasoned veterans on the flanks. Hannibal allowed the Roman forces to advance, and as they surged forward and engaged, Hannibal slowly pulled back his main battle line to draw in more of the enemy. Around this time, Hannibal then sent his veteran forces around the flank on both sides of the Romans to perform a full double envelopment of the enemy. [124]

Hannibal's flanking maneuvers at Cannae created a scenario where the Roman's numerical advantage became a disadvantage. As a result, the Roman soldiers panicked, and the army lost an estimated 50,000 soldiers while Hannibal lost only 6,000 men. [124]

Image 41: Source: Battle Cannae destruction.png: The Department of History, United States Military Academy. Second Punic

War, The Battle of Cannae; destruction of the Roman
army (red color) by Hannibal's forces (blue). [125]

While most of us are not engaged in warfare, the lessons of identifying and attacking the weak flanks remain as powerful and relevant as ever. Whatever the challenge is that you face, there are always several options available to overcome it. The trick is having the right mindset to use your skills, knowledge, courage, and humility to uncover hidden possibilities.

In a business context, attacking the flanks can be interpreted as leaders thinking creatively to rise past the perceived and real constraints that they face. Time and again in business, we see small start-up companies bring large, entrenched incumbents with giant customer bases and deep pockets to their knees. At first glance, it would seem that small start-ups are at a massive disadvantage. Their success comes from attacking the flanks —they don't try to attract customers with the same products that the large incumbents offer but instead offer innovative new products or new processes. Most of us, however, do not have an endless checkbook or an unlimited amount of time. Pursuing the flanks is a smart option to bypass unnecessary hurdles to increase progress and decrease the cost of any initiative.

The innovation-focused mindset of attacking the flanks is useful because even if we have identified the right battle or opportunity to pursue, we must still be conscious of how to use our advantages to the greatest effect and, at the same time to minimize our disadvantages.

When you think like a leader, you will develop and execute the strategies that overcome even overwhelming disadvantages and turn the competition's advantages into liabilities.

Thinking like a leader also means attacking the challenges within your company. Targeting the pressure points of a big nasty problem will cause it to fold unto itself so that you can build anew.

What Attaching the Flanks looks like in action in your company is keeping in mind the law of nature:

1. Instead of spending time and money trying to fix old systems under the sunk-cost fallacy, scrap the process and build something new using tools that an ordinary person can understand.

2. Learn a new skill or technology to automate processes and free up time from non-value-added tasks.

3. Bring together the people involved in a dispute to talk through the challenges instead of passively accepting non-conformance.

4. Asking peers in other companies how they overcome similar challenges.

Going Too Far? The Maverick and The Heretic

"Vision without execution is hallucination."

- Thomas Edison

When defining different types of innovation-minded leaders, two different personifications often appear, which we'll refer to as the maverick and the heretic. While both personalities are similar in their eagerness to drive change and share their ideas with a bias towards action, what differentiates them is their long-term success and tenure at their organizations.

Let's cover the definitions first:

1) A maverick is: "an unorthodox or independent-minded person who is no longer content to sit back and merely accept the traditional way of doing things."

2) A heretic is: "a person holding an opinion at odds with what is generally accepted. A Nonconformist."

After a quick read, it may seem that the maverick and heretic think the same way. But, be careful here.

Both heretics and mavericks possess visionary leadership and are unafraid of operating outside of conventional thinking and bending the rules to make things happen. However, what matters a great deal and determines success or failure is how the maverick or heretic interacts with others and adapts to their environment.

Typically, mavericks will be dynamic and open to criticism and collaboration while heretics are steadfast with their vision: It is either their way or the highway. Mavericks are open to new ideas wherever they come from, but heretics have their own definition of the solution and are unbending in their approach. What is often the differentiating factor is whether the mavericks or heretics can convince others to buy into their vision for change to ensure that improvements have a long-lasting benefit—rather than a quick uptick, then a reversal.

There is a fine line between being hailed as a maverick versus being vilified as a heretic. **While execution leadership requires risk-taking and challenging the status quo in ways that shock others into a Sense of Urgency, there is a right way and a wrong way to go about it.**

While mavericks may exhibit some of the same traits as heretics, they are much more strategic and intentional with their actions. Characterized by strategic risk-taking behavior, mavericks become incredibly valuable because they are unafraid to make changes that will improve the organization and advance its mission. To do this, they challenge rules, persevere with grit, and demonstrate resilience and resourcefulness to overcome challenges and win support. For organizations steeped in tradition or maintaining the status quo, mavericks may be essential to moving forward.

Mavericks succeed much more than heretics in organizations because they don't have a bull-in-a-china-shop mentality. They charge blindly about with no concept of what they might be destroying. Instead, a leader with a maverick mentality is willing to embrace strategic planning, influence building, and preparation to put ideas into action. Mavericks are drivers in creating and maintaining a culture that celebrates experimentation and improvement. Rather than see the world as me versus them, mavericks phrase challenges as "us versus the problem."

Heretics, on the other hand, wind up causing chaos instead of results in the end. Despite having potential and maybe some early wins, their inappropriate behavior and incapability with others will undermine the organization's values and damage its culture. Heretics typically don't always get along well with others as they often think of challenges as "me versus the problem, instead of us. As a result, they often cause friction and conflict due to their quirky ways, strong wills, and outspoken demeanor. They make others uncomfortable and say things that make others grit their teeth due to a lack of awareness. Over time, a heretic-styled leader will offend enough people and break enough sacred corporate laws to the point that they are deemed dangerous.

What happens, in the end, is the maverick becomes celebrated for effectively leading change and Getting Shit Done. The heretic will be ostracized, marginalized, and rejected by the corporate immune system or colleagues who want harmony or simplicity. While the heretic presented an illusion of Getting Shit Done, their downfall is a difference between Getting Shit Done and Getting Shit Done right.

Throughout history, the reaction to heretics is the same; they are censored, excommunicated, and exiled.

Image42: The "baptism by fire" of Old Believer leader Avvakum
in 1682- Public Domain [126]

Accordingly, if you want to think like a leader, you need to demonstrate a maverick's behaviors and avoid the heretical pitfalls. If you don't approach challenges with the right mind-set, all of your work will ultimately be undone.

TEACH A MAN
TO FISH

"Give a man a fish, and you feed him for a day; teach a man to fish, and you feed him for a lifetime."

- Unknown

"Strategy without process is little more than a wish list."

- Robert Filek

The mastery of chess has many lessons to teach us about thinking like a leader. But there is one major difference between chess and leaders. Chess is a solitary game; leadership is a team sport. In this final section, we'll explore the notion that leaders' success is measured by the success of those who work for them. And that success occurs when leaders scuttle the old thinking of command and control. Leadership today requires the mentality of a teacher and coach, not a general.

The concept of teaching a man to fish instead of giving him a fish goes back thousands of years and is manifested in one form or another in cultures all across the world. If a man is given a fish, he will eat it, and the next day he will be hungry and search for yet another free meal. The man who seeks resources but does not contribute to them becomes a drain on a community. The community must then spend time and resources tending to those who could otherwise meet their own needs and add value. The lesson from this teaching is to build a strong community; people must be taught to become self-sufficient, or better yet, a teacher of others.

The man who asks for a fish is not incapable of fishing. He just did not know how to go about it. Somewhere along the line, a lack of leadership, education, or design saw that this person fell through the cracks. However, a leader will quickly step up to fix ongoing resource drains by teaching others, which leads to a strong organization or community. Taking ownership and sacrificing time to teach others or adjust systems to be self-reliant can pay huge dividends over time. Each distraction slowly siphons resources, and a "death by a thousand cuts" is felt. Fixing these issues once they reach a crisis point can be a real challenge. Instead, by teaching each person to meet their own needs, any resources available can be diverted where they are needed most.

For example, colleagues may often ask for information they could have easily collected themselves if given the right training and have the necessary skill set. Often, we default to sharing that information because we believe it is initially faster and easier than teaching them how to collect that information. By doing this, you have given them a fish, which is not thinking like a leader. Your time that could have been spent on higher-value activities is lost, and the drain on the resources will remain so long as the process remains in place. The challenge with teaching another person to fish for or solve their own demands requires the use of the word "no." "No, I will not do what you ask without first understanding. Instead, I will take the extra step to understand your needs and teach you." What may take 2 hours to teach once saves 20 mins each day in perpetuity.

The trick with teaching others to fish, though, is that we must first become master fishermen. If you haven't learned how to catch the fish yourself, bait a hook, or filet the catch, we will not be effective teachers. Leadership here is about setting the example and mastering the material ourselves before we can then help others. Being a leader with fantastic soft skills is pointless if you've never caught a fish yourself, just the same as being focused on only technical skills may find you frustrated and impatient while trying to share knowledge. You must have both.

In our world of strategy-execution, "teaching a man to fish" means that we must strive to build self-sustaining behaviors, processes, and systems with an emphasis on design thinking. Each process must be built in a way so that it consumes the least amount of resources, time, and attention possible so that time can be spent on what matters. Each process or workflow that is inefficient causes the organization to cannibalize its resources; the organization takes one step forward and two steps backward. If we can view the world with a firm grasp of design thinking, then the initial efforts that we put into work will be sustained and will allow us to accelerate progress forward. We do not want to commit to regularly sacrificing energy, time, and other resources to ensure that what has been done stays done.

Strategy-execution is better facilitated when the organization does not regularly play whack-a-mole and can apply focus and resources to reach their goals and project milestones. A good leader identifies the processes that should produce more and consume less and know who to involve. Awareness, education, and technical adeptness are useful to differentiate among problems and potential solutions. We can solve this dilemma by investing a small amount of time teaching the man to fish. A master fisherman is a leader who can connect the dots in the organization to drive increased productivity.

What teaching people to fish looks like in business:

1) Create self-serve solutions that allow users to ask and answer their own questions.

2) Understand the nature of requests.

3) Linking systems together. One master solution instead of 100 individual "solutions."

In fewer words, would you rather have this?

Image 43: Whack-a-male

Or this?

Image 44- Teach a man to fish

When you think like a leader, you aren't just interested in giving orders and micro-managing underlings. Instead, you teach others to fish to focus on the leadership actions and decisions that create the most value for your organization.

Takeaways

1. Strategy and execution require different types of thinking. Strategic thinking is long-term thinking, usually in the context of 3-5 years out. Execution

thinking is action-oriented thinking, focused on the present or near future.

2. To close the strategy-execution gap and build operational and professional excellence in our organizations, we must act differently and think differently.

3. Approach strategy-execution like a chess master. Never lose sight of the end objective, protect what matters, and be ready to adapt to your opponent and circumstances. Be proactive, prepared, focused, & innovative.

4. The strategy-execution mindset is about making the best decision possible with the available facts and information and committing to action.

5. In working to reach a decision, collaboration is essential, deliberation is vital, but there needs to be a cutoff point where people move forward in a co-ordinated effort. A strong leader intuitively knows where this point lies. A good decision executed quickly beats a brilliant decision implemented slowly.

6. Look at execution through the lens of the Serenity Prayer- can a leader accomplish the possible, say no to the impossible, and know the difference between the two?

7. Be proactive and ready to face your challenges. Being proactive means that you're prepared to act, and being reactive means that you're ready to blame. Look forward, not backward.

8. Anticipate for the likely, the unlikely, and the near impossible to avoid surprises. Preparedness will improve the strength of the project.

9. Pick your battles wisely to win the war. Find the critical path through strategy-execution to deliver

outstanding results in a reasonable timeframe.

10. Be prepared to identify and attack the flanks of an opportunity. Use your strengths and advantages at precisely the point where your opponent or target has the most vulnerabilities.

11. There is a fine line between being hailed as a maverick versus being vilified as a heretic. While execution leadership requires risk-taking and challenging the status quo in ways that shock others into a Sense of Urgency, there is a right way and a wrong way to go about it.

12. Think of strategy-execution as teaching a man to fish instead of giving the man a fish. Work done should be self-sustaining and add momentum to the overall body of work, not detract from it.

Reflection

1. How many times have you been caught off guard by being unprepared? Look back at each scenario, consider what you could have done differently, and then consider what you must do to prepare for the next challenge.

2. Are you playing whack-a-mole to put out fires continually, or are you teaching others to fish by training others to think for themselves and create self-sustaining systems?

3. How often do you get lucky and were unprepared for the unforeseen recently? If it's often, then find ways to anticipate and prepare for the unknown.

4. Do you look at work through the lens of a checkers or chess player? Do you see work as a chessboard or battlefield where your objective is to win by finding the critical path where your advantages are paired against your adversary's disadvantages?

5. Are you decisive and move to address challenges, or do you wait for others to step up and do something?

6. Are you reactive or proactive? Do you make things happen, or do things happen to you?

Maverick vs. Heretic

7. Are you bringing up problems, or are you offering to drive solutions?

8. Are you inspiring people to challenge the status quo or harassing people?

9. Are you inspiring others to embrace management's goals or objectives, or are you criticizing the administration openly?

10. Are you a Maverick or a Heretic in your organiza-

tion? Does your view of who you match the perceptions of others?

CHAPTER 9

Getting Shit Done by Executing Like a Leader

"Do or do not; there is no try."

-Yoda

"Decide. Commit. Act. Succeed. Repeat."

-Tim Grover

"Leadership without the discipline of execution is incomplete and ineffective. Without the ability to execute, all other attributes of leadership become hollow."

-Larry Bossidy, Execution

INTRODUCTION

If Getting Shit Done were your typical business or management book, at this point in the story, I would carefully select and share several soon-to-be-dated examples of corporate heroism that serve to back up my thesis in a meaningful way.

I'd cherry-pick examples and stories to tell you what an executive or their team did, leading that executive to become an American household name. Like hundreds of authors before me, I could reference the likes of Steve Jobs at Apple, Jack Welch at GE, or even Jeff Skilling at Enron.

But... there's a big problem here.

Depending on which company or stock you look at and at which point in time, the entire narrative changes. Take, for example, in 2001, when Enron was the darling of Wall Street. For years they were hailed as one of the best and most innovative companies to work for; in that same year, the company would fall apart due to a massive fraud scheme. Without a doubt, you will still find books and magazines published around their heyday glorifying Enron's business model and leadership team.

The problem with many of these sorts of corporate quasi-case studies is that they are so incomplete with their short-sided nature and incomplete narrative that they are laughable.

The flaw with using corporate "heroism" storytelling is that no outsider will ever have an accurate and full picture of what really went on inside an organization. Even when we get stories worth sharing, it's almost always only good news as companies spin the truth to pursue an agenda. PR and legal departments are a bit leery of sharing tales of failure, negligence, and other faults that could lead to investor class-action lawsuits.

In my humble opinion, no one should give a shit about what Enron executives and their PR departments said about what made Enron such a fantastic work environment; you're buying into someone's narrative, not the facts and truth.

Enron

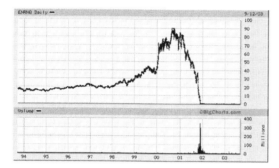

Fortune: *"The #1 Company to work for in the top 100"*

Ken Lay: *"My personal belief is that Enron stock is an incredible bargain at current prices, and we will look back a couple of years from now and see the great opportunity that we currently have."*

Instead, true leadership lessons are timeless. They never falter or become obsolete through the years, centuries, or even millennia. Just ask the Greek hoplite soldiers featured in Chapter 4. As we've learned throughout this book, we should look for other ways to learn from what others have done and the lessons that could be shared.

So, where, then, should we look to find the stories, examples, and case studies that illuminate timeless leadership lessons?

Military history, of course!

Military history helps us understand what has worked in the past to continue to apply those lessons today. Military examples work well because they are so spartan—either one army or the other commands the battlefield at the end of the day. The casualties are counted, the damage is surveyed, and the winner is declared. We can study past events and understand Who did What and When to put the lessons into an educational context.

Even more, military history teaches people to accept ambiguity, to become comfortable with it, and to reject cut-and-dry formulas. History offers a framework, a way of thinking, a way to search for patterns that recur from one situation to another to more broadly assess the parameters of what's possible, the boundaries of likely action, or possible success.

By looking back to our shared history of military conflicts, it is here that we find a rich source of information because history is an objective study of what actually happened. Because so many different people capture the same events from multiple viewpoints, we are left with a complete, accurate, and meaningful story of the events that transpired. Here, a general can say whatever they wish after a conflict, but facts and figures rule the day and set the narrative. You either won or you didn't, and these claims can be independently verified.

Too often, management authors try and apply a new theory to explain the world around them, but as the saying goes, "There is nothing new under the sun." There is no point in reinventing the wheel. Each time we face what we think is a new challenge, others have faced the same dilemma many times before in one form or another. To study and master strategy-execution, we must find events, examples, and stories where time has thoroughly vetted the truth.

With that being said, buckle up; we are headed back in time to 1861.

THE US CIVIL WAR

**"Those who cannot remember the past
are condemned to repeat it."**

- George Santayana, The Life of Reason

If you truly want to understand the importance of leadership in strategy-execution, you must spend time studying the American Civil War. Here, we find one of the most compelling case studies between competing organizations whose fate is determined by leadership quality in their organization. If you stop and think about it, no case study comes close in terms of scale, importance, or the impact of outstanding leadership.

If you're not familiar with US history, the Civil War spanned from 1861-1865 and encompassed more than 10,500 battles: small and big. The war involved nearly four million soldiers (2.6 million Union vs. 1.2 million Confederates or CSA). It ultimately claimed the lives of more than 750,000 of those soldiers, making it the deadliest military conflict in US history.

Both sides were overconfident in their abilities leading into the conflict. They expected a quick end to the dispute, and most Americans anticipated an easy, bloodless victory for their respective sides. The Union felt confident since they possessed more abundant resources in every material category; more men, better rifles, and a more robust economy. Still, their adversary, the CSA (Confederate States of America), was confident in their cause's righteousness and proved formidable in using their limited resources coupled with more capable and experienced generals.

Objectively, each side's strategy was simple; beat the competition by winning more battles than the opponent so that the enemy would lose all taste for war and concede. With most things, what happens after strategy (or war) is declared is what matters most.

When war erupted, many of the best generals with training from the West Point military academy and experience in the recent Mexican-American War sided with their home states and pledged their efforts to the Confederacy. The Union forces were instead left with a power vacuum at all levels. In 1860, just one year before war was declared, the entire US Army numbered only 16,367 men. [127]

Photo by Chris Chow on Unsplash

Suddenly, a grand experiment in building and leading an organization was underway as both armies' command structures, strategy, and culture were built on the fly. Top Union roles were not filled with military veterans but mostly civilian volunteers and politicians who used their influence and wealth to gain rank to fill in the leadership roster.

Though lacking in resources, the advantage of capable leaders saw the Confederacy generate an early, consistent, and stunning trail of victories that almost led to them winning the entire thing. By being more effective in their ability to master the pairing of strategy with execution, they delivered results for their people. They would deliver defeats to enemy forces that were more than twice their size on many occasions.

Alternatively, the leadership deficiency at the Union helm was disastrous for the Eastern Potomac Army throughout the early years of the war. Each general and their actions (or inactions) disappointed the country with their strategy, execution, or a combination of both. The body count quickly rose to staggering levels, which diminished the national will to continue the fight.

Then...just as the war looked darkest, the Union found in General Ulysses S. Grant, a man who espoused many of the lessons and values that we have learned in Getting Shit Done, the leader who could lead them to victory.

Follow along to learn the lessons from both sides of this great conflict. Without a doubt, you'll find once again that strategy-execution was a critical element in separating the winners from the losers at the center of our nation's greatest conflict. We'll explore the more important battles and generals, the power of culture, and the actions of individuals that coalesced to shape destiny.

By the end of this chapter, **you'll find that the Civil War isn't just a poignant history lesson but a story of how an organization with every disadvantage can come out on top (or vice-versa) when led by great leaders who understand both strategy and execution.**

ANTIETAM

The first battle that we will explore is the battle of Antietam, which took place in northern Maryland in September 1862. This battle of Antietam Creek (or Sharpsburg) became famous as it is known as one the bloodiest battles in US history in terms of the rate of casualties: 23,000 casualties fell between the two forces in just 12 hours. [128]

Leading up to the battle of Antietam, Union General George McClellan held the numerical advantage and outnumbered his opponent by a staggering 87,000 soldiers—all of whom were well supplied, prepared, and drilled for the coming engagement compared to the exhausted Confederates 41,000-man army.

In addition to far superior resources in men and equipment, McLellan had another major advantage that most generals in battle can only dream of: he knew the Confederate's battle plans.

Image: McClellan Libaray of Congress. https://
www.loc.gov/item/2018669889/

Ahead of the battle, Confederate forces under General Robert E. Lee had divided their army into four parts and planned to invade the North after capturing the arsenal at Harper's Ferry only days before. However, Confederate scouts had accidentally dropped the Confederate troop movement plan (Special Order No. 191) on the roadside. [129]

In a stroke of bad luck, the plans were found and given to the Union leadership, who could profit from this chance discovery to defeat the enemy and drive them back down South.

As both armies took positions on the field on the day of battle, McClellan waited too long and allowed the Confederates to take strong defensive positions to assail the Union forces with ease later. The piecemeal and staggered frontal assaults from Union forces led to many casualties as men were marched into fortified and waiting enemy troops throughout the day. Although the Union was able to gain ground and push the Confederates back to the line known as The Sunken Road, the price of each foot of ground was costly. The Confederate line wavered but did not break.

As the Union sought to bring their remaining forces to the

field on the far side of the battlefield, a fiasco unfolded. What became known as Burnside's Bridge is an example of how the Union squandered its advantage in battle while the Confederate forces, on the other hand, often overcome overwhelming odds.

While the Union Army's top leadership struggled to break the Confederate line, McClellan sent an order to divisional commander General Burnside and requested that his 6,000 soldiers cross a narrow bridge at Antietam Creek and join the primary battle right of the Sunken Lane. If successful, Burnside's men could add the weight to win the day and overwhelm the enemy. [130]

https://www.loc.gov/pictures/resource/ppmsca.19393/?co=civwar

Instead, what followed was chaos. Burnside hesitated after receiving his orders. After junior officers pushed him to do something, he ordered a headfirst and uncoordinated attack to cross a single, narrow bridge. The men, bunched in a large group formation, became easy targets for slaughter, and the situation turned into a bloody bottleneck.

Burnside's entire IX Corps was pinned down by just 500 confederate sharpshooters placed high on the ledge overlooking the narrow crossing for three full hours. The Union repeatedly tried, in uncoordinated efforts, to advance their large force through the small and well-defended bridge.

Source: http://historynet.com/wp-content/uploads/2012/09/
battle-of-antietam-map.jpg

By the time the Union finally crossed the bridge three hours later, the Confederates had inflicted around 600 casualties on the Union troops while losing only 120 men of their own. More importantly, Burnside Bridge's defense bought precious time for the Confederate army to avoid defeat and reinforce their faltering line. When the Union soldiers finally crossed the river, it would be too late for Burnside's large force to have much of an impact in the fight.

The Battle of Antietam Ends

As the first day closed, McClellan still had significant numbers of uncommitted troops held in reserve. Porter's Federal V Corps waited East of the Antietam Creek while Pleasonton's cavalry division waited West of the creek on the Boonesboro Pike. Meanwhile, the Confederate Army had been fought to a standstill where Lee had virtually no reserves left. His casualties had been substantial, and several vital brigades had virtually ceased to exist as fighting entities. [131]

Lee and General Stonewall Jackson examined the options for a counter-attack on the positions on the Union left, but the Federals had heavily reinforced their positions. That night the ravaged Confederate army withdrew across the Potomac into Virginia. McClellan, surprisingly, did nothing and allowed Lee to retreat without resistance.

Although McClellan knew when the enemy would be on the field and where to find them, the Union could not seize the opportunity to ambush and route the Confederate Army of Northern Virginia and end the war. McClellan's lack of leadership capabilities and lack of strategy-execution skills would leave the Union grasping at victory. After the general repeatedly refused Lincoln's orders to pursue Lee's retreating troops, Lincoln removed McClellan from command.

From McClellan's perspective, he had accomplished his mission of forcing Lee's troops from Maryland and preventing a Confederate win on Union soil. McLellan's refusal of his orders to pursue Lee's retreating troops was the final straw. Despite Lincoln repeatedly ordering McClellan to pursue the retreating Confederates and finish the fight, the battle ended in a tactical draw.

President Lincoln was deeply displeased with McClellan, and shortly after, he was removed from command.

Good Strategy - Poor Execution

The advantages of the Union Army at Antietam should have guaranteed victory. Because of a leadership failure, Antietam was inconclusive. Worse, the failure to win would cost tens of thousands of unnecessary casualties over the next few years. Had McClellan and the Union Army gotten shit done at Antietam, there would have been no Gettysburg, Chickamauga, or Chancellorsville. Much of the death and destruction that made the Civil War America's bloodiest conflict could have been avoided altogether.

The loss at Antietam fell squarely on McClellan's lack of both strategy and execution leadership.

McClellan's leadership style was characterized by:

- Distrust of others:
    - General McClellan found himself politically embroiled with others in the government and army as the battle loomed and the strategy and tactics were being set. McClellan distrusted others and failed to invite his generals to provide their input and observations for the coming battle to keep his hold on power and authority.

    - Even if McClellan had a drive to execute the strategy effectively, the right leaders were not in place or inclined to execute it. For example, Burnside's Bridge did not have to be a mistake. Getting the troops onto the field through several other alternative paths was possible. Burnside's unimaginative execution of the order - bottlenecking his forces at the bridge and turning them into sitting ducks- was the mistake. A good leader understands the objective and executes it effectively and efficiently.

    - Few operational commanders understood their strategic role at Antietam and couldn't or wouldn't operate outside of rigid commands to deliver results. Thousands of Union soldiers were marched into and cut down by enemy defenses without firing a shot before the next regiment was called up to follow in their tracks.

- An outsized ego:
  - McClellan believed that he knew best, always.
  - He was reluctant to listen to the counsel of others.
  - McLellan was all command-and-control: he gave the orders, you followed them. Troop orders were often dispatched and arrived at a pace far too slow and too late to have the necessary effect of sweeping the day.
- Excessive Caution:
  - Lacking input from others and untrusting intelligence, McClellan was cautious, almost paranoid. McClellan conceived the battle plan and strategy for Antietam in a vacuum based on the assumption that there were two to three times more rebels on the field than there were. McClellan saw every hill as about to be overrun with the enemy swarming into his open flank.
  - Excess troops were kept in reserve to check a phantom threat instead of being deployed to win the battle. Ultimately, the Confederates deployed 100 percent of their fighting force while the Union only deployed 75 percent. Just as Confederate lines were about to break during the second day, the reserves were called to a halt.

Due to a lack of trust, ego, and excessive caution, Antietam was not a great Union success. The Union had more men, the coordinates on the enemy position, more supplies, more and better cannons, more everything, but did not use those resources properly to execute the mission.

Alternatively, the Confederates seized what few advantages

they had much more effectively. Using fewer men, they took better ground; they created logistical bottlenecks for the enemy, and they concentrated fighting on opportunities that would yield results. As the battle heated up, their regiments did not break and retreat as the Union was oft to do. Fighting forces of hundreds were whittled down to sometimes tens of men who would not yield the line. At several points in the battle, the Confederate generals were in disbelief that the enemy had called off the attack, knowing that one more coordinated assault would break them. [78]

Overall, the Confederates were better organized, better led, and supported by a command structure that encouraged decentralization and initiative-taking. Each commander, each officer, each soldier, and each artilleryman understood their purpose and significance on that day, and as a result, they fought harder.

At Antietam, **the takeaway is that every advantage can be squandered if not used properly and promptly.** The right strategy and the proper execution of that strategy would have turned Antietam into a Union victory, ended the war, and saved tens of thousands of American lives. When victory or defeat hung in the balance at Antietam, strategy-execution was the key.

Great Execution > Great Strategy

Overall, McClellan's strategy focused more on not losing than winning.

FREDERICKSBURG

A second compelling example of poor leadership and strategy-execution was the battle of Fredericksburg, which occurred not long after Antietam in December 1862. With McClellan gone and few worthy replacements available to take the top role in the army, President Lincoln asked that General Burnside accept the position, despite Burnside's objections.

The campaign began when General Burnside sensed an opportunity to sneak past Lee and advance towards Richmond. He combined the various Federal army divisions and then marched southwards.

However, the Union Army's progress ground to a halt when they suffered a critical delay in crossing the Rappahannock River just shy of Fredericksburg, Maryland, as the necessary pontoon bridges were absent. While a supply commander in D.C. had promised the vital pontoon bridges to be in place ahead of the troop's arrival, their absence was undeniable. It took more than a week before Burnside's army finally received the pontoon bridges as they waited in a massed formation. Despite being only about two hundred feet from their destination, poor internal leadership and communication flaws in the Union army bureaucracy kept 120,000 men frozen in place and unable to cross the river. [132]

General Lee quickly ordered all his army divisions to take strong defensive positions on the town's outskirts with the Union army stuck in place. While Lee and his generals were initially alarmed and surprised to observe Burnside's troop movement through Maryland, they quickly adapted and reformulated a strategy that aggregated the dispersed Confederate Army units into a powerful force around Fredericksburg. The Confederates used the time caused by the Union's delay to work uncontested in digging strong and nearly impenetrable defensive positions to prepare for the coming battle.

The Union river crossing efforts were further hindered by the garrisoned Confederates defenders whose sharpshooters were led by Brigadier General William Barksdale's Mississippi brigade. For a full twelve hours, scores of Union engineers worked to assemble the bridges across the river so that the army could move again. However, the unprotected men fell prey to Confederate snipers hidden in positions throughout the town's infrastructure. As losses to the engineers mounted, the Union adapted the plan and sent several transport boats full of soldiers across the river, finally breaching the town limits.

Source: https://www.loc.gov/pictures/resource/ppmsca.22479/?co=civwar

Even though General Lee asked Barksdale to hold the town for just two hours to allow the Confederate to finish their preparations, Barksdale instead took ownership of the task and surpassed all expectations in the town's defense. Barksdale seized the initiative and executed a stubborn defense that bought Lee extra time to create an impregnable defensive perimeter. Because Barksdale took ownership of achieving his piece of the strategy, the Confederate Army's chances for success soared. [78]

When the Union Army finally crossed the river, what transpired afterward led to one of the most demoralizing defeats for the Union at the time. The decisive moment of the struggle came when General Burnside decided that the Union would still commit to their original and nearly defunct strategy. He would literally charge his men uphill without cover across an open field into a fortified stone wall. Despite circumstances where the enemy held all conceivable advantages, the Union haphazardly launched their attack.

Looking down towards the town, the Confederate Army, which in some sections counted six soldiers for each linear foot of the wall, patiently waited as Union brigades marched, one after the other, into formation and straight towards their secure position. The Confederates must have watched in disbelief as waves of blue charged headfirst towards the waiting defenders behind their embattlements. Volley after volley echoed as the Union forces melted away.

Not one soldier from fifteen Union brigades would reach the enemy position as 12,600 men were counted dead. The day was lost for the Union while the Confederates counted only 5,600 casualties, with many suspected as deserters headed home for the Christmas holidays in a jubilant mood.

Poor Strategy & Poor Execution

At Fredericksburg, General Burnside paid the price for his weak leadership capabilities with the lives of countless men. While Burnside could boast that he did have a strategy, he lacked the ability, like McClellan before him, to execute it. However, where McClellan was cautious, Burnside was reckless.

First, poor communication skills caused the pontoons' delay, alerting the enemy to his position. Despite having an initial strategy, Burnside committed a significant error in not adapting to the current circumstances.

As we have learned in Getting Shit Done, sometimes the best course of action is to do nothing or retreat; action for action's sake is useless. As we have learned from master Sun Tzu, we must pick the battles that we fight. Rarely is the best fight, one where the enemy is waiting and prepared for you. At Fredericksburg, Burnside's strategy held no advantage, and yet he still attacked. In the same breath, we have to remember that doing something or looking busy is not the same as execution. **Strategy-Execution begins with a strategy where the benefits outweigh the risks and then applying focused discipline to remove all obstacles in its path.**

We've also learned in Getting Shit Done that while plans are useless, planning is everything. A plan to attack must be worth pursuing, but at the same time, we need the humility to recognize if it's attainable or whether we made a mistake and must change course. We shouldn't throw good money, resources, or men after bad. At Fredericksburg, there was no need to throw so many lives against that stone wall. **Execution is not blindly following a strategy; it's finding and doing the thing that works as quickly as possible.**

WHY THE SOUTH WAS WINNING: THE 13 PRINCIPLES OF STRATEGY-EXECUTION

At this point in the war, the Union Army's efforts had been a major disappointment. Despite abundant resources and capabilities, the Union Army couldn't get things right or catch a break. The war was headed in the wrong direction, and it was fair to say that after Fredericksburg, the Confederates were winning the war.

Winning one battle against unlikely odds is probably luck. Twice might be chance. But to win a majority of both minor and significant contests with inferior resources in each is something entirely different.

What was is it that the Southern Army got right and did right to produce such results?

Let's look at both camps and compare using the 13 Principles of the Strategy-Execution Framework.

1	Strategy	
2	Planning	
3	Focus	
4	Decentralization	
5	Ownership & Accountability	Who
6	Communication	Will
7	Culture	Do
8	Leadership	What
9	Experience	and
10	Skills	By
11	Professionalism	When?
12	Continuous Improvement Mindset	
13	Execution	

Image12- Strategy-Execution GSD Framework Illustration

Confederate

1. Strategy

The South understood that they did not need a complex strategy to achieve their vision. By fighting defensive battles on favorable ground, they could inflict devastating casualties on the Union. Their war strategy was to avoid the capture of Richmond and other major cities and push back the Union invaders each time they reassembled.

They would not have to defeat the enemy army to win the war but rather break their people's will to continue the fight. If the Union had enough of the war, they would remove Lincoln from office and sue for peace. The end goal, the vision, was simple, and for that reason, it worked.

The battle strategy was to hit the enemy's flank where they were not suspecting to be attacked. Rather than face the enemy force's full might, they would reveal and press maximum pressure onto those vulnerable spots. When executed correctly, the full enemy army would be routed and retreat.

2. Planning

Lee's decisions and actions in the first part of the war demonstrated a balance of planning and adaptation. Through meticulous planning, such as placing his troops in advantageous positions (such as hilltops) where they could overcome their numeric inferiority Lee successfully implemented the defensive strategy described above. At the same time, Lee had the agility to set aside plans and react to unforeseen circumstances, such as the Union Army stalling at the Rappahannock River.

Lee frequently divided his forces and trusted his general's judgment. Separating his forces maximum flexibility, mobility and confused the enemy. When the time came to reassemble his forces, the subordinate generals understood Who had to do What and by When.

3. Focus

Lee rarely took his eye off his most significant threat, the Army of the Potomac. Most of the time, the Confederates knew where the enemy was positioned and understood their disposition. Whenever the Union marched South, Lee would head the enemy off and wait for them in a strong position.

Lee understood the aim of the army's strategy and was tactful in creating battles that would favor the Confederates. He understood what the Confederates were good at and stuck with it.

Only later at Gettysburg would Lee lose focus from the defensive plan, and in that battle, he took a decisive loss that, as a result, marked what turned out to be the Confederacy's farthest advance against the Union.

4. Decentralization

Leaders of units were allowed to exercise discretion in securing an objective.

At the battle of White Oak Swamp, the famous Stonewall

Jackson defied Lee's orders and halted the advance of his division against the enemy. He had realized that he was about to lead his men straight into the high ground protected by Union infantry and cannon and that they would be cut down for minimum gain. Jackson would take responsibility for defying Lee's orders upon finding unfavorable ground. That decision forever earned him the soldiers' respect and loyalty.

In another example, the army's cavalry arm, led by Jeb Stuart, was often provided an end goal and allowed to choose which route and side objectives they would take based on the enemy's showing. The battle plan was developed on the go as circumstances revealed themselves. Jeb rewarded Lee for his freedom by routinely returning to camp from the North with hundreds of stolen horses, prisoners, and wagon trains while scarcely losing a man. The cavalry raids would cause chaos by targeting Union rail and logistics depots and cause millions in damages.

Decentralization was crucial for developing a resourceful fighting force, capable commanders, and obtaining supplies and military intelligence. From his headquarters, Lee would have been incapable of ordering troops as well as ground commanders could have. Lee preferred to disperse his army over a wide area and then converge in force similar to Napoleon to retain flexibility of response.

5. Ownership & Accountability

The Confederates saw themselves as patriots of a new country that they could shape in their image, free from the Federals' influence. They would own the land and the legislature that governed it. That, in itself, was highly motivating to the Southern people. The Confederacy was succeeding because it believed in empowering individuals throughout the organization.

As a result of the ownership mindset, there were many examples of courageous and ingenious actions taken by Confederate generals, corporals, sergeants, and soldiers alike throughout the war. With the strategy clear and compelling, the fertile ground was seeded and bore fruit to gallant creativity and strategic risk-taking—leaders who could seize the initiative wherever possible to yield enormous rewards for their cause.

Also, as the army was often short on supplies like food, shoes, and horses, they were encouraged by necessity to put in the extra effort to take what was required from the enemy. If they didn't win, they might not eat that day.

In the following year after Fredericksburg, for example, the rebel spirit on ownership and initiative-taking was seen in full display at the battle of Chancellorsville, Virginia. Against the new Union General Hooker, who possessed a two-to-one manpower advantage, the Confederates led by Lee and Jackson achieved a massive tactical victory by combining deception and courage. Lee feigned troop movements that confused and delayed their enemy. Meanwhile, Jackson led a third of Lee's army to break off, sneak behind the Union lines, and then smash into their unprotected flank, which routed them from the field. [133]

During the battle of Fredericksburg, one great of ownership was John Pelham. Pelham was a 24-year-old junior officer responsible for commanding a small cannon battery stationed on the flank when he observed a large mass of Union forces beginning to move onto the battlefield. By quickly grasping the magnitude of the threat to his comrades and cause, Pelham decided to take ownership of present circumstances. He then burst towards bold action- he quickly worked with his men to move two cannons forward to attack the exposed Federal. Without a few moments, Pelham's actions caused massive confusion on the enemy, critically wound a key enemy general, and divert an entire Union division. [78]

Pelham was found still firing away even after one of his two cannons was disabled by counter-battery fire when General Jeb Stuart observed Pelham's actions. The general sent word that Pelham should feel free to withdraw from his dangerous position at any time. To this, Pelham courageously retorted, "Tell the General I can hold my ground." The effect of Pelham's action was that an entire division of the Union army reacted, sprung backward, and then cautiously repositioned themselves to deal with this perceived threat of a more massive, yet imaginary, enemy on their flank.

Pelham's ownership of his role effectively removed 120,000 opposing soldiers from the field of battle. It provided the rest of his army the opportunity to score a massive victory, which they did. Pelham's actions followed what we had learned about the 80/20 Pareto Principle, where choosing the best action could yield tremendous results.

6. Communication

The South excelled at maneuvering troops and armies around enemy positions without taking losses. They employed experienced cavalry scouts and spies to ascertain enemy positions and then communicate that information to the appropriate parties quickly. When armies were dispatched, Lee ensured that leaders understood the objective and what to do if an obstacle was presented. (Hint, see #5.) It was uncommon for a unit of the army to not be coordinated with the plan for the day. Due to the South's limited resources, they had to coordinate battles with excellent communication to ensure the full force was affected carefully.

The South was also mindful to disrupt and cut communication for Northern troops whenever possible. The calvary frequently targeted telegraph lines and undertook missions to acquire prisoners who revealed valuable information.

Again, only when communication was lost would the South lose. When Jeb Stuart uncoupled from the Army in Pennsylvania to pursue glory by sacking towns, Lee lost his eyes and ears. As his generals forced battle on the uncertain ground at Gettysburg, Lee had to bet big on unknown probabilities.

7. Culture

The Southern culture was better suited to producing soldiers leading into the war. A slightly smaller percentage of white Southerners were literate than their Northern counterparts, and Southern children tended to spend less time in school. As adults, Southern men gravitated toward military careers as well as agriculture. Next to the West Point Military Academy, the Virginia Military Institute was the next most prestigious school for aspiring military leaders. Many past heroes from the Revolutionary War had a home in the South. The military culture in the South led to a broader and deeper pool of candidates to choose from to build their organization. [134]

In battle, the South was creative in adapting their culture to create unique Ways of Working. For example, to overcome their lack of physical resources, including ammunition, the Confederates relied on human intellect to fill the gap. The "Rebel Yell" became a signature trademark that the Confederates would use before a charge to instill terror into the enemy. Unable to fight the Union man for man, the Confederates relied on their men's veterancy and courage. Seeing and hearing the screaming Rebels rush towards them, the Union soldiers would typically drop their supplies and arms and flee the field.

8. Leadership

Effective leadership enabled the Army of Northern Virginia to punch above its weight. Lee built a unified, trusting, and motivated command team that seldom disappointed.

To facilitate building a leadership pipeline, the South had a robust system for identifying high potential leaders in the army and advancing the best men into top leadership positions. While some political figures were in the army structure, most of the top roles were earned through meritocracy by demonstrating leadership, courage, and initiative-taking on the field.

After each battle, all the commanding officers and Lee prepared a detailed analysis and report to understand what happened during the encounter and learn from it. Mistakes and incompetent officers were identified and rectified. [78]

9. Experience

Because the Confederates often fought a defensive battle, they lost fewer men than the Union did in most battles. Over time, the Confederates' veterancy created highly effective and renowned brigades skilled in maneuvering, marksmanship, and battlefield composure. Each Confederate soldier was considered to be worth two or more Union men in battle as a result.

There were strong leadership candidates in all arms of service who had experience effectively leading men in battle. When one leader would fall, another equally good replacement would take command and continue the fight. Many of the leaders and soldiers in the army also had previous battle experience from the Mexican-American War.

10. Skills

The men of the Confederacy benefited from a rural life that translated directly to soldiering. Many men had experience with firearms and animal husbandry, and the South, in general, was strong in military tradition. As the South won more battles, the veterans within the army became highly skilled with their rifles. A skilled soldier could probably load and fire between 3 and 5 aimed shots a minute.

As for leadership skills, many officers and generals had attended West Point or one of the Southern military academies for their formal training. Skilled leaders did not make rookie mistakes that would lead to their men's quick capture or deaths. Highly skilled leaders could use an inferior force to secure objectives.

11. Professionalism

To create a professional army from volunteers, Confederate leadership was diligent in the frequent drilling of troops. In battle and under duress, they could maneuver effectively with minimal losses. Desertion and straggling were condemned and punished harshly with court-martials and execution of the worst offenders. In battle, the Confederates very infrequently broke and fled a position. [78]

When called to reach ambitious goals such as walking 30 or 40 miles a day to escape or flank an enemy, the Confederates prevailed. Often, in haste with little food, little rest, and no shoes, the men obliged. Night and early morning marches were not uncommon to keep the enemy off-kilter.

Southern generals, Jackson especially, was diligent in maintaining high discipline and professionalism in the army. To uphold the highest standards of professionalism, no one could be exempt. Stonewall Jackson, on several occasions, placed other generals under arrest for perceived insubordination.

12. Continuous Improvement Mindset

While lacking in resources and men, the Confederacy was creative in finding innovative ways to continue their fight. The examples below illuminate some of the creativity that was deployed.

Ironclad ships

The Merrimack (C.S.S. Virginia) was launched and initiated in March 1862 while participating in history's first naval battle between ironclad warships. It was part of a Confederate effort to break the Union blockade of Southern ports, including Norfolk and Richmond, Virginia, imposed at the start of the war. The USS Monitor's design was so innovative that the ship featured more than 40 different newly patented inventions when it was launched. [135]

Naval mines and torpedoes

The Confederates developed naval mines to counteract the Union's blockades of Southern ports. Mines and later torpedoes were very effective in sinking forty Union ships. These mines' success led to the creation of land mines and grenades used in later wars.

13. Execution

As you have read above, the Confederates became a skilled and determined fighting force. Because they could satisfy all dimensions of the Principles of Strategy-Execution Framework, they could execute their strategy and almost won the war.

From general to soldier, each man understood the vision, strategy and accordingly took ownership of their responsibilities and performed their utmost to deliver results. Where resources were lacking, initiative-taking filled the void. In battle after battle, the Confederate army was victorious.

If the Union continued with the tactics and organization currently in place, history might have been different. However, as you will learn, General Ulysses Grant would soon enter the picture and change everything.

The Union

"Without execution, the breakthrough thinking breaks down, learning adds no value, people don't meet their stretch goals, and the revolution stops dead in its tracks. What you get is a change for the worse because failure drains the energy from your organization. Repeated failure destroys it."

- Larry Bossidy, *Execution*

1. Strategy

The strategy of the Union army was complex and broad. The Union's strategy to win the war did not emerge all at once. By 1863, however, the Northern military plan consisted of five primary goals:

1. Fully blockade all Southern coasts. This strategy, known as the Anaconda, would eliminate the possibility of Confederate help from abroad.

2. Control the Mississippi River. The river was the South's major inland waterway. Also, Northern control of the rivers would separate Texas, Louisiana, and Arkansas from the other Confederate states.

3. Capture Richmond. Without its capital, the Confederacy's command lines would be disrupted.

4. Shatter Southern civilian morale by capturing and destroying Atlanta, Savannah, and the heart of Southern secession, South Carolina.

5. Use the numerical advantage of Northern troops to engage the enemy everywhere to break the Confederate Army's spirits. [136]

While ambitious, the plan required extensive resources and manpower to accomplish. Without a clear prioritization, all five points of the strategy were initiated in a similar timeframe. Owing to the advantage of defense in military technology at this time, the capture of land objectives and defeating the enemy armies was incredibly challenging and costly.

The Union army almost had to be everywhere at once against an entrenched and determined enemy.

2. Planning

The Union Army's planning was dismal on many occasions. How does an army arrive at an unfordable river two weeks before the pontoon bridges? And then there's the Burnside Bridge's disaster at Antietam. When a far superior military force loses consistently, lack of planning is one of the major culprits.

Union generals frequently relied on a command-and-control structure for issuing plans and orders. However, due to a lack of information and communication speed, the original context had often changed when orders were received. Generals ordered regiments to counter phantom forces and ordered men to their death without firing a shot. Without flexibility in planning, the Union could not and did not use their resources to maximum effect.

Union generals and leaders were often promoted on their ability to move and feed an army, not fight.

3. Focus

The Union efforts lacked the focus necessary to be effective. While trying to achieve all five strategic objectives simultaneously, they could make little progress other than the blockade. By trying to maintain everything at once, the essential details were elusive.

The large displacement of men on the battlefield led to commanders overlooking critical junctures of when the enemy was about to route them or when they could press for the advantage. Commanders focused on the logistical challenges of moving and supporting their fighting forces, not winning battles.

Because Union generals had abundant resources and always more men to fill in for the fallen, they did not focus on maximizing what they had to the greatest effect.

Union generals would focus on not losing and winning. They would focus on what General Lee could do and not take the fight and initiative against the enemy.

4. Decentralization

If you were to step back into history and peer into the organization, you would find a system controlled by bureaucracy governed by rules, procedures, and tradition. Low-quality generals set the tone and expectations at the top. The tendency to follow military protocol ingrained soldiers' worst characteristics; they embraced the status quo and limited creativity and initiative-taking conditions.

As we learned in Fredericksburg, the rule was that orders were not to be interpreted but strictly followed. A great example of this was McClellan ordering Burnside to join the fight while prescribing the bridge as the only means of travel instead of asking Burnside to find the most practical and least costly means of getting his men to battle.

The large number of Union troops involved in battles and the lack of visibility into the battlefield's current conditions as they transpired resulted in frequent missteps from both army generals and unit commanders.

5. Ownership & Accountability

Because the Union was a well-supplied invading force in a foreign land, many officers and soldiers were more inclined to follow orders than take the initiative and demonstrate ownership of their tasks and accountability for their results.

The culture that the Union leadership created up to this point led to a fighting force that did not believe in or understand the war strategy. Many soldiers pondered questions such as: "Why are we here? Why are we fighting? How will we win?" went unanswered. Even more demoralizing, the Union strategy seemed to shift on political whims more than common sense tactics. It was not clear if this was a war on slavery, states' rights, or preserving the Union, and the internal divisions only grew wider after each loss as the fight needed a reason to continue. Soldiers were fighting a war they didn't feel was theirs.

Throughout the various campaigns, soldiers watched as weak leaders sacrificed their men's lives due to poor strategy or poor execution without facing repercussions. By setting an example, soldiers were not inclined to take extraordinary risks in battle other than required.

A few ownership breakthroughs did occur. One of the best examples is Chamberlain at Gettysburg.

On July 2nd, the 20th Maine regiment under the command of Joshua Chamberlain found itself positioned on high ground known as Little Round Top. General Meade tasked the regiment to hold the line at the Union extreme left "at all costs." With a small force of 386 men, including 120 deserters from another Maine regiment that Chamberlain had been given the option to guard or shoot, Chamberlain had to work quickly and creatively to increase his odds. Instead of sidelining the deserters, Chamberlain instead used empathy to convince most of the 120 disaffected soldiers to rejoin the fight. Under his command, Chamberlain surveyed the field with a now more potent force and then tasked his men to build defensives to steel themselves behind. [137]

It was not long after Hood's division arrived and began their assault on Little Round Top. Chamberlain, quickly grasping the gravity of the regiment's burden, implored his men to stand bravely and put up the most vigorous defense possible- to the last man if need be. During this encounter, time and time again, the Confederates struck with ferocity, and the 20th Maine was almost pushed back. Despite the odds, Chamberlain's men stood their ground and beat back each charge. As victory looked possible, disaster struck as ammunition ran dangerously low.

Had Chamberlain retreated here, no one would have blamed him- he put in a reasonable effort.

However, Chamberlain would not waver on the objective and fail his country. He took ownership and committed to execution. Chamberlain faced dire circumstances and acted to reform his line with all able body men left, ordered that they fix bayonets, and prepared to charge. He personally initiated the charge as the 20th Maine swept down the hill, with the left-wing wheeling continually to make the charging line swing like a hinge. The order created a simultaneous frontal assault and flanking maneuver and captured nearly 100 of the exhausted Confederate soldiers and successfully saving the Union flank and likely turning the battle and war.

6. Communication

Communication breakdowns between the Union army were frequent occurrences. The Army of the Potomac frequently acted less like an army and more like a collection of divisions that happened to be in the same place at the same time. The results for the Union were often disastrous.

When orders were received, sometimes they were enacted slowly, sometimes ignored, and sometimes bungled to the advantage of the enemy. The Union was often ill-equipped to navigate unfamiliar territory and walk into the Confederates' traps set for them. The Union rarely caught the Confederates off guard or in a vulnerable position as a result.

Confederate forces ran circles around their invaders in unfamiliar territory, and cut/intercepted telegraph cables at will. The Union was intimidated in facing Stuart's cavalry due to a lack of skills and experience and preferred to keep themselves at a distance.

7. Culture

The culture established in the Union army was often the result of the ego of the commanding generals. The tone and examples set at the top of an organization are critical. As lower-ranking generals would notice that those who didn't ask too many questions and did as they were told, the culture was set.

Weak leaders created a weak organization. Culture is defined not only by what is said but what is done.

8. Leadership

The Union Army was in a sorry state up to this point. The lack of a strategy and execution were byproducts of the organization.

In McClellan, the Union found a leader who could prepare but not act.

In Burnside, the Union found a leader who could act but not think.

9. Experience

The staggering casualties on the Union side required the constant recruitment of citizens to join the army. New regiments and replacements for old ones were filled with green recruits, many of whom had never held a rifle before.

In the leadership ranks, few excellent leaders presented themselves at this point in the war. Those who rose quickly were more inclined to the logistical aspects of leading an army and not the tactical. Many people used political skills and connections to obtain a leadership role, and many of these men had no or limited battlefield experience. Contrary to the Confederate force, Union commanders would typically stay far in the rear away from war's danger and realities.

Experienced soldiers and leaders in the Union were lacking.

10. Skills

As many Northern citizens lived in an urban environment, fresh recruits lacked all the skills required to fight a war in the country. It would take time to learn the life and responsibilities of a soldier. Live-fire drills were seldom performed, owing to the cost of powder and bullets, and many soldiers never properly learned how to use their sights for aiming.

Many officers came into their positions unskilled and unprepared. Few had training from a military academy or experience in battle or leading men.

11. Professionalism

The Union army struggled to assemble a cohesive and professional fight force.

The class divide didn't help the situation much. Elite men would voluntarily join the war as Union officers or generals by leveraging their elite class statuses and connections to obtain their positions. The officers, lacking proper training, were unskilled or unwilling to put in the time and attention to drill and instill discipline in their troops.

Meanwhile, the typical Union soldier was fighting because many had no choice or (legal) alternative. It wasn't uncommon for recruits to lack a common culture or language since many new Irish and German immigrants were forced into the war effort almost fresh off the boat. While many early soldiers were volunteers, as the war progressed, many soldiers who comprised the bulk of the fighting force were draftees called up to fill the gaps from the fallen.

The lack of professionalism in the Union army was such that frequently in battle, and at critical points, Union soldiers would melt under pressure and retreat.

On multiple occasions throughout the war, Confederates attacked Union soldiers in the morning while their rifles were stacked and their breakfast was cooking.

12. Continuous Improvement Mindset

The Union did have an advantage with their numerous factories in improving their armaments. The Union developed and utilized better and more extended-range cannons than their opponent. These were readily available in abundant quantity for the army.

By 1863, there was also an improvement to the typical muzzle-loaded rifle, the repeating rifles, or weapons that could fire more than one bullet before needing a reload. The most famous of these guns, the Spencer carbine, could fire seven shots in 30 seconds. However, in the end, military leadership determined the new technology was far too expensive, and the armies were concerned with wasting ammunition, so they saw limited use.

Where it mattered most, innovation was lacking in the Union, and the camp conditions made the soldier's experience no better. Two-thirds of soldiers in both armies died from disease rather than battle wounds as hygiene was non-existent; disease spread rapidly as a result. It was not until late in the war that the latrines (toilets) were properly built downstream, preventing the drinking water from being contaminated with human waste.

13. Execution

Due to the combination of a poor culture and lack of cohesion within the army, Union regiments discontentment led to an inconsistent performance on the field. Some units like the Iron Brigade earned an excellent reputation, but too many other units would flee the field once a certain amount of pressure was applied. Numbers would count for nothing if entire units were quick to scatter in the face of adversity and death. Even though the Union had more resources, they lacked much in the factors that made their enemy so formidable: a robust culture, brilliant strategy, and execution-obsessed leadership.

The good news, though, is that the Union was preparing to make a change shortly, with men like Generals Grant and Sherman entering the picture.

TURNING POINT: ULYSSES S. GRANT TAKES OVER

"If various members and groups within the organization don't have a commitment to change, it will never happen."

- Gil-li Vardi

"In war, anything is better than indecision. We must decide. If I am wrong, we shall soon find it out and can do the other thing. But not to decide wastes both time and money and may ruin everything." [138]

- General Ulysses Grant

"The Art of War is simple enough. Find out where your enemy is. Get at him as soon as you can. Strike him as hard as you can, and then move on."

- General Ulysses S. Grant

Our journey into the Civil War isn't over yet. We step forward to 1864, where the Union recently found a major strategic and tactical victory at Gettysburg. However, in the aftermath, President Lincoln had lost faith in the newest general, George Meade. Acting with an abundance of caution in the army's typical fashion, Lee and his devastated forces slipped away after the crucial battle.

In Meade's place, General Ulysses S. Grant was placed in charge of leading the Army of the Potomac. Coming fresh from victories in subduing Vicksburg, Mississippi, and Nashville, Tennessee, Grant was confident and knowledgeable of his opponent.

Even better, he was decisive.

The Wilderness

The first test of Grant commanding the Army of the Potomac was the Battle of the Wilderness located West of Fredericksburg, Virginia. Here, Grant led the last big push against Confederate General Robert E. Lee's Army of Northern Virginia. Grant started toward the Confederate capital at Richmond with 118,000 men and hoped to get around Lee's line and capture Richmond. However, his large army could not move fast enough to outmaneuver the smaller Confederate force. [139]

As Grant's plan became clear to Lee on May 4, Lee knew that it was imperative to fight in the Wilderness for the same reason as the year before: his army was massively outnumbered. His artillery's guns were fewer and inferior to those of Grant's. Fighting in the tangled woods would eliminate Grant's advantage in artillery. The close quarters and ensuing confusion there could give Lee's outnumbered force better odds. Lee, therefore, ordered his army to intercept the advancing Federals in the Wilderness.

Thus, Grant met Lee's army of 64,000 on May 5, in a thick forest known as the Wilderness. The clash that followed horrified even the most experienced soldiers. Men charged blindly through the dense thickets, often firing at the enemy at close range, as the woods constantly hummed with both shot and shell. When the smoke cleared, nearly 19,000 Union and 12,000 Confederate casualties were counted. Although both armies lost roughly the same percentage of men based on their armies' size and both armies remained on the field after the two days of fighting, the battle was a tactical draw. However, unlike Grant, Lee had minimal opportunity to replenish his losses.

Although the opening of the two-day battle was bloody and the Union had been pushed back, Grant did something that no other Civil War general before him had done: **Grant didn't give up.** And because of this, Grant would significantly impact both the Union Army's culture and its ability to formulate and execute its strategy. Here was the turning point of the war: Lee had failed to turn back the invasion for the first time.

After the Battle of the Wilderness, the onward advance of General Ulysses Grant marked the first time in the Civil War that the Army of the Potomac had continued to fight after the initial offensive in a Virginia campaign. Instead of retreating, Grant took stock of his circumstances and made the best of it. He sought counsel from his subordinates, maneuvered, and ordered his men to continue the fight on the second day.

As the Confederates worked to turn the Union flank at one point in the battle, an officer is said to have rushed to Grant and have exclaimed that soon, Lee would split his army and make retreat impossible. To this, Grant is credited with replying, "Oh, I am heartily tired of hearing about what Lee is going to do. Some of you always seem to think he is suddenly going to turn a double somersault and land in our rear and on both of our flanks at the same time. Go back to your command and try to think what we are going to do ourselves instead of what Lee is going to do." [140]

In Grant, finally, the army had a general with leadership capabilities that would pair strategy with execution. Although he would suffer losses, Grant learned from each opportunity to make himself and his troops better.

Grant finally leveraged the Union's advantages: it had men and ammunition with which to resupply, and the Confederates didn't. Each battle would become more desperate for the rebels the harder they were pushed. Meanwhile, the Union army's morale soared.

Just two days later, on May 8, 1864, Grant and Lee clashed again at a crossroads called Spotsylvania Courthouse. After that came Spotsylvania, Cold Harbor, and then Petersburg, which Grant sieged for nine months. Finally, in April 1865, Grant took the city and then quickly took Richmond, as well. Later that same month, Lee offered terms of surrender.

The war had been won.

Who was Grant?

Who was Grant? And what did he do differently than all the men before him?

To answer this question, perhaps the best judge of a man's character is not what he says about himself but how others describe him. General Sherman, Grant's most trusted subordinate commander, noted that Grant had a "simple faith in success," which proved infectious. Grant had confidence and determination that made others believe in themselves as well.

Sherman wrote to Grant:

> "When you have completed your best preparations, you go into battle without hesitation...no doubts, no reserve." "I tell you that it was this that made us act with confidence. I knew wherever I was that you thought of me, and if I got in a tight place, you would come—if alive."

Sherman went on to explain to his fellow officer James Harrison Wilson,

> "I am a damned sight smarter man than Grant. I know a great deal more about war, military history, strategy, and grand tactics than he does. I know more about organization, supply, and administration and about everything else than he does. But I'll tell you where he beats me and where he beats the world. He don't care a damn for what the enemy does out of his sight, but it scares me

like hell!"

These words are telling. Grant was not a genius, and he owned this. He put his ego aside to make room for execution and results. In both Strategy and Execution, Grant was neither a mystic nor was he reckless.

Source: Ulysses S. Grant and his Generals on horseback.
1865, Library of Congress.

Here, in Grant, the Union finally found strategy and execution. To Grant, Lee was just another obstacle to be overcome by applying the Getting Shit Done Framework. Grant had leadership talent that secured the Union. His strategy and style still offer valuable lessons for today's employees, managers, directors, and executives.

1. Strategy

As Bossidy stated in *Execution*, "Execution is a systematic way of exposing reality and acting on it," We can apply that same truth to the Civil War and Grant. Grant found the facts, ignored the rumors, and built a strong team around him to execute his strategy.

The generals who came before Grant did not seek to embrace reality. McClellan overestimated the enemy's strength at Antietam. Burnside sent thousands of men to their death in an impossible attack at Fredericksburg. Meade did not recognize that the Confederates were on their last legs after Gettysburg. In Lee and his army, each Union general saw an unstoppable force.

Grant realized that the strategy and the highest priority should be to destroy Lee's army. He made this his primary objective.

2. Planning

Grant was a fan of flexible planning. He focused on attacking the enemy on his terms to maximize Union advantages and reveal Confederate weaknesses. As events transpired, the enemy shifted, and opportunities revealed themselves, Grant created new plans on the go.

When Lee dug in soldiers around Richmond, Grant moved his army further south to the unprotected Petersburg. Grant put Lee on the defensive constantly. Lee could not continue to stretch his limited forces further to keep pace. Grant didn't give up, but he wasn't foolish, either; he returned to the fight with a plan for success.

In the victory over Vicksburg, after repeated frontal tasks failed to take the city, Grant came up with a new plan. He sailed his forces past the city and landed them down river. Vicksburg had no defenses in this direction, and the city soon fell.

3. Focus

Grant had a great strategic sensibility and knew how to prioritize objectives. He understood that the Union had more men and resources than the Confederacy and would maximize that advantage by constantly attacking. But he also knew that the secessionists could win by not losing — that is, by hanging on until the Northern states lost the will to fight.

Grant focused on bringing the fight to the enemy relentlessly. Wherever they would go, he would be. Under pressure, Lee would make mistakes.

Accordingly, he adopted an aggressive strategy that relied on corralling the enemy by cutting its forces off from the territory needed to maneuver, the resources needed to fight, and one another. And then, after mustering the largest force possible, Grant attacked to destroy or capture the enemy armies.

4. Decentralization

Grant adopted decentralization and trusted his commanders to do the right thing as events progressed. Grant trusted his generals to act as he would with very limited guidance.

General Sherman would lose contact with Grant for extended periods during his march across the South to Atlanta, but the operation was very successful. Despite the separation, Sherman was trusted and understood the strategic priority and guidelines for achieving results. Working under general guidance, Sherman issued Special Field Orders No. 120 informing his officers what they were and were not permitted to do and how they should conduct themselves in this operation using only around 500 words. [141]

5. Ownership & Accountability

Grant took the blame from subordinates when things went wrong and praised them when things went right. After the failure of the Petersburg Crater, he "[attached] no blame to Burnside...but I do to myself for not having had a staff officer with him" and "to [Sherman] belongs the credit of [his campaign's] brilliant execution" of his subordinate generals. [142]

Grant took Extreme Ownership and realized that good or bad; he was responsible for the outcomes.

6. Communication

In working to fill the gaps of what he did not know, Grant relied on honesty in his communications to build trust and accountability through Ways of Working with others within his team and organization. What he lacked in knowledge of military art and science, he made up for with perseverance and grit as he did not let go of his enemy, pushing them hard enough so that, for the first time, they began to make tactical errors.

Perhaps what else contributed to Grant's extraordinary success was his ability to synthesize information quickly. Grant was an expert listener, one staff officer proclaimed. For example, faced with a dire situation on arriving in the besieged city of Chattanooga in late 1863, Grant sat "as silent as the sphinx" while officers delivered their reports, according to an eyewitness. Then, after firing "whole volleys of questions," he proceeded to write out a series of dispatches. [143]

7. Culture

Establishing a cultural change — such as the mindset of refusing to give up — becomes real when your aim is execution.

For his part, Sherman recognized in Grant a rare ability to draw the best from lieutenants. "General Grant possesses in an eminent degree that peculiar & high attribute of using various men to produce a Common result," he observed in the summer of 1863, "and now that his Character is well established, we can easily subordinate ourselves to him with the absolute assurance of serving the Common Cause of our Country." [144]

He encouraged alternative viewpoints from subordinate generals and welcomed criticism, understanding that conveyance of humility and delegation of responsibility was essential to efficient operations.

8. Leadership

Ulysses S. Grant was far from perfect, encountered many demons daily (alcoholism), and had peaks and valleys on his climb to success mountain. What is evident in Grant's wartime behavior—and above all in his deathbed memoirs—is an unusual degree of self-awareness. Grant was neither confessional nor overly introspective. He had taught himself who he was far more accurately than any good- or ill-wishers could hope to match in addressing his drinking. When he looked inward, Grant had no illusions and few delusions.

Grant saw beyond battles, writes Chernow, "to a boldly expansive blueprint for taking state after state and terminating hostilities. His great strength was that he thought in terms of sequence of battles." And the cadence of battles was as important to Grant's strategic vision as the sequence. "Momentum was everything for Grant," adds Chernow. [105]

Steady confidence, unshakable will, and tenacity, together with a willingness to shoulder ultimate responsibility, provided a calming framework for the Union.

9. Experience

Grant was promoted because he had demonstrated success in the War's Western theatre. Grant got better at commanding and strategy-execution as he commanded larger numbers of troops in more significant battles.

He made his reputation in Tennessee, at Fort Donelson, and the Battle of Shiloh. Later major victories that stood out were the Vicksburg, Chattanooga, and the Overland campaigns.

10. Skills

Grant was trained at West Point and had fought in the Mexican-American War, but he did not presume that these qualifications would make him a better decider in battle. A striking attribute about Grant was his low-key management style. He assumed leadership by building trust rather than asserting authority.

Grant became a skilled general by leading troops through both victories and losses. As he gained more experience, he became more adept and comfortable leading soldiers and officers. Grant looked for opportunities to continue to learn and improve as a leader.

11. Professionalism

Grant was respectful of others, fair, and even-tempered, but never lax in expectations or accountability. Finding an alarming lack of discipline in his new regiment of volunteers, Grant acted promptly — ordering that no one was to leave the camp without a pass, punishing deserters, and instituting daily drills. "I found it very hard work for a few days to bring all the men into anything like subordination," he wrote, "but the great majority favored discipline, and by the application of a little regular army punishment, all were reduced to as good discipline as one could ask."

12. Continuous Improvement Mindset

In a final push to end the war, Grant took a creative approach to capture Petersburg quickly.

After the initial attacks on Petersburg by Union forces ended on June 18, a portion of the IX Corps picket line, built under fire, was established only four hundred feet from Elliot's Salient, part of the main Confederate line. The Federals decided to construct and explode a mine underneath the salient to surprise and overwhelm the Confederates and then seize the heights above Petersburg.

The Union sent unit after unit into the 200-foot-wide gap created in the Confederate line. The poorly led Federal soldiers end up heading into the crater and not around it as planned. [145]

Burnside was relieved of command for the final time for his role in the fiasco. He was never again returned to command, and to make matters worse, Ferrero and General James H. Ledlie were observed behind the lines in a bunker, drinking liquor throughout the battle.

The botched battle of the Crater It may have been Grant's best chance to end the siege of Petersburg; instead, the soldiers settled in for another eight months of trench warfare. Grant assumed full responsibility for the failure.

13. Execution

Grant's willingness, even need, to act was one of the qualities that distinguished him from many other Union military leaders. As the war's final push resulted in more Union casualties, even those calling him "The Butcher," there were many calls for Grant's removal. Lincoln never wavered in his support of the man he had made a major general less than two months earlier. "I can't spare this man," he reportedly said of Grant. "He fights." [105]

Grant combined all Getting Shit Done Framework elements to create a winning combination that ended the war for the Union and reunited the country.

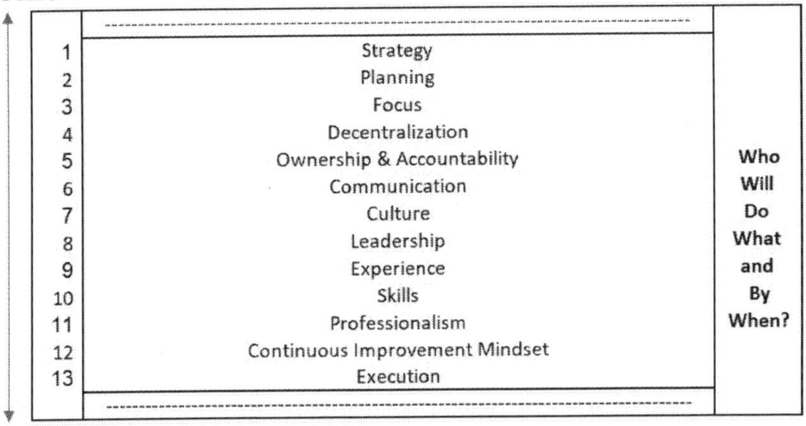

1	Strategy	
2	Planning	
3	Focus	
4	Decentralization	
5	Ownership & Accountability	Who
6	Communication	Will
7	Culture	Do
8	Leadership	What
9	Experience	and
10	Skills	By
11	Professionalism	When?
12	Continuous Improvement Mindset	
13	Execution	

Image12- Strategy-Execution GSD Framework Illustration

TAKEAWAYS

By this point, you should grasp the power and impact that leaders have on the world around them. Leaders are vital because they can have a defining factor in many aspects of life and our world, not just historical battles. Whether you are working to overcome a challenging business environment, drive results on improvement projects, or even reinventing an industry in the face of new technology and competitors, success hinges on great leaders who can inspire and drive teams. Great leaders don't just get lucky once; they are obsessed with building an organization, a supporting team that will allow them to consistently deliver outstanding results by masterfully pairing and coordinating strategy and execution.

On the other hand, poor leaders create other weak leaders. They poison the culture; they negate all organizational advantages and turn them into disadvantages. They keep good ideas away.

Even though the final battles for the Union were costly, the soldiers were appreciative to finally have leadership that believed in them and was capable of ending the conflict and saving many more lives. The men, at all levels, rose to the challenge when the proper man took the top leadership role.

REFLECTION:

1. Do your leaders have the ability to understand, prioritize, and disseminate strategy? Do your leaders have the ability, strength, and courage to challenge a bad strategy? Do they have the experience, knowledge, or capability to develop a winning strategy?

2. Do your leaders rigidly plan the execution of strategy, or do they give people flexibility and freedom to determine the best and most efficient execution path?

3. Do your leaders know how to identify the priorities that require the most focus? Are they capable of maintaining focus and driving resources towards that priority?

4. Do your leaders hoard responsibility for themselves, or do they share responsibility and seek out smart, talented, and driven people who are more knowledgeable in their areas of expertise?

5. Do your leaders take ownership of the results, good or bad? Or do they look for who to blame and punish?

6. Do your leaders communicate effectively on strategy, execution, and all the elements in between? Do your leaders listen and think before they speak?

7. Do your leaders champion and set the tone at the top to create an execution culture? Do they set an example of acceptable and unacceptable behaviors?

Do they reward and punish the proper behaviors consistently?

8. Do your leaders have the right leadership behaviors? Do they set the organization in the right direction and inspire others towards action? Do they support their people when needed and remove obstacles?

9. Do your leaders have the experience to execute the strategy? Are they familiar and knowledgeable of the elements of the strategy-execution gap, and do they have a plan to remedy each item? Do you leaders how technical and business knowledge to understand the challenges and solve them?

10. Do your leaders have the proper skills or know what skills are required to execute strategy? Are people encouraged and supported to maintain and upgrade their skills along the way?

11. Do your leaders set clear standards of professionalism to guide acceptable behaviors and expectations?

12. Do your leaders inspire and encourage a continuous improvement mindset where innovative ideas are celebrated?

13. Do your leaders champion execution? Are they focused on results and empowering people to achieve them? Do they understand the obstacles and accelerants of strategy-execution?

CHAPTER 10

Getting Shit Done

"The best time to plant a tree was 20 years
ago. The second-best time is now."
-Chinese Proverb

"Unless you try to do something beyond what you
have already mastered, you will never grow."
– Ronald E. Osborn

"Efficiency is a process. It doesn't happen the first or second
time you do something. Which means to be productive
in the fullest sense, you have to commit to the process of
always looking for ways to improve over the long term."
-Parkinson's Law

INTRODUCTION

The question that I've thought much about when reading and researching this book is, "If there are already other books, consultants, and courses out there in the world on the subject of strategy-execution, then why hasn't the problem been solved?"

Why are we still struggling to close the strategy-execution gap?

The real answer is that closing the strategy-execution gap is hard; really, really hard. Building a great organization, attracting and retaining the right people, and building and maintaining excellence throughout an organization are challenges that can't be solved quickly.

There is no simple color-by-numbers solution to fill in structural gaps for a prize so large in our organizations' health, profitability, and economies.

It isn't one thing or three things that we must get right once. Strategy-Execution is about getting the critical elements right all the time.

What I've discovered in the process of writing this book is that **strategy-execution isn't an objective; it's a discipline**. Like any discipline, strategy-execution depends on an earnest and wholehearted adoption, not choosing sections a la carte that fits best into your worldview. Each block builds upon the others to create a lasting structure.

After nearly a year of thinking, reading, and writing accompanied by nearly a decade of hands-on experience, the path to closing the strategy-execution gap has flushed itself out in the steps below. If you and your organization want to Get Shit Done, you must be able and willing to check off and "own" each item.

1. Build and maintain high employee engagement levels demonstrated around ownership of Who, What, and When. Explain the Why.

2. Establish ownership in the organization. Hire the right people, trust them, and compensate them for aligning them with the organization's goals.

3. Demand high levels of professionalism by encouraging a disciplined structure of personal development, growth, and learning. Through deliberate practice, encourage others to develop grit and tenacity to persevere against challenging goals. Continuous learning is a must.

4. Set Expectations of Excellence to create and maintain an environment where full accountability and excellence are the norms. A highly skilled workforce with a focus on a continuous improvement mindset will beat a centralized command-and-control policy. Build Accountability Chains to increase accountability—reward excellence.

5. Ingrain a Sense of Urgency. Define what the real priorities are and get people are resources pointed in the right direction.

6. Acknowledge tradeoffs are required between resources. An organization must be deliberate in choosing what to do and not do. Avoid unrealistic expectations.

7. Separate strategy-execution into two categories; the Big What and Little Whats. To prepare for achieving large and complex goals, individuals and teams obtain experience leading projects and improving work in their teams, departments, and functions.

8. Avoid static planning methodologies and embrace decentralization to allow those closest to the work to build the best solutions.

9. Set clear expectations and avoid assumptions.

10. Track and measure progress against realistic goals that have clear owners.

11. Incorporate design thinking into the Who, What, and When. Systemize and automate where possible to free time for value-added work. Remove friction wherever possible.

12. Foster excellent communication demonstrated by candor, feedback, alignment, and frequent check-ins. Be mindful in determining how we communicate to increase speed, increase accountability, and avoid confusion.

13. Build a unique and robust culture manifested through Ways of Working.

14. Minimize distractions and embrace simplicity. Focus on what matters and minimize what doesn't with the Pareto Principle.

15. Encourage individuals to learn and think like leaders and to act accordingly. Encourage creativity and innovation to build systems and processes that e. Being forward-looking, prepared, and proactive are valuable characteristics. Build leadership at all levels.

16. Execute, assess, iterate. Repeat.

In this book, we've explored the pieces of the puzzle that must come together to build a more vibrant and successful organization. These 13 Principles of Strategy-Execution are:

THE FRAMEWORK

1. STRATEGY
2. Planning
3. Focus
4. Decentralization
5. Ownership & Accountability
6. Communication
7. Culture
8. Leadership
9. Experience
10. Skills
11. Professionalism
12. Continuous Improvement Mindset
13. EXECUTION

FINAL WORDS

The Strategy-Execution framework introduced in this book is an integrated, organization-wide framework that entails establishing the required strategies for success and effectively executing those strategies. The right strategies lay the foundation for the future of the organization. Effectively executing the wrong strategies is a swift path to failure.

Once the right strategy is in place, the focus shifts fully to execution. More than mere tactics, execution is *the* fundamental bridge between strategy and performance. It must be approached as a systematic process for rigorously reviewing and challenging strategic imperatives, operational directives, underlying capabilities, accountabilities, and performance outcomes.

When managed as a disciplined process, strategy-execution is an iterative, adaptive, and robust method for running a business. Without this discipline — this systematic process — the strategy-execution lessons might remain only good ideas left sitting on a bookshelf.

While many managers and professionals may think of improving strategy-execution as identifying and removing the few, big, identifiable roadblocks like filling in a pothole in the middle of a highway, there is way more to it. Working towards strategy-execution is a multi-faceted process.

Because progress has been slowed by years of compounded neglect and unintentionality in an organization, obvious quick fixes are not the remedy- we must look deeper. Imagine sand caught in many gears at the same time that eventually causes a machine to sputter out of control. Unless you specifically look for the damage, the destruction can almost be unseen until it is too late. Likewise, by the time organizations acknowledge a strategy-execution issue, the cost of repairs is unmanageable. According to the Harvard Business Review Advisory Council, senior executives wholeheartedly agree that an organization's architecture — which includes the very structures, processes, and systems supposed to enable work — is their most significant obstacle to strategic execution.

Poor architecture, leadership, and command structures slow down decision-making in a morass of reporting relationships, regulations, approvals, and other bureaucratic tendrils. They confuse and impede progress through inefficient resource flows, process inefficiencies, conflicting priorities, and finger-pointing. And they muddy rather than elucidate decision-making with incomplete or distorted information. To close the strategy-execution gap, we now understand that goals are only met by embracing an intentional and systematic strategy-execution framework, not a patchwork of tools and policies.

We also must champion the fact that people hold the knowledge and the answers, whether they know it now or not. Each person in your organization needs to be empowered to grow and share their skills and knowledge with others, especially those who make decisions.

On the human resource side, strategy-execution isn't just about focusing on productivity but also attracting, developing, deploying the best human capital, raising skill levels, and ensuring that the organization possesses the knowledge, skills, skills, and abilities appropriate for the task.

Rather than command-and-control, we need flexible structures and sophisticated information systems to support work processes that fit the tasks and strategy. More agile, cross-functional structures accompanied by easy access to the right information at the right moment create the capacity to meet shifting demands quickly.

To Get Shit Done (and get it done right), combine the thirteen strategy-execution elements presented in this chapter and in this book to create a powerful synergy and help you find best practices that work for your organization. Getting Shit Done is about making each day better than the last. A little faster, a little more efficient, a little bit more savings. At one point, you will turn around and will have built an organization, a project, and a career to be proud of. It is never too late to get started. As the Chinese saying goes, "the best time to plant a tree was 20 years ago; the second-best time is now."

As Larry Bossidy explained in *Execution*, "Strategy-execution is an unending process that requires constant attention."

In short, to close the strategy-execution gap, you must always seek to answer these three central questions again and again (AND AGAIN):

1. What needs to be done?
2. Who is going to do it?
3. When is it going to be done?

The journey to strategy-execution starts here, with you.

CHAPTER
REFERENCES

CHAPTER 1

8.   Maister, David. Strategy and the Fat Smoker: Doing What's Obvious but Not Easy. Boston, MA: Spangle Press, 2008.

26.   "What Is Strategy?" Harvard Business Review, November 7, 2019. https://hbr.org/1996/11/what-is-strategy.

43.   Sunzi. The Art of War: the Oldest Military Treatise in the World. New Delhi: The Readers Paradise, 2019.

29.   Mainardi, Cesare R., and Paul Leinwand. Strategy That Works. Harvard Business Review, 2016.

25.   Hussey, David E. The Implementation Challenge. Chichester: Wiley, 1996.

CHAPTER 2

5.   Connors, Roger, Tom Smith, and Craig R. Hickman. The Oz Principle: Getting Results through Individual and Organizational Accountability. New York, NY: Portfolio, 2010.

11.   Hardy-Vallee, Benoit. "The Cost of Bad Project Management." Gallup.com. Gallup, October 20, 2020. https://news.gallup.com/businessjournal/152429/cost-bad-project-management.aspx.

30.   "5 Ways the Best Companies Close the Strategy-Execution Gap." Harvard Business Review, February 7, 2020. https://hbr.org/2017/11/5-ways-the-best-companies-close-the-strategy-execution-gap.

18.   Kahneman, Daniel. Thinking, Fast and Slow. New York: Farrar, Straus and Giroux, 2013.

122. History.com Editors. "First Battle of Bull Run." History.com. A&E Television Networks, April 1, 2011. https://www.history.com/topics/american-civil-war/first-battle-of-bull-run.

34.   "Udemy In Depth: 2018 Workplace Distraction Report." Udemy Research, April 30, 2020. https://research.udemy.com/research_report/udemy-depth-2018-workplace-distraction-report/.

23.   Davidson, Lauren. "Is Your Daily Social Media Usage Higher than Average?" The Telegraph. Telegraph Media Group, May 17, 2015.https://www.telegraph.co.uk/finance/newsbysector/mediatechnology-andtelecoms/11610959/Is-your-daily-social-media-

usage-higher-than-average.html.

24.   NEWPORT, CAL. DEEP WORK: Rules for Focused Success in a Distracted World. GRAND CENTRAL PUB, 2018.

53.   "Beware the Busy Manager." Harvard Business Review, November 18, 2014. https://hbr.org/2002/02/beware-the-busy-manager.

35.   "What Is Flow in Psychology? Definition and 10+ Activities to Induce Flow." PositivePsychology.com, March 10, 2021. https://positivepsychology.com/what-is-flow/.

20.   Summaries, Must Read. A Sense of Urgency - John Kotter. Primento Publishing, 2011.

48.   Deane, Morgan. "Top 8 Inventions & Innovations of WWII." WAR HISTORY ONLINE, December 10, 2018.   https://www.warhistoryonline.com/instant-articles/inventions-and-innovations-wwii.html.

146. Bungay, Stephen. The Most Dangerous Enemy: a History of the Battle of Britain. London: Aurum Press, 2015.

CHAPTER 3

15.   Roberts, Andrew. Napoleon: A Life. Penguin Books, n.d.

69.   Merchant, Nilofer. The New How: Building Business Solutions through Collaborative Strategy. Sebastopol, CA: O'Reilly Media, 2014.

8.   Maister, David. Strategy and the Fat Smoker: Doing What's Obvious but Not Easy. Boston, MA: Spangle Press, 2008.

39.   "Making Your Strategy Work on the Frontline." Harvard Business Review, August 12, 2015. https://hbr.org/2010/06/making-your-strategy-work-on-t.

3.   Bossidy, Larry, and Ram Charan. Execution: the Discipline of Getting Things Done. London: Random House Business, 2011.

41.   McChrystal, Stanley. Team of Teams: New Rules of Engagement for a Complex World. Troy, MI: Business News Publishing, 2016.

19.   Willink, Jocko, and Leif Babin. Extreme Ownership: How U.S. Navy SEALs Lead and Win. Sydney, N.S.W.: Macmillan, 2018.

52.   "Mission Command Requires Sharp Commander's Intent." www.army.mil. Accessed March 31, 2021. https://www.army.mil/article/215297/mission_command_requires_sharp_commanders_intent.

146. Bungay, Stephen. The Most Dangerous Enemy: a History of the Battle of Britain. London: Aurum Press, 2015.

22.   Harter, Jim. "4 Factors Driving Record-High Employee Engagement in U.S." Gallup.com. Gallup, January 18, 2021. https://www.gallup.com/workplace/284180/factors-driving-record-high-employee-engagement.aspx.

56.   Maunz, Shay. "The Great Hanoi Rat Massacre of 1902 Did Not Go as Planned." Atlas Obscura. Atlas Obscura, June 6, 2017. https://www.atlasobscura.com/articles/hanoi-rat-massacre-1902.

CHAPTER 4

8.   Maister, David. Strategy and the Fat Smoker: Doing What's Obvious but Not Easy. Boston, MA: Spangle Press, 2008.

6.   Michie, J., and L. Lobao. "Ownership, Control and Economic Outcomes." Cambridge Journal of Regions, Economy and Society 5, no. 3 (2012): 307–24. https://doi.org/10.1093/cjres/rss015.

54.   TAYLOR, FREDERICK WINSLOW. PRINCIPLES OF SCIENTIFIC MANAGEMENT. DIGIREADS COM, 2020.

55.   Bauer, Tim, Cassandra Estep, and Emily E. Griffith. "Does Psychological Ownership Improve Team Member Contributions?" USC Marshall, n.d. https://www.marshall.usc.edu/sites/default/files/2018-11/Does%20Psychological%20Ownership%20Improve%20Team%20Member%20Contributions.pdf.

117.   "APA PsycNet." American Psychological Association. American Psychological Association. Accessed March 31, 2021. https://psycnet.apa.org/record/2010-26312-008.

3.   Bossidy, Larry, and Ram Charan. Execution: the Discipline of Getting Things Done. London: Random House Business, 2011.

66.   Holiday, Ryan. Daily Stoic: 366 Meditations on Self-Mastery, Perseverance and Wisdom: Featuring New Translations of Seneca, Marcus Aurelius and Epictetus. Penguin Publishing Group, 2016.

5.   Connors, Roger, Tom Smith, and Craig R. Hickman.

The Oz Principle: Getting Results through Individual and Organizational Accountability. New York, NY: Portfolio, 2010.

19.   Willink, Jocko, and Leif Babin. Extreme Ownership: How U.S. Navy SEALs Lead and Win. Sydney, N.S.W.: Macmillan, 2018.

11.   Hardy-Vallee, Benoit. "The Cost of Bad Project Management." Gallup.com. Gallup, October 20, 2020. https://news.gallup.com/businessjournal/152429/cost-bad-project-management.aspx.

57.   Chappell, Bill. "Outsourced: Employee Sends Own Job To China; Surfs Web." NPR. NPR, January 16, 2013. https://www.npr.org/sections/thetwo-way/2013/01/16/169528579/outsourced-employee-sends-own-job-to-china-surfs-web.

58.   "10 Easy Ways To Look Busy At Work." Thought Catalog, January 20, 2014. https://thoughtcatalog.com/tamara-jenkins/2014/01/10-easy-ways-to-look-busy-at-work/.

CHAPTER 5

25.   Hussey, David E. The Implementation Challenge. Chichester: Wiley, 1996.

24.   NEWPORT, CAL. DEEP WORK: Rules for Focused Success in a Distracted World. GRAND CENTRAL PUB, 2018.

CHAPTER 6

29. Mainardi, Cesare R., and Paul Leinwand. Strategy That Works. Harvard Business Review, 2016.

49. "What Is Organizational Culture? And Why Should We Care?" Harvard Business Review, August 7, 2014. https://hbr.org/2013/05/what-is-organizational-culture.

70. "Leading Change: Why Transformation Efforts Fail." Harvard Business Review, July 13, 2015. https://hbr.org/1995/05/leading-change-why-transformation-efforts-fail-2.

14. "The Seven Virtues of Bushido." English Shotokan Academy. Accessed March 31, 2021. https://www.englishshotokan.net/history-of-karate/virtues-of-bushido.

4. Horowitz, Ben. What You Do Is Who You Are. Harper Collins UK, 2019.

15. Roberts, Andrew. Napoleon: A Life. Penguin Books, n.d.

16. Callahan, Shawn. "What Might Amazon's Six-Page Narrative Structure Look like?" Anecdote. Anecdote, December 2, 2020. https://www.anecdote.com/2018/05/amazons-six-page-narrative-structure/.

17. Classicalycourt. "Jeff Bezos' 'Two Pizza Rule' Can Help You Hold More Productive Meetings." CNBC. CNBC, April 30, 2018. https://www.cnbc.com/2018/04/30/jeff-bezos-2-pizza-rule-can-help-you-hold-more-productive-meetings.html#:~:text=Jeff

%20Bezos'%20'two%20pizza%20rule'%20can
%20help,you%20hold%20more%20productive
%20meetings&text=While%2C%20sadly%2C
%20the%20rule%20does,t%20feed%20the%20entire
%20group.

8.   Maister, David. Strategy and the Fat Smoker: Doing What's Obvious but Not Easy. Boston, MA: Spangle Press, 2008.

3.   Bossidy, Larry, and Ram Charan. Execution: the Discipline of Getting Things Done. London: Random House Business, 2011.

45.   Garfinkle, Joel, Amit Maimon, and Ron Ashkenas. "Why We Should Be Disagreeing More at Work." Harvard Business Review, April 17, 2018. https://hbr.org/2018/01/why-we-should-be-disagreeing-more-at-work.

44.   Rajkumar, S. (2010). Art of communication in project management. Paper presented at PMI® Research Conference: Defining the Future of Project Management, Washington, DC. Newtown Square, PA: Project Management Institute.

59.   "Three Keys to Effective Execution." Harvard Business Review, July 23, 2014. https://hbr.org/2008/02/three-keys-to-effective-execut.

37.   "Simplicity-Minded Management." Harvard Business Review, August 1, 2014. https://hbr.org/2007/12/simplicity-minded-management.

40.   Ashkenas, Ronald N. Simply Effective: How to Cut through Complexity in Your Organization and Get Things Done. Boston, MA: Harvard Business Review Press, 2010.

42.   Bodell, Lisa. Why Simple Wins: Escape the Complexity Trap and Get to Work That Matters. New York:

Bibliomotion, Inc., 2017.

CHAPTER 7

8.   Maister, David. Strategy and the Fat Smoker: Doing What's Obvious but Not Easy. Boston, MA: Spangle Press, 2008.

64.   PricewaterhouseCoopers. "24th Annual Global CEO Survey." PwC. Accessed March 31, 2021. https://www.pwc.com/gx/en/ceo-agenda/ceosurvey/2020.html.

119. Dunning, D. (2011). The Dunning-Kruger effect: On being ignorant of one's own ignorance. In J. M. Olson & M. P. Zanna (Eds.), Advances in experimental social psychology. Advances in experimental social psychology, Vol. 44 (p. 247–296). Academic Press.

120. Duckworth, Angela. Grit: the Power of Passion and Perseverance. United States: Paula Wiseman Books, 2020.

71.   Gladwell, Malcolm. Outliers: Why Some People Succeed and Some Don't. New York: Little Brown & Co., 2008.

66.   Holiday, Ryan. Daily Stoic: 366 Meditations on Self-Mastery, Perseverance and Wisdom: Featuring New Translations of Seneca, Marcus Aurelius and Epictetus. Penguin Publishing Group, 2016.

121. Cattell, Raymond Bernard. Intelligence: Its Structure, Growth and Action. Amsterdam: North Holland, 1987.

63.   "Where Companies Go Wrong with Learning and Development." Harvard Business Review, January

20, 2021. https://hbr.org/2019/10/where-companies-go-wrong-with-learning-and-development.

CHAPTER 8

123. Covey, Stephen R. The 7 Habits of Highly Effective People. Provo, UT: Franklin Covey, 1998.

66.   Holiday, Ryan. Daily Stoic: 366 Meditations on Self-Mastery, Perseverance and Wisdom: Featuring New Translations of Seneca, Marcus Aurelius and Epictetus. Penguin Publishing Group, 2016.

43.   Sunzi. The Art of War: the Oldest Military Treatise in the World. New Delhi: The Readers Paradise, 2019.

124. Andrews, Evan. "Ancient Rome's Darkest Day: The Battle of Cannae." History.com. A& E Television Networks, August 2, 2016. https://www.history.com/news/ancient-romes-darkest-day-the-battle-of-cannae.

CHAPTER 9

127. "The Mexican-American War and the Civil War." Encyclopædia Britannica. Encyclopædia Britannica, inc. Accessed May 2, 2021. https://www.britannica.com/topic/The-United-States-Army/The-Mexican-American-War-and-the-Civil-War.

78.   Lee's Lieutenants A Study in Command. Touchstone Books, 2001.

129. Bowman, Tom. "Antietam: A Savage Day In American History." NPR. NPR, September 17, 2012. https://www.npr.org/2012/09/17/161248814/antietam-a-savage-day-in-american-history.

131. "Home." British Battles. Accessed May 2, 2021. https://www.britishbattles.com/american-civil-war/battle-of-antietam/.

132. History.com Editors. "Battle of Fredericksburg." History.com. A&E Television Networks, November 9, 2009. https://www.history.com/topics/american-civil-war/battle-of-fredericksburg.

133. "Battle of Chancellorsville Begins." History.com. A&E Television Networks, November 13, 2009. https://www.history.com/this-day-in-history/battle-of-chancellorsville-begins.

134. "North and South." American Battlefield Trust, April 13, 2021. https://www.battlefields.org/learn/articles/north-and-south.

135. History.com Editors. "Battle of Hampton Roads."

History.com. A&E Television Networks, November 9, 2009. https://www.history.com/topics/american-civil-war/battle-of-hampton-roads.

136. "Northern Plans to End the War." ushistory.org. Independence Hall Association. Accessed May 2, 2021. https://www.ushistory.org/US/33h.asp.

137. "Defense of Little Round Top." American Battlefield Trust, March 26, 2021. https://www.battlefields.org/learn/articles/defense-little-round-top.

138. II, Julian Hayes. "3 Timeless Principles of a Winner's Mindset From Ulysses S. Grant." Inc.com. Inc., December 27, 2018. https://www.inc.com/julian-hayes-ii/what-civil-war-general-us-president-ulysses-s-grant-can-teach-you-about-adopting-a-winners-mind-set.html.

139. "Grant's Greatest Battles." PBS. Public Broadcasting Service. Accessed May 2, 2021. https://www.pbs.org/wgbh/americanexperience/features/grants-greatest-battles/.

140. Porter, General Horace. Campaigning with Grant. United States: Pickle Partners Publishing, 2015.

143. Samet, Elizabeth D. "7 Reasons Ulysses S. Grant Was One of America's Most Brilliant Military Leaders." History.com. A&E Television Networks, May 13, 2020. https://www.history.com/news/ulysses-s-grant-civil-war-general-strengths.

144. Chan, Amy. "The Supreme Partnership: Grant and Sherman." HistoryNet. HistoryNet, May 17, 2017. https://www.historynet.com/supreme-partnership-grant-sherman.htm.

145. "The Crater." National Parks Service. U.S. Department of the Interior. Accessed May 2, 2021.

105. CHERNOW, RON. GRANT. HEAD OF ZEUS, 2018.

ALL REFERENCES

1. "The 5 Pillars of Strategy Execution." Smarter With Gartner. Accessed March 31, 2021. https://www.gartner.com/smarterwithgartner/the-five-pillars-of-strategy-execution/.

2. "Turning Great Strategy into Great Performance." Harvard Business Review, September 15, 2015. https://hbr.org/2005/07/turning-great-strategy-into-great-performance. Bossidy, Larry. Execution (p. 41). Crown. Kindle Edition.

3. Bossidy, Larry, and Ram Charan. Execution: the Discipline of Getting Things Done. London: Random House Business, 2011.

4. Horowitz, Ben. What You Do Is Who You Are. Harper Collins UK, 2019.

5. Connors, Roger, Tom Smith, and Craig R. Hickman. The Oz Principle: Getting Results through Individual and Organizational Accountability. New York, NY: Portfolio, 2010.

6. Michie, J., and L. Lobao. "Ownership, Control and Economic Outcomes." Cambridge Journal of Regions, Economy and Society 5, no. 3 (2012): 307–24. https://doi.org/10.1093/cjres/rss015.

7. "WHAT IF? - Community-Wealth.org: Wealth-Building ..." Accessed March 31, 2021. https://community-wealth.org/sites/clone.community-

wealth.org/files/downloads/report-scearce-et-al.pdf.

8. Maister, David. *Strategy and the Fat Smoker: Doing What's Obvious but Not Easy.* Boston, MA: Spangle Press, 2008.

9. "Promise-Based Management: The Essence of Execution." Harvard Business Review, August 1, 2014. https://hbr.org/2007/04/promise-based-management-the-essence-of-execution.

10. "Why Your Agile Projects Fizzle Out." Harvard Business Review, April 3, 2020. https://hbr.org/2018/11/making-process-improvements-stick.

11. Hardy-Vallee, Benoit. "The Cost of Bad Project Management." Gallup.com. Gallup, October 20, 2020. https://news.gallup.com/businessjournal/152429/cost-bad-project-management.aspx.

12. Ukleja, Mick. "Closing The Execution Gap - Convene: Christian CEO Peer Advisory Groups, Executive Coaching and Business Consulting." Convene. Convene | Christian CEO Peer Advisory Groups, Executive Coaching and Business Consulting, September 14, 2015. https://www.convenenow.com/blog/2015/09/14/closing-the-execution-gap.

13. "Samurai." Japanese Warriors. Accessed March 31, 2021. https://www.japan-guide.com/e/e2127.html#:~:text=The%20samurai%20(or%20bushi)%20were,and%20symbol%20was%20the%20sword.

14. "The Seven Virtues of Bushido." English Shotokan Academy. Accessed March 31, 2021. https://www.englishshotokan.net/history-of-karate/virtues-of-bushido.

15. Roberts, Andrew. Napoleon: A Life. Penguin Books, n.d.

16. Callahan, Shawn. "What Might Amazon's Six-Page Narrative Structure Look like?" Anecdote. Anecdote, December 2, 2020. https://www.anecdote.com/2018/05/amazons-six-page-narrative-structure/.

17. Classicalycourt. "Jeff Bezos' 'Two Pizza Rule' Can Help You Hold More Productive Meetings." CNBC. CNBC, April 30, 2018. https://www.cnbc.com/2018/04/30/jeff-bezos-2-pizza-rule-can-help-you-hold-more-productive-meetings.html#:~:text=Jeff%20Bezos'%20'two%20pizza%20rule'%20can%20help,you%20hold%20more%20productive%20meetings&text=While%2C%20sadly%2C%20the%20rule%20does,t%20feed%20the%20entire%20group.

18. Kahneman, Daniel. Thinking, Fast and Slow. New York: Farrar, Straus and Giroux, 2013.

19. Willink, Jocko, and Leif Babin. Extreme Ownership: How U.S. Navy SEALs Lead and Win. Sydney, N.S.W.: Macmillan, 2018.

20. Summaries, Must Read. A Sense of Urgency - John Kotter. Primento Publishing, 2011.

21. "Timeline: Consulate/1st French Empire." napoleon.org. Accessed March 31, 2021. https://www.napoleon.org/en/young-historians/napodoc/timeline-consulate1st-french-empire/.

22. Harter, Jim. "4 Factors Driving Record-High Employee Engagement in U.S." Gallup.com. Gallup, January 18, 2021. https://www.gallup.com/workplace/284180/factors-driving-record-high-

employee-engagement.aspx.

23. Davidson, Lauren. "Is Your Daily Social Media Usage Higher than Average?" The Telegraph. Telegraph Media Group, May 17, 2015. https://www.telegraph.co.uk/finance/newsbysector/mediatechnologyandtelecoms/11610959/Is-your-daily-social-media-usage-higher-than-average.html.

24. NEWPORT, CAL. DEEP WORK: Rules for Focused Success in a Distracted World. GRAND CENTRAL PUB, 2018.

25. Hussey, David E. The Implementation Challenge. Chichester: Wiley, 1996.

26. "What Is Strategy?" Harvard Business Review, November 7, 2019. https://hbr.org/1996/11/what-is-strategy.

27. "Turning Great Strategy into Great Performance." Harvard Business Review, September 15, 2015. https://hbr.org/2005/07/turning-great-strategy-into-great-performance.

28. "Research: Do People Really Get Promoted to Their Level of Incompetence?" Harvard Business Review, April 10, 2018. https://hbr.org/2018/03/research-do-people-really-get-promoted-to-their-level-of-incompetence.

29. Mainardi, Cesare R., and Paul Leinwand. Strategy That Works. Harvard Business Review, 2016.

30. "5 Ways the Best Companies Close the Strategy-Execution Gap." Harvard Business Review, February 7, 2020. https://hbr.org/2017/11/5-ways-the-best-companies-close-the-strategy-execution-gap.

31. Diduch, Maria Konnikova Produced by Mary. "What If Your Company Had No Rules? (Bonus Episode)." Freakonomics, March 22, 2021. https://freakonomics.com/podcast/book-club-hastings/.

32. "The 5 Pillars of Strategy Execution." Smarter With Gartner. Accessed March 31, 2021. https://www.gartner.com/smarterwithgartner/the-five-pillars-of-strategy-execution/.

33. Oppong, Thomas. "To Get Better Results, Do Less But Do It Better." Thrive Global, June 29, 2018. https://thriveglobal.com/stories/to-get-real-stuff-done-focus-on-the-20-of-your-work-that-leads-to-80-of-your-results/.

34. "Udemy In Depth: 2018 Workplace Distraction Report." Udemy Research, April 30, 2020. https://research.udemy.com/research_report/udemy-depth-2018-workplace-distraction-report/.

35. "What Is Flow in Psychology? Definition and 10+ Activities to Induce Flow." PositivePsychology.com, March 10, 2021. https://positivepsychology.com/what-is-flow/.

36. Bellis, Rich. "Read This Google Email About Time Management Strategy." Fast Company. Fast Company, December 29, 2016. https://www.fastcompany.com/3054571/the-better-time-management-strategy-this-googler-taught-his-coworkers.

37. "Simplicity-Minded Management." Harvard Business Review, August 1, 2014. https://hbr.org/2007/12/simplicity-minded-management.

38. "CMO by Adobe." Adobe Blog. Accessed March 31,

2021. https://cmo.adobe.com/articles/2016/1/good-ideas-are-important-but-execution-is-key.html#gs.bb7p3w.

39. "Making Your Strategy Work on the Frontline." Harvard Business Review, August 12, 2015. https://hbr.org/2010/06/making-your-strategy-work-on-t.

40. Ashkenas, Ronald N. Simply Effective: How to Cut through Complexity in Your Organization and Get Things Done. Boston, MA: Harvard Business Review Press, 2010.

41. McChrystal, Stanley. Team of Teams: New Rules of Engagement for a Complex World. Troy, MI: Business News Publishing, 2016.

42. Bodell, Lisa. Why Simple Wins: Escape the Complexity Trap and Get to Work That Matters. New York: Bibliomotion, Inc., 2017.

43. Sunzi. The Art of War: the Oldest Military Treatise in the World. New Delhi: The Readers Paradise, 2019.

44. Rajkumar, S. (2010). Art of communication in project management. Paper presented at PMI® Research Conference: Defining the Future of Project Management, Washington, DC. Newtown Square, PA: Project Management Institute.

45. Garfinkle, Joel, Amit Maimon, and Ron Ashkenas. "Why We Should Be Disagreeing More at Work." Harvard Business Review, April 17, 2018. https://hbr.org/2018/01/why-we-should-be-disagreeing-more-at-work.

46. Block, Peter. The Answer to How Is Yes Acting on What Matters. San Francisco, Calif: Berrett-Koehler, 2003.

47. Block, Peter. Stewardship. San Francisco, CA: Berrett-Koehler Publishers, 1993.

48. Deane, Morgan. "Top 8 Inventions & Innovations of WWII." WAR HISTORY ONLINE, December 10, 2018. https://www.warhistoryonline.com/instant-articles/inventions-and-innovations-wwii.html.

49. "What Is Organizational Culture? And Why Should We Care?" Harvard Business Review, August 7, 2014. https://hbr.org/2013/05/what-is-organizational-culture.

50. Feloni, Richard. "The 16 Best Ways to Sabotage Your Organization's Productivity, from a CIA Manual Published in 1944." Business Insider. Business Insider, November 5, 2015. https://www.businessinsider.com/oss-manual-sabotage-productivity-2015-11.

51. 262588213843476. "1944 OSS Simple Sabotage Field Manual." Gist. Accessed March 31, 2021. https://gist.github.com/kennwhite/467529962c184258d08f16dae-c83d5da.

52. "Mission Command Requires Sharp Commander's Intent." www.army.mil. Accessed March 31, 2021. https://www.army.mil/article/215297/mission_command_requires_sharp_commanders_intent.

53. "Beware the Busy Manager." Harvard Business Review, November 18, 2014. https://hbr.org/2002/02/beware-the-busy-manager.

54. TAYLOR, FREDERICK WINSLOW. PRINCIPLES OF SCIENTIFIC MANAGEMENT. DIGIREADS COM, 2020.

55. Bauer, Tim, Cassandra Estep, and Emily E. Griffith. "Does Psychological Ownership Improve Team Member Contributions?" USC Marshall, n.d. https://www.marshall.usc.edu/sites/default/files/2018-11/Does%20Psychological%20Ownership%20Improve%20Team%20Member%20Contributions.pdf.

56. Maunz, Shay. "The Great Hanoi Rat Massacre of 1902 Did Not Go as Planned." Atlas Obscura. Atlas Obscura, June 6, 2017. https://www.atlasobscura.com/articles/hanoi-rat-massacre-1902.

57. Chappell, Bill. "Outsourced: Employee Sends Own Job To China; Surfs Web." NPR. NPR, January 16, 2013. https://www.npr.org/sections/thetwo-way/2013/01/16/169528579/outsourced-employee-sends-own-job-to-china-surfs-web.

58. "10 Easy Ways To Look Busy At Work." Thought Catalog, January 20, 2014. https://thoughtcatalog.com/tamara-jenkins/2014/01/10-easy-ways-to-look-busy-at-work/.

59. "Three Keys to Effective Execution." Harvard Business Review, July 23, 2014. https://hbr.org/2008/02/three-keys-to-effective-execut.

60. "APA PsycNet." American Psychological Association. American Psychological Association. Accessed March 31, 2021. https://doi.apa.org/record/1999-15054-002?doi=1.

61. Jacobson, Linda. "Duckworth: 'Deliberate Practice' Is an Important Element of Grit." K-12 Dive, April 18, 2018. https://www.educationdive.com/news/duckworth-deliberate-practice-is-an-important-

element-of-grit/521559/.

62. "Articles." davidmaister.com > Why (Most) Training is Useless. Accessed March 31, 2021. https://davidmaister.com/articles/why-most-training-is-useless/.

63. "Where Companies Go Wrong with Learning and Development." Harvard Business Review, January 20, 2021. https://hbr.org/2019/10/where-companies-go-wrong-with-learning-and-development.

64. PricewaterhouseCoopers. "24th Annual Global CEO Survey." PwC. Accessed March 31, 2021. https://www.pwc.com/gx/en/ceo-agenda/ceosurvey/2020.html.

65. "Skills Matter: Further Results from the Survey of Adult Skills." OECD instance. Accessed March 31, 2021. https://www.oecd-ilibrary.org/education/skills-matter_9789264258051-en.

66. Holiday, Ryan. Daily Stoic: 366 Meditations on Self-Mastery, Perseverance and Wisdom: Featuring New Translations of Seneca, Marcus Aurelius and Epictetus. Penguin Publishing Group, 2016.

67. Vinney, Cynthia. "Fluid Versus Crystallized Intelligence: What's the Difference?" ThoughtCo. Accessed March 31, 2021. https://www.thoughtco.com/fluid-crystallized-intelligence-4172807.

68. Cherry, Kendra. "What Are Fluid Intelligence and Crystallized Intelligence?" Verywell Mind, December 7, 2019. https://www.verywellmind.com/fluid-intelligence-vs-crystallized-intelligence-2795004#:~:text=Such%20factors%20represent%20what%20psychologists,that

%20are%20acquired%20throughout%20life.

69. Merchant, Nilofer. The New How: Building Business Solutions through Collaborative Strategy. Sebastopol, CA: O'Reilly Media, 2014.

70. "Leading Change: Why Transformation Efforts Fail." Harvard Business Review, July 13, 2015. https://hbr.org/1995/05/leading-change-why-transformation-efforts-fail-2.

71. Gladwell, Malcolm. Outliers: Why Some People Succeed and Some Don't. New York: Little Brown & Co., 2008.

72. Bungay, Stephen. The Art of Action: How Leaders Close the Gaps between Plans, Actions and Results. London: Nicholas Brealey, 2012.

73. DOSHI, NEEL. Primed to Perform: How to Build the Highest Performing Cultures through the Science of Total Motivat. NEW YORK: HARPERBUSINESS, 2015.

74. Mintzberg, Henry. The Rise and Fall of Strategic Planning: Reconceiving Roles for Planning, Plans, Planners. New York: Free Press, 2013.

75. Willink, Jocko, and Leif Babin. The Dichotomy of Leadership: Balancing the Challenges of Extreme Ownership to Lead and Win. New York: St. Martin's Press, 2018.

76. Simons, Robert. Seven Strategy Questions A Simple Approach for Better Execution. Boston: Harvard Business Review Press, 2014.

77. Simons, Robert. Control in an Age of Empowerment. Boston, Mass: Harvard Business Press, 2008.

78. Lee's Lieutenants A Study in Command. Touchstone Books, 2001.

79. Hunger, J. David, and Thomas L. Wheelen. Essentials of Strategic Management. Essex: Pearson, 2014.

80. Speculand, Robin. Beyond Strategy: The Leader's Role in Successful Implementation. John Wiley & Sons, 2009.

81. Pijl, Jacques, Mischa Hoyinck, Robert Chesal, Aad Goudappel, and Klis Hans van der. Strategy = Execution. Deventer: Management Impact, 2020.

82. Speculand, Robin. Excellence in Execution: HOW to Implement Your Strategy. New York, NY: Morgan James Publishing, 2017.

83. Mellon, Elizabeth, and Simon Carter. Strategy of Execution: a Five-Step Guide for Turning Vision into Action, 2014.

84. MacLennan, Alex. Strategy Execution: Translating Strategy into Action in Complex Organizations. London: Routledge, 2011.

85. Lynch, Stephen. Business Execution for Results: a Practical Guide for Leaders of Small to Mid-Sized Firms. United States: Stebian.com, 2013.

86. Huff, Darrell, and Irving Geis. How to Lie with Statistics. New York: W.W. Norton & Co., 2006.

87. Canic, Michael. Ruthless Consistency: How Committed Leaders Execute Strategy, Implement Change, and Build Organizations That Win. New York: McGraw-Hill, 2021.

88. Stepping Up: How Taking Responsibility Changes Everything Ed. 2. Berrett-Koehler Publishers, 2020.

89. Goodwin, Doris Kearns. Leadership in Turbulent Times. Thorndike, ME: Large Print Press, a part of

Gale, a Cengage Company, 2019.

90. McCausland, Jeffrey D., and Tom Vossler. Battle Tested!: Gettysburg Leadership Lessons for 21st Century Leaders. New York: Post Hill Press, 2020.

91. Kaplan, Robert S., and David P. Norton. Execution Premium: Linking Strategy to Operations for Competitive Advantage. Boston, MA: Harvard Business Press, 2009.

92. Orlick, Terry. In Pursuit of Excellence. Champaign, IL: Human Kinetics, 2016.

93. Senge, Peter, Charlotte Roberts, Richard B. Ross, Bryan Smith, and Art Kelner. The Fifth Discipline Fieldbook: Strategies and Tools for Building a Learning Organization. London: Nicholas Brealey, 2009.

94. McKeown, Greg. Essentialism: the Disciplined Pursuit of Less. London: Virgin Books, 2021.

95. Meier, J. D. Getting Results the Agile Way: a Personal Results System for Work and Life. Bellevue, WA: Innovation Playhouse, 2010.

96. Trulock, Alice Rains. In the Hands of Providence Joshua L. Chamberlain and the American Civil War. Chapel Hill: The University of North Carolina Press, 2013.

97. 7 HABITS OF HIGHLY EFFECTIVE PEOPLE. SIMON & SCHUSTER LTD, 2017.

98. Sutherland, Jeffrey Victor. Scrum: the Art of Doing Twice the Work in Half the Time. London: Random House, 2019.

99. Holiday, Ryan. The Obstacle Is the Way: the Timeless Art of Turning Trials into Triumph. New York: Portfolio/Penguin, 2014.

100.	Godin, Seth. Tribes We Need You to Lead Us, 2014.

101.	Scott, Kim Malone. Radical Candor: How to Be a Kickass Boss without Losing Your Humanity. New York: St. Martin's Press, 2019.

102.	Bailey, Chris. Hyperfocus. Penguin USA, 2019.

103.	Coleman, Peter T., and Robert Ferguson. Making Conflict Work: Harnessing the Power of Disagreement. Boston, NY: Mariner Books, Houghton Mifflin Harcourt, 2015.

104.	R., Covey Stephen M, and Rebecca R. Merrill. The Speed of Trust: the One Thing That Changes Everything. New York: Free Press, 2018.

105.	CHERNOW, RON. GRANT. HEAD OF ZEUS, 2018.

106.	PETERS, TOM. EXCELLENCE DIVIDEND: the Rules of Excellence from a Lifetime in Pursuit of Perfection. NICHOLAS BREALEY PUB, 2018.

107.	Morgan, Mark, William A. Malek, and Raymond E. Levitt. Executing Your Strategy. Boston, MA: Harvard Business School Press, 2008.

108.	Hessler, James A. Sickles at Gettysburg: the Controversial Civil War General Who Committed Murder, Abandoned Little Round Top, and Declared Himself the Hero of Gettysburg. El Dorado Hills, Cal.: Savas Beatie, 2015.

109.	Pierce, Jon L., and Iiro Jussila. Psychological Ownership and the Organizational Context: Theory, Research Evidence and Application. Cheltenham: Edward Elgar, 2012.

110.   Blanchard, Kenneth H., and Mark Miller. The Secret: What Great Leaders Know and Do. New York, NY: MJF Books, 2014.

111.   Schmidt, Terry. Strategic Project Management Made Simple: Practical Tools for Leaders and Teams. Hoboken, N.J: Wiley, 2009.

112.   Harpst, Gary. Six Disciplines Execution Revolution: Solving the One Business Problem That Makes Solving All Other Problems Easier. Findlay: Six Disciplines Publishing, 2015.

113.   McKnight, Richard, Tom Kaney, and Shannon Breuer. Leading Strategy Execution: How to Align the Senior Team, Design a Strategy-Capable Organization, and Get All Employees on-Board. Philadelphia: TrueNorth Press, 2010.

114.   FLANDER, JEROEN DE. ART OF PERFORMANCE: the Surprising Science behind Greatness. PERFORMANCE FACTORY, 2019.

115.   Leadership and Self-Deception: Getting out of the Box. Oakland, CA: Berrett-Koehler Publishers, Inc., 2018.

116.   Weisinger, Hendrie, and J. P. Pawliw-Fry. Performing under Pressure: the Science of Doing Your Best When It Matters Most. New York: Crown Business, 2015.

117.   "APA PsycNet." American Psychological Association. American Psychological Association. Accessed March 31, 2021. https://psycnet.apa.org/record/2010-26312-008.

118.   Carnegie, Dale. How to Win Friends and Influence People by Dale Carnegie. Simon & Schuster, 1936.

119. Dunning, D. (2011). The Dunning-Kruger effect: On

being ignorant of one's own ignorance. In J. M. Olson & M. P. Zanna (Eds.), Advances in experimental social psychology. Advances in experimental social psychology, Vol. 44 (p. 247–296). Academic Press.

120. Duckworth, Angela. Grit: the Power of Passion and Perseverance. United States: Paula Wiseman Books, 2020.

121. Cattell, Raymond Bernard. Intelligence: Its Structure, Growth and Action. Amsterdam: North Holland, 1987.

122. History.com Editors. "First Battle of Bull Run." History.com. A&E Television Networks, April 1, 2011. https://www.history.com/topics/american-civil-war/first-battle-of-bull-run.

123. Covey, Stephen R. The 7 Habits of Highly Effective People. Provo, UT: Franklin Covey, 1998.

124. Andrews, Evan. "Ancient Rome's Darkest Day: The Battle of Cannae." History.com. A& E Television Networks, August 2, 2016. https://www.history.com/news/ancient-romes-darkest-day-the-battle-of-cannae.

125. "File:Battle Cannae Destruction.-Ca.svg." Wikimedia Commons. Accessed April 25, 2021. https://commons.wikimedia.org/wiki/File:Battle_cannae_destruction.-ca.svg.

126. "Death by Burning." Wikipedia. Wikimedia Foundation, April 21, 2021. https://en.wikipedia.org/wiki/Death_by_burning#/media/File:Avvakum_by_Pyotr_Yevgenyevich_Myasoyedov.jpg.

127. "The Mexican-American War and the Civil War." Encyclopædia Britannica. Encyclopædia Britannica, inc. Ac-

cessed May 2, 2021. https://www.britannica.com/topic/The-United-States-Army/The-Mexican-American-War-and-the-Civil-War.

128. "The Ten Bloodiest Battles of the Civil War." The Great Courses Daily, October 9, 2020. https://www.thegreatcoursesdaily.com/ten-bloodiest-battles-civil-war/.

129. Bowman, Tom. "Antietam: A Savage Day In American History." NPR. NPR, September 17, 2012. https://www.npr.org/2012/09/17/161248814/antietam-a-savage-day-in-american-history.

130. "Burnside Bridge (U.S. National Park Service)." National Parks Service. U.S. Department of the Interior. Accessed May 2, 2021. https://www.nps.gov/places/antietam-battlefield-burnside-bridge.htm.

131. "Home." British Battles. Accessed May 2, 2021. https://www.britishbattles.com/american-civil-war/battle-of-antietam/.

132. History.com Editors. "Battle of Fredericksburg." History.com. A&E Television Networks, November 9, 2009. https://www.history.com/topics/american-civil-war/battle-of-fredericksburg.

133. "Battle of Chancellorsville Begins." History.com. A&E Television Networks, November 13, 2009. https://www.history.com/this-day-in-history/battle-of-chancellorsville-begins.

134. "North and South." American Battlefield Trust, April 13, 2021. https://www.battlefields.org/learn/articles/north-and-south.

135. History.com Editors. "Battle of Hampton Roads." History.com. A&E Television Networks, November 9, 2009. https://www.history.com/topics/american-civil-war/battle-of-hampton-roads.

136. "Northern Plans to End the War." ushistory.org. Independence Hall Association. Accessed May 2, 2021. https://www.ushistory.org/US/33h.asp.

137. "Defense of Little Round Top." American Battlefield Trust, March 26, 2021. https://www.battlefields.org/learn/articles/defense-little-round-top.

138. II, Julian Hayes. "3 Timeless Principles of a Winner's Mindset From Ulysses S. Grant." Inc.com. Inc., December 27, 2018. https://www.inc.com/julian-hayes-ii/what-civil-war-general-us-president-ulysses-s-grant-can-teach-you-about-adopting-a-winners-mindset.html.

139. "Grant's Greatest Battles." PBS. Public Broadcasting Service. Accessed May 2, 2021. https://www.pbs.org/wgbh/americanexperience/features/grants-greatest-battles/.

140. Porter, General Horace. Campaigning with Grant. United States: Pickle Partners Publishing, 2015.

141. Mark. "Sherman's Plan for His March to the Sea: Special Field Orders Numbers 119 and 120." Iron Brigader, April 20, 2019. https://iron-brigader.com/2019/11/15/shermans-plan-for-his-march-to-the-sea-special-field-orders-numbers-119-and-120/.

142. Lively, Matt. "To Lead, Be Humble-Ulysses S. Grant." Medium. The Startup, August 31, 2019. https://medium.com/swlh/to-lead-be-humble-ulysses-s-grant-b3374233a99f.

143. Samet, Elizabeth D. "7 Reasons Ulysses S. Grant Was One of America's Most Brilliant Military Leaders." History.com. A&E Television Networks, May 13, 2020. https://www.history.com/news/ulysses-s-grant-civil-war-general-strengths.

144. Chan, Amy. "The Supreme Partnership: Grant and Sherman." HistoryNet. HistoryNet, May 17, 2017. https://www.historynet.com/supreme-partnership-grant-sherman.htm.

145. "The Crater." National Parks Service. U.S. Department of the Interior. Accessed May 2, 2021. https://www.nps.gov/pete/learn/historyculture/the-crater.htm?fullweb=1.

146. Bungay, Stephen. The Most Dangerous Enemy: a History of the Battle of Britain. London: Aurum Press, 2015.

COPYRIGHT:

GETTING SHIT DONE was edited by Chris Murray

A former journalist, newsletter editor, and international management consultant, Chris is a developmental editor and editorial coach specializing in non-fiction books on a variety of business and self-development topics, including corporate strategy, customer relationships, entrepreneurship, marketing, employee engagement, and leadership.

Perhaps you have great ideas for a book, but you find yourself struggling to convert them into well-organized chapters.
Or perhaps you have a half-written book that you cannot quite seem to finish.
Or you may have a general theme or concept in your mind and are looking to take the first step in writing a book.
Whatever your need, hiring a professional book editor will help.

For more information, please visit:

www.chrismurrayeditor.com

All illustrations done by Na'toria Marketing & Design Solutions.

GLOSSARY

1. Sense of Urgency
2. Little Whats
3. Big What
4. Accountability Chain
5. Mental Ownership
6. Physical Ownership
7. Under Estimation Ratio
8. Eisenhower Box
9. Planning Fallacy
10. Flow
11. Crystallized Intelligence
12. Fluid Intelligence
13. Grit
14. Decentralization
15. Commander's Intent
16. Accountability Chains
17. SMART
18. KPIs
19. Bushido
20. Memo Approach
21. Two-Pizza Rule

Made in the USA
Monee, IL
20 February 2022

91511003R00230